>>Expert internet searching

FIFTH EDITION

>>Expert internet searching

FIFTH EDITION

Phil Bradley

Published by Facet Publishing
7 Ridgmount Street, London WC1E 7AE
www.facetpublishing.co.uk

Facet Publishing is wholly owned by CILIP: the Library and Information Association.

British Library Cataloguing in Publication Data
A catalogue record for this book is available from the British Library.

ISBN 978-1-78330-247-5 (paperback)
ISBN 978-1-78330-248-2 (hardback)
ISBN 978-1-78330-249-9 (e-book)

First published (as *The Advanced Internet Searcher's Handbook*) 1999
Second edition 2002
Third edition 2004
Fourth edition 2013
This fifth edition 2017

Text printed on FSC accredited material.

Typeset from author's files in 10.5/14 pt Bergamo and Myriad Pro by Flagholme Publishing Services.
Printed and made in Great Britain by CPI Group (UK) Ltd, Croydon, CR0 4YY.

Contents

List of figures

Preface

Welcome to this, the fifth edition of *Expert Internet Searching*, which began its life back at the beginning of the century, when it was called *The Advanced Internet Searcher's Handbook*. That very first edition, published towards the end of 1999, didn't even mention Google. Most of the search engines that I wrote about no longer exist and over the years functionality has waxed and waned.

We're now in a world of user-generated content, access to data not just at the touch of a button but by simply asking the question into our living rooms where our mobile assistants can research and answer the question as soon as we have finished speaking it. 'News' now means things that happened in the last few seconds, instead of the last few hours or the last day or week, and we've seen the rise of 'fake news'. While we have such easy access to information, and everyone can contribute to it, the other side of that coin is that everyone does it, only not for the greater good, but to promote their own political or religious agenda, and in doing so accuracy and truth become immediate casualties.

We all still see the rather silly claim that 'it's all on Google, so why do we need libraries and librarians?' but I firmly believe that information professionals are needed now more than ever. It's in part our role to help stem the tide of fake news, to open people's eyes to the rich abundance of information available in so many different formats, and to assist them in working out what they need to know and the best way of getting it. When I was a child and I told my careers officer that I wanted to be a librarian she said 'is it because you like books?' and I said 'No, it's because I want the power'. It's even more true today than it was rather too many decades ago. The more information that we have at our fingertips, the more useful and powerful we become. However, we don't get that by simply visiting Google at every opportunity. We need to know how Google works inside and out of course, but we also need to understand what other search engines are better than Google, which engines provide access to material that Google doesn't, and how best to utilise those resources. That's really what this book is all about – providing you with the information that you need to play with other search engines, explore their capabilities, strengths and weaknesses and appreciate when to use one over another. The more we can get the information we need quickly, the more we can help our clients and make their lives easier. While it may be argued that's perhaps something of a 'Pollyanna' view to take, I can balance that out with the rather more cynical view that the more we can find material that other people can't, the more important information professionals become, and the more we will all be valued.

Talking of valuing people, over my career I have been helped by some marvellous, wonderful people, and I'd like to take a moment to recognise them:

Tara Calishain's enthusiasm with her site 'ResearchBuzz' astonishes me with what she is able to find and her generosity in sharing it.

Sarah Houghton (the Librarian in Black) leaves me awestruck by her compassion, her strength, her values and her resilience to never stop fighting for what is right.

Marydee Ojala who knows more about search than I ever will, and is just so enthusiastic about it!

Greg Notess was one of the very first search engine experts I met, and he helped show me what a rich and fascinating area it was.

David Lankes has been my personal 'guru' for many years, and I have been encouraged and excited by his view of librarians, and librarianship.

Gary Price who has always amazed me with his breadth of knowledge in the field of information.

Michael Stephens has a generous and positive view of our profession, and has so often shown me by words and deeds how caring for people benefits us all.

Then there are all of my British colleagues, who over the course of my career helped, aided, assisted and turned me into a better person, and hopefully better information professional! Jo Alcock, Ian Anstice, Barbara Band, Karen Blakeman, CILIP colleagues, Hazel Edmunds, Biddy Fisher, Hazel Hall, Beverley Humphrey, Lisa Jeskins, Alison McNab, Professor Charles Oppenheim, Dave Pattern, Nick Poole, Caroline Roche, Val Skelton, all of the 'Voices of the Library', Arthur Weiss, Nicky Whitsed, and so, so many others. It's little by the way of 'thanks', but this book is dedicated to each and every one of you.

Phil Bradley

Acknowledgements

Working with people in the information community is a real joy, since they are some of the most interesting, helpful and committed professionals on the planet. I have been fortunate enough to work in many countries around the world and have only to walk into the nearest library to feel at home, with new friends waiting to be met. Conferences are a joy to attend since they provide me with inspiration, ideas and unique insights into many different communities. Social media platforms such as Facebook and Twitter allow me to interact with information professionals all day and every day and I can reach out, ask a question and receive a helpful answer within minutes. So thanks to all of the many hundreds of people who have helped increase my knowledge of the world around me.

I'd also like to thank the people – most of whom I don't know and have never (and will never) have chance to meet – who spend their time crafting search engines, tools, apps and helpful websites for the rest of us to make use of. Of course, the staff at Facet Publishing and CILIP are a great group of people to work with – enthusiastic, helpful and informative; it's invidious to name too many names, but particular thanks to Natalie and Damian.

Finally, friends and family, information professionals already mentioned, and you the reader, many thanks for your continual support – even when you don't realise you're providing it!

Every effort has been made to contact the holders of copyright material reproduced in the text, and thanks are due to them all for their kind permission to reproduce the material indicated. If there are any queries, please contact the publisher.

Phil Bradley

CHAPTER 1

An introduction to the internet

Introduction

When writing a new edition of an existing book, one of the decisions that you have to take is how much to change, and how much to keep the same. In all of the previous editions of this title I've included an introduction to the internet, and clearly I'm doing so again – why change a winning formula? However in truth, it's not really about that, it's rather more to do with the fact that I strongly believe that an introduction really IS required. As you might imagine, I talk to people all of the time about the internet, and the majority of them are not internet or information professionals, they are the average person on the street, or in my case, out walking their dogs in the park. Their knowledge of the internet is about as limited as my knowledge of the way in which the internal combustion engine works, which is to say, limited in the extreme. Of course, if you're someone who works with the internet on a regular, daily basis you're probably far more aware of the internet and what it does and doesn't do. However, it's always a good idea to have a refresher every now and then, and even if you read this chapter in a previous edition of the book it's worth scanning through it again because information does change year on year.

What doesn't change, however, is the old time-worn phrase 'It's all on Google'. Having spent some time in 2016 looking at two big political events, the British European Union referendum and the American Presidential election, it's very easy to see that not only is it not all on Google but Google may very well just provide you with the information that it thinks you want to see, limiting your choice even further than what is available in its databases. Once we add in the data flooding on the internet from the users of social media platforms, live video streaming and the hidden and dark webs (two different but related concepts I'll talk about later) we can safely say that it's most certainly not all on Google. A figure that I have often seen referenced is that Google only indexes 5% of the internet. Now of course for this figure to have any validity we'd need to know just how much information IS available and quite simply we don't. However, we can say that search engines (and I want to broaden this discussion out to all engines rather than just one) don't index any content that requires a password to access it, websites that have files that request engines not to index their content, sites without links, customised content, blacklisted sites, sites that just haven't been found, intranets and much more. Indeed, we need to define what we're actually talking about; web pages, total content by bytes, static IP addresses and so on.

There is a battle that is being waged right in front of us to get our eyeballs on their adverts; Google, Microsoft, Facebook, Apple, Amazon and many others want us to use their services so that we may now and then click on one of those adverts and make the giants some money. In this decade we have seen the rise of the smartphone and in 2016 devices such as Amazon's Alexa, which sits quietly in the living room waiting to respond to every spoken command. We still have to see if smart watches and glasses reach their potential, to say nothing of virtual reality systems.

However, I'm in danger of getting ahead of myself, so let's take a step back and address some of the fundamentals of the internet.

An overview of the internet

The UK Office of National Statistics in their 2011 release 'Internet access, households and individuals' estimates that 77% of UK households had access to the internet, and 45% of users had used a mobile phone to connect to it. By May 2016 this figure had risen to 87.9% of adults in the UK who had recently used the internet, compared with 86.2% in 2015. The number of people who had never used the internet had dropped from 11.4% to 10.2% between 2015 and 2016.

Virtually all adults aged between 16 and 24 used the internet (99.2%) while only 38.7% of adults aged 75 and over had used it. Interestingly enough, however, women aged 75 and over had seen the largest rise in recent internet use, up 169% on 2011 (www.ons.gov.uk/businessindustryandtrade/itandinternetindustry/bulletins/internetusers/2016). It's useful to remember, though, that many older and disabled people are still not online, so it is still very much a 'black hole' for specific groups.

People use the internet for everything that they have always done in the past, most particularly e-mail and search, and these activities have been constant over time. However, communication is now often by social media platform, with real-time chat face to face via video. People watch films via their smart televisions, ensure the safety of their houses by internet connected security systems, listen to books as their home assistants read them aloud and so on. In fact, if we look at the key internet activities for UK users in 2016:

- sending and receiving e-mail is undertaken by 79% of users
- finding information about goods and services by 76%
- social networking such as Twitter and Facebook by 63%
- reading online news, newspapers or magazines by 60%
- looking for health-related information also by 60%.

Less common activities include creating websites or blogs, making appointments with health practitioners, selling goods or watching video on demand (www.ons.gov.uk/peoplepopulationandcommunity/householdcharacteristics/homeinternetandsocialmediausage/datasets/internetaccesshouseholdsandindividualsreferencetables). Of course, these figures will already be changing as people connect more and more devices to the internet and continue to

Did you know?
50.2% of internet users live in Asia, 17.2% in Europe, 9.3% in Africa and 8.6% in North America (www.internetworldstats.com/stats.htm).

find other uses for it.

Irrespective of the number of people engaged in specific activities, it's clear that the internet – at least in the developed world – is an essential element of everyday life. Moreover, everyone searches, from the professional who is capable of using a complex nested logic search using a specific database to the individual who wants to know where they can get their smartphone screen replaced and posts to a local Facebook group. To that extent, we are all searchers; it's just that some are better than others.

What the internet is and is not

It's not a single network

When I originally wrote this particular section I spent my time explaining how the internet was put together, how one computer connected to another and how different networks were 'plugged in' to each other. The internet is sufficiently advanced that we can essentially almost completely ignore this; the only time that you will probably have any interest in how your device connects to any other device is if you want to secure your own privacy, and I talk about privacy settings and search engines in appropriate chapters.

However, the point is still valid, and increasingly so as social networks create their own infrastructures and make it difficult, if not impossible, for search engines to explore them and index the content. For example, if you explained the internet from scratch to someone who had never used it and then showed them Facebook they could – and should – be forgiven for thinking that Facebook was the internet and vice versa. After all, people can communicate directly with each other, they can share information, companies create their own presence, people can view images and videos and so on. However, Facebook is its own entity and much of the information is inside a walled-off garden, and until you create your own account and get involved much of that information is invisible to you. We have dozens of social media networks all doing their own thing, with people communicating, sharing and engaging in many different ways. On Pinterest, for example, people will interact over the common ground of images, and much the same can be said of Instagram or WhatsApp. On Spotify people will create their own networks so that they can listen to the music that their friends enjoy and people on Google+ will similarly share things with friends and colleagues over their networks. It's of course true to say that some of these platforms do allow search engines to index content, but it's not always the case, so we're seeing a situation in which people can very easily create their own social systems that have limited communication with others using different platforms.

As far as the searcher is concerned, our job has become much harder; not only can we not use one single search engine to return the information that we need, we may well need to create accounts on different platforms before searching them effectively. Far from the internet bringing information to our fingertips via the medium of the search engine, quite the opposite has occurred, and we have to let our fingers do the walking, hunting out the information that we need based on our own knowledge and expertise.

It's both local and global

Did you know?
The penetration of internet use is highest in North America at 88.1%, followed by Europe 77.4% and Oceania/Australia at 68.1%. Lowest is Africa, with 27.7% of the population (www.internetworldstats.com/stats.htm).

When I started teaching people about the internet over 20 years ago my explanation here was simple – information was ubiquitous and it didn't matter where you were. If you had access to the internet you could reach the information that you needed; you weren't tied to your own internal network. Nowadays of course we mean something entirely different; our smartphones mean that we're connected to the internet and when we search for information our devices are intelligent enough to work out where we are and to respond accordingly. I don't have to say to Amazon Alexa 'What's the weather like in Basildon Essex?' I can simply ask it 'What's the weather like' because it knows where I am, to within two houses. If I search on Google for 'libraries' or 'plumbers' the search engine will return results to me based on my location, assuming (rightly in most cases) that I want a plumber to come to my house to fix something, so there's no point in giving me details on plumbers in Idaho. Alternatively, I can find the information that I need from a localised search engine, or check via Twitter's geographic search function. In all probability, however, I'll visit my favourite social network and ask my question there, since I'm less interested in a random collection of websites (however well a search engine arranges them) and more interested in what my friends, colleagues and local experts can tell me. This is in fact a very important point, and one that I'll return to at various points in the book – the increasing role of the individual in social networks and the decreasing value of websites and the news and information you can get from them.

It isn't a single entity

Did you know?
The most popular country domain is .tk, with over 18 million sites ending in it (http://research. domaintools.com/statistics/tld-counts). It is the domain for Tokelau, a territory of New Zealand.

This really does follow on from my previous point, which is to say that there is no such thing as 'the internet' to which you can point. Back in the late 1990s or early 2000s we would dip in and out of newsgroups or mailing lists, and these were seen as being very different to the recently emerging websites and web pages. However, even in those days we could see the beginnings of social networking and user-generated content as people began to create their own weblogs. People were beginning to realise that they could say what they wanted to without having to author websites and buy domains. These days we don't tend to focus on newsgroups and mailing lists any longer (though they still exist of course), but we spend our time in blogs, wikis, photograph-sharing websites, forums on book-sharing websites like GoodReads, Twitter streams and postings to say nothing of watching films and television series available on Netflix via our smart televisions.

Over the last decade the internet has slowly but surely morphed into a resource that allows individuals to share whatever they wish, from their innermost thoughts to photographs of their suppers. Moreover, they can do this with virtually no technical background knowledge or skill. The way in which people share this information has also changed as well. When I wanted to find people in my local area who were dog owners and walkers I didn't for a moment consider running a search on a traditional search engine to see if I could locate anyone – I went straight to Facebook. Once I found that no such group existed I created it in a matter of moments. It's now a thriving group of almost 2000 members and has proved to be extremely helpful and informative. With respect to search, the key thing to keep in mind, therefore, is that no one single search engine can do the job. If you want to search the internet effectively and quickly then it is necessary to have a good grasp and understanding of a wide variety of different search engines and an awareness of their strengths and weaknesses. Moreover, you need to have experience in, and an understanding of, many different social media platforms.

It's possible to use a wide variety of hardware and software

Once again, for a heading that's now about 15 years old, it's still as relevant today as it was when I first wrote it. As previously mentioned, an increasing number of people are using their smartphones to connect to the internet. There are many figures to illustrate this (and of course they're all different!), but it's a fair estimate to assume that at least 80% of internet users have a smartphone and use it to search the internet (www.smartinsights.com/mobile-marketing/mobile-marketing-analytics/mobile-marketing-statistics/).

However, people can also use their smart televisions, games consoles, smart watches and smart wristbands, to say nothing of household devices such as Amazon Alexa and Google Home. Finally, we must not forget the access that we have via various tablet devices as well as the more traditional laptop and desktop devices.

We should not underestimate the importance that this multiplicity of access is having to the way in which we search for, and find information. For instance, on 21 April 2015 Google expanded its use of mobile friendliness as a ranking factor. This is so important it's been named 'Mobilegeddon', 'Mobilepocalypse' and 'Mobocalypse'. Simply put, the more friendly that a website is to mobile devices, the higher it will rank in search results. Of course, pages with high-quality content will still show up in results, irrespective of how mobile-friendly they are, but it's a new factor that searchers should contend with.

Since we are now using a wider variety of both soft- and hardware, as well as the ubiquitous 'cloud' to store our data, we must once again remember that no single search engine is going to do it all for us.

It's difficult to say who is in charge

We have moved from a digitally lawless Wild West into an internet which is more controlled, as governments seek to impose their will on what users can do and see. Under the 'right to be forgotten', search engines have to be far more responsive to removing search results which are an unduly prominent part of an individual's internet footprint. Google has a page on their site which provides details of the requests that it receives to remove information from its products: www.google.com/transparencyreport/removals/government.

This figure continues to rise, from 1062 requests in December 2009 to almost 5000 in December 2015. The reasons for asking Google (and other search engines, to be fair) to remove content are varied; content that may be defamatory, content that violates local laws prohibiting hate speech or adult content, privacy and security or national security. Since Google started reporting on removal requests....in 2010 more than 33% of government removal requests have cited defamation as the reason for removal.

Google receives requests from all levels of government, such as court orders, local government agencies and law enforcement professionals. Sometimes these requests will ask for the removal of one specific piece of content, or perhaps multiple pieces. Google does not automatically remove links to the content in question, since some requests might not be specific enough, the content may already have been removed or they have not been made through the correct channels, or even because court orders are actually forgeries! Requests usually concern content on Blogger, Search and YouTube, but may be from any of Google's other products.

Some governments may wish to go further and limit what citizens are able to do or see on the internet. At the time of writing the British government is keen to limit access to pornographic material to only those sites that require some proof of age, although quite how that can be made to work is open to some doubt.

People are increasingly finding, to their cost, that they are legally responsible for the information that they share across their preferred social media platforms. Jurors have been chastised for sharing details of cases, individuals have been taken to court for making unsubstantiated claims on Twitter and others have been sent to jail for harassment.

On the other hand, people are making greater use of the 'dark web' to share information and to sell or buy illegal material. I'm sure that none of my readers have any interest in purchasing drugs or fake passports, but the dark web is the place to go for such items, and they can be paid for with bitcoins, making the transactions untraceable. People use virtual personal networks to view material and websites that they don't want others to know they have seen, and various browsers will mask the addresses that they are visiting.

Did you know?
Approximately 96% of the internet is dark or hidden (http://expandedramblings.com/index.php/internet-statistics).

Consequently, the struggle for control continues unabated, and as soon as one side thinks it has got the upper hand, someone will produce a new piece of technology to circumvent the restriction. As searchers we need to remember that what we see on the results page are not necessarily all that there is to be found and simply because a search engine or indeed a number of them do not return results on a particular person, company or event, that doesn't mean that information doesn't exist – simply that the engines are not displaying the links to it.

It's fast and effective

Given the existence of social media platforms, we have to revisit what the idea of 'news' really means. In pre-internet days news would be what you could find on the radio every hour, on the television news that evening or in the newspaper the next day. Professional news and updating might be once a month, or every quarter, depending on when the journal was released. However now, with tools and resources such as Twitter, 'news' is anything that happened about a second ago. Speaking from personal experience, I get most of my news reports from either Twitter, Facebook or text messages from various organisations that I have given my details to. It's a matter of a few moments to look at Facebook's 'Trending' section and I can get a quick overview of all the top stories or those in entertainment, sport, politics or science and technology (see Figure 1.1 on the next page).

TRENDING

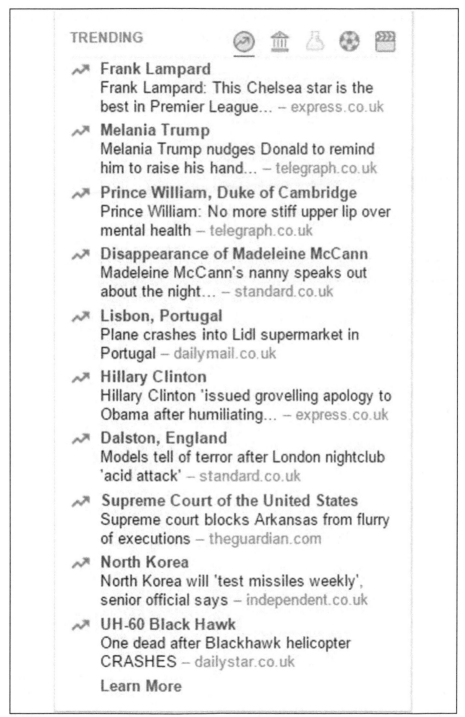

Frank Lampard
Frank Lampard: This Chelsea star is the best in Premier League... – express.co.uk

Melania Trump
Melania Trump nudges Donald to remind him to raise his hand... – telegraph.co.uk

Prince William, Duke of Cambridge
Prince William: No more stiff upper lip over mental health – telegraph.co.uk

Disappearance of Madeleine McCann
Madeleine McCann's nanny speaks out about the night... – standard.co.uk

Lisbon, Portugal
Plane crashes into Lidl supermarket in Portugal – dailymail.co.uk

Hillary Clinton
Hillary Clinton 'issued grovelling apology to Obama after humiliating... – express.co.uk

Dalston, England
Models tell of terror after London nightclub 'acid attack' – standard.co.uk

Supreme Court of the United States
Supreme court blocks Arkansas from flurry of executions – theguardian.com

North Korea
North Korea will 'test missiles weekly', senior official says – independent.co.uk

UH-60 Black Hawk
One dead after Blackhawk helicopter CRASHES – dailystar.co.uk

Learn More

Figure 1.1 *Trending topics in Facebook, Friday 13 January 2017*

I can then click on any of those links and read in more detail about the story, pulling content from a variety of different news websites.

News now comes from a wide variety of different sources as well. It used to be the province of the news reporter on the scene, with their cameraman, relaying the events 'back to the studio', and if we were really lucky the report would be live. However, since almost all of us have smartphones with cameras and video recording options, and we're linked via 4G networks to our social media accounts, we have all become journalists, only without the training and sensitivity that they may have. We seldom think 'Is it a good idea to share this?' and rather more consider how quickly we can get information out to a wider audience. Some people seem to want to get the news out quickly in the hope that it's going to go viral and they will have their own two minutes in the spotlight. As a result they may well be rather economical with the truth. Older images and videos are rebadged as happening a few moments ago, images are photoshopped to make a scene more interesting or exciting and news stories are quite simply invented.

The searcher has something of a dilemma at this point because we want to make sure that we have the most current information to give to our enquirer, so speed is of the essence. However – so is accuracy! 2016 saw the rise of fake news stories, particularly surrounding the US Presidential election and the word of the year, according to Oxford Dictionaries, was 'post-truth', an adjective meaning 'relating to or denoting circumstances in which objective facts are less influential in shaping public opinion than appeals to emotion and personal belief' (https://en.oxforddictionaries.com/word-of-the-year/word-of-the-year-2016). 'Just because it's on the internet doesn't mean that it is true' is something that we're all aware of, but we now have to remember that some sites have been created with the express purpose of trying to disseminate false information in the guise of news for various reasons. I'll look in more depth at this phenomenon, and discuss ways of dealing with it, in Chapter 10.

It's easy to talk to individuals or groups

If the internet is about anything, it's going to be about communicating. As I previously mentioned, I created a dog-walking group on Facebook for my local town. It's a very busy group, with people sharing a wide variety of things – pictures of their pets, advertising their dog-related services, asking for advice, setting up walks and so on. If I'm out on a walk and I see something particularly interesting I can photograph or video it, and share it directly with the group almost instantly. In the last few years technology has advanced apace, so it's now even easier to set up chatrooms, either textual or video-based, to have discussions, run training sessions or simply hang out with friends. Traditional blogs are being challenged by vlogs – video logs – and podcasts are still thriving. Moreover, we can do this on our smartphones or tablets, so 'outside broadcasting' is perfectly acceptable and easy to achieve.

If you want to have a discussion with a group the main problem these days is simply to decide how best to do this. Is it via Skype, Facebook video, Messenger, chatroom, or Twitter chat? All of these have their own unique advantages and disadvantages, and some of them allow the conversations to be archived and searched. As information professionals we can use this to our advantage by going straight to our clients and discussing their needs face to face, even if they are on the other side of the world. Of course, we could always do this with telephones, but visual communication conveys so much more, and we can quickly and easily share screenshots, live views of our monitors and so on.

It's not all hard work

I used to take this to mean that there were plenty of resources available on the internet for people to indulge in their hobbies. I think these days we can take that as a given, but if we start to look at this in terms of internet search and the effect that has we can very quickly see that people who have an interest in a particular subject or hobby are able to produce content and make it available on the web. Therefore, an increasing amount of authoritative content may well be produced by hobbyists or skilled amateurs and they will be making this information available in a variety of ways on a variety of platforms. Effective searchers must therefore once again be able to work out the authority and validity of content, not by the relatively simple means of assessing a website but by the far more difficult method of evaluating the information provided by specific individuals. Once again, search is becoming inextricably bound up with social media resources and if a search engine is going to succeed it has to be able to take individuals into account at least as much as, if not more than, traditional websites.

We also need to decide where to go in order to get the information that we need. I was recently asked to assess the merits of a particular airgun, which isn't something I have any knowledge of. I went to the manufacturer's website, which of course gave me lots of positive information about the product, but then they would. While it was useful to know the weight of the gun, and how powerful it was, that was only one part of the equation. I then looked on various enthusiasts sites before moving onto YouTube to check out some videos. There I was able to see the gun being fired and the thoughts and opinions of the people who had used it. It certainly took longer to get an answer than perhaps it might have done years ago, but I was able to get a far more rounded picture of facts, figures and opinions than would have been possible.

It's not just for 'geeks'

It used to be quite complicated to put information onto the internet, due to complicated HTML (hypertext mark-up language, the code used to create web pages) and so on. However, we have moved on since then and it's now extremely easy to share content, photographs, videos and so on. Moreover, with the general ease of use of smartphones, people can add content to the internet quickly and easily without even thinking about it. Not only are we all journalists, we are instant reporters and able to provide information on newsworthy events as they are occurring. The influence that this has had on search engines is quite profound, since they have to weigh up the various merits of the immediacy of the data with the uncertain authority of the person or organisation producing it. Late in 2016 Google came in for a great deal of criticism for posting a link to a news site reporting on the results of the US Presidential election which was giving completely inaccurate information. Their top news link for a search on 'final election results' went to a website that suggested Donald Trump had won both the popular and electoral college votes. No one is clear on why Google included that news story and website, but they did, resulting in considerable embarrassment for the search engine company.

So people can produce content, real or otherwise and make it available on the web for anyone to search for, find it and then use it. The search engines are caught in a cleft stick, because they want to make the results accurate, speedy and helpful, but also accurate. Furthermore, this information needs to be available to unskilled and technically illiterate users who don't know how to create a complicated search. This isn't a criticism of most users – it's only a tiny fraction of a single per cent of users who care about search; most people don't want to search, they just want to find. Consequently engines are now engaged in personalisation – particularly Google. They want to ensure that anyone can go to run a search and get exactly what they need with as little input as possible. Of course, in order to do this, they need to understand what searchers are interested in, so that when a user searches for 'apple' they are able to take the term, work out what the user is interested in and display results where the search term is used in the correct context. This has several implications. First, search engines have to watch and remember what searchers look for, and the sort of result that they click on. So in order for the searcher to get accurate results quickly they have to surrender some of their privacy. Secondly, the engine will create what Eli Pariser has termed 'filter bubbles' (www.ted.com/talks/eli_pariser_beware_online_filter_bubbles) and this basically means that searchers will see results that the search engine thinks that we want, without exposing us to different or alternative viewpoints. Now, that's not a problem for the average user who simply wants to check basic facts and figures, but when they are researching a subject it's not enough to get material that supports a pre-existing position. Thirdly, there may well be times when the searcher wants to look for information about a different type of 'apple' and they have to fight against the search engine's assumptions as to what they want.

As a result, it becomes more and more difficult to respond to an enquirer by giving them information couched in the terms 'do a search for your keyword and you'll find the result that you need is the third one down' since the third result down for them is not necessarily the same third result as seen by the searcher. There are of course many ways around this – not least by using search engines that do not personalise results or track searches. Even simply logging out of a Google account will to some extent reduce this risk. It's all too easy to forget this however, but skilled searchers will always keep in the back of their mind the fact that they are often searching on behalf of other users rather than themselves, and the personalised results that they may receive are not necessarily the best results for the original enquirer.

It's not well organised

This should not come as a surprise to anyone, and it is as true today as it has ever been. In fact, I would go so far as to say that the longer the internet exists, the more disorganised and chaotic it becomes, and I see no sign of this stopping. It's a simplification to say that we used to just have web pages, e-mail and newsgroups, but it's not too far off the mark. Now, however, we have multimedia, social networks, apps on smartphones, home hubs, hundreds if not thousands of domain extensions, the 'internet of things' and more. All of these are being added without any reference to anyone else and although there are a few bodies that oversee the development of the internet such as ICANN (the Internet Corporation for Assigned Names and Numbers), these are few and far between. This is both an advantage and a disadvantage for the searcher. It's an advantage because it makes our job more interesting and challenging and more difficult because it means that we have to search in an ever-increasing number of places using a wider variety of tools than ever before.

It's growing at an enormous rate

Did you know?
74.8% of the top 10 million websites are English, Russian, Japanese, German and Spanish (https://en.wikipedia.org/wiki/Languages_used_on_the_Internet).

It's almost pointless to try and give you any kind of statistics about internet growth, since any figures I find at the time of writing will be completely inaccurate at the time of reading. However, rather than do nothing, if I provide some figures now you can, if you are so inclined, compare them with the figures that are accurate to the time when you are reading this. 3.2 billion people use the internet, 44% of the world population has access to the internet, 82.2% of people in developing countries have internet access and 96% of the internet is 'dark' or hidden (http://expandedramblings.com/index.php/internet-statistics). Facebook has over 1.79 billion users, making it the largest 'country' in the world if users were equated to populations, and 1.13 trillion 'likes' have been pressed. Facebook sees 100 million hours of daily video watch time and if one person wanted to emulate that, it would take 11,415 years. Twitter users send 500 million tweets per day and it has 317 million monthly active users. Two new professional accounts are created on LinkedIn every second and 40% of users check it daily. 95 million photographs and videos are posted to Instagram every single day and the average user spends 25 minutes a day on the platform. The average number of monthly searches on Pinterest is 2 billion and 75 billion pins have been created. 400 million Snapchat stories are created every day, and it has 150 million users active on a daily basis (https://socialpilot.co/blog/151-amazing-social-media-statistics-know-2017). Google processes over 40,000 searches every second, which works out to 3.5 billion per day and 1.2 trillion searches per year (www.internetlivestats.com/google-search-statistics). I could continue in a similar vein for the rest of the chapter, if not the entire book, but I'm sure that you get the point that I want to make.

Consequently, it's simply not possible for a single search engine, or even a dozen search engines to index, arrange and make available all of that information. Unfortunately, however, it's our job as skilled researchers to try and do rather better! Rather than making things simpler and easier the easy access to applications which make us all content creators has in actual fact made it that much harder to find the information that we require. In order to solve this thorny problem search engines have to improve, people have to help others, and searchers need to explore an ever-increasing number of avenues to find the information that they need.

Did you know?
10.2% of adults in the UK in 2016 had never used the internet (www.ons.gov.uk/businessindustryandtrade/itandinternetindustry/bulletins/internetusers/2016).

Search engines

I would like to be able to say that the search engine industry is flourishing, and that we are experiencing a golden age of access to data in a quick simple and easy manner. However, this is far from the truth, and in fact, I think that as searchers, we are going through very lean times indeed. However, before I get into that, let's make one point perfectly clear from the outset – search engine companies are not interested in search. They do not have as their core mission statement 'Let's help people find the information that they need quickly and easily'. In fact, what they are interested in is making money. Search is merely the way in which they have decided to put adverts in front of us. If there was no money to be made from advertising there would be no Google or Facebook. Google got to their position of prominence because they were the first company to really understand the link between the search that someone was running and the adverts that could be put in front of them. If someone was running a search on mobile phones, giving them a link to mobile phone companies may well result in a clicked advertising link, resulting in money for the engine. In fact, if you think about it, search engines have a real problem due to this model. If they are really good at search, and you can find what you want quickly and easily, you're not going to need to see adverts – you can just go direct to the page or company site that you're interested in; the search engine company has made no money out of you or your search. On the other hand, if the searcher can't find what they want, they are more likely to look around the page, see an advert that they think may answer their query and click on the link. Bingo! The search engine has just made a small amount of money. So why should search engines spend a lot of money and engineers time making search more effective?

A second, and equally cynical, point that also needs to be made is that you, as the searcher, are not a user of search engines; the users of search engines are the advertisers, and all of us are simply the fodder that is required in order to make them money. So search engines are not your friends, and never assume that they have your interests at heart.

Following on from this, search engines do not have to be excellent at search – they simply have to be good enough for the vast majority of users. Don't forget that these people, and that includes all of us for most of the time, don't want to search, they want to find. They're not interested in the intricacies of search; they just need to know the name of the plumber down the road, the 12th President of the United States or the GDP of Thailand. Search engine developers will only introduce new functionality and techniques if and when this will increase their revenue streams. Conversely, anything that doesn't do that is liable for the chop. Google has not developed its search engine functionality for years – in fact what it has been doing for the last six or seven years is actually cut away at search functionality, bit by bit. It used to be possible to direct Google to search for synonyms by using the tilde symbol, so a search for *~beginner* would return that word, but also similar words such as 'tutorial' and 'training', for example. Users were able to limit results to particular reading levels, or to see which sites linked to the page or site that they were interested in. They could limit results to pages that they had already looked at, or those that they hadn't. None of this functionality is available today, and it would not surprise me at all if by the end of this year Google cuts more search functions – I'd certainly be astonished if they actually brought in any new ones!

So what does this mean for the searcher? The key point here is not to have any loyalty whatsoever to any search engine; remember my earlier point – you are the fodder, not the user. Their only interest in you is as someone who can make them some money. The idea of brand loyalty for search engines simply should not exist, and while I understand the temptation to 'Google it', that's not always going to be the best course of action. Instead, exhibit the behaviour of a discerning shopper in a large mall; go from counter to counter, shop to shop to seek out the best bargains, or in our case from engine to engine to find the best functionality that you can. If you don't get what you want with one search engine, go onto the next until you do find what you seek. By all means go back to your favourite shop/search engine, but don't let that be your only choice.

Also remember that new search engines appear all the time; I hear about new ones on a weekly basis. It's always worth exploring a new engine to see what it does differently. Have a few favourite searches that you're familiar with and that you know will give you good results, and try them out on anything new. Yes, I know that it takes a few minutes of your time, and sometimes that time will be wasted, but if you don't explore and don't try out new things you will be destined to continue along the same old paths. If you don't change what you've always done you'll only ever have what you've already got. Be ruthless in your approach and once a search engine fails to deliver on a consistent basis, just drop it and move onto something else. Don't get attached to search engines – you're simply getting attached to familiarity, and although most people don't like change, in the fast-moving world of the internet and search, change is the normal way of doing business. Once you start to rely on a particular search engine you will become a less than successful searcher. That does not of course mean that you can't have your preferences, because we all do, but it does mean that your head needs to rule your heart.

In the last paragraph I mentioned that I hear about new search engines every week, but in the previous edition of the book I mentioned that I heard about new ones on a daily basis. I think that the search engine industry as a whole is not nearly as healthy now as it was a few years ago. Looking back over my blog for the last couple of years (www.philbradley.typepad.com), I have spent longer talking about search engines that have closed their doors than I have with new ones opening up. We've lost engines such as Socialmention, Smashfuse, ChaCha, Alternative.to, 10x10, Sulia, Silobreaker, Eye.in, Swayy, Mahalo, Blekko, Infomine and so on. Of course, that has to be balanced against the new ones that have come into play, some of which I'll be focusing on in the book, but overall I think that the market does look particularly bleak at the moment for anyone who is thinking of starting a new search engine venture.

Having said all of that, I don't want to paint a completely bleak picture of internet search engines, or to be overly cynical. Internet search is still a vibrant and exciting area, and one that is constantly changing. For the last 20 years or so I have run a course entitled 'Advanced Internet Searching' and it is still as popular today as it has ever been. There's very little that I teach now which is the same as when I started however, and I am always updating my presentation to take account of new changes in the landscape. As we shall see in later chapters, there are many opportunities to explore different resources, many of them far more powerful now than we would have thought possible even a few years ago.

Failing resources

As well as search engines, plenty of other resources are going out of fashion. There is no point in devoting entire chapters to resources such as USENET newsgroups or mailing lists, as I did in earlier editions; these days they are worth little more than footnotes. There are many reasons why resources fail. People like to move onto the 'latest thing', and that may well be something that is mobile which they can use in the form of an app on their smartphone. Newsgroups have been largely superseded by Facebook groups or LinkedIn groups; indeed, I can't remember the last time that I looked at a newsgroup –

it was probably when I was researching the previous edition! Intelligent agents were at one point touted as the next best thing to sliced bread, and they were supposed to hunt out new information for us on the internet and bring it back to us. That never really came to fruition, and the role has now been commandeered by various news apps that you can get, both online and mobile. Many users will be familiar with tools such as Flipboard which they use on their tablets, although my personal favourite Zite died a death a few years ago.

People don't use bookmarking services such as Delicious any longer; there's very little interest in them and I don't see much reference to them any longer. Once again the role of storing your favourite places online has been taken over by tools such as Pinterest, Google Keep and Facebook Saved items, to say nothing of other tools such as Symbaloo and Pearltrees that are far more elegant and easy-to-use tools.

Mailing lists continue to exist, although I think that it is fair to say that they are in the main within the realm of academia rather than more general public use. They flourished in the past due to the prevalent use of e-mail, as it was very easy for people to disseminate the messages that they wished to larger groups of people, and to have general discussions. Nowadays however people are using apps such as WhatsApp, Kik, Instagram and instant messaging to communicate with friends and colleagues. Nonetheless, we cannot and should not forget about the existence of these resources because, depending on the enquiry that we have their archival value is still very important.

The information mix

Effective internet searching is part science, part art, part skill and part luck. Most of all, however, it's an effective blend of different resources, search engines, apps, websites and a willingness to look for information wherever it might be, and for however long it takes. This comes as no surprise to an information professional, of course, but the average user will in all probability not have the experience, knowledge, understanding or tenacity to blend those together into a successful search. Once you add into the mix the increase in user-generated content, and the fake and false news that is pumped out on an hourly basis, it becomes increasingly difficult to get anything but the simplest of information quickly and easily.

In this book I'm really not going to spend any time at all on traditional resources, but we should never forget that traditional resources such as books, databases on CD-ROM, or even microfiche still have an important part to play. Therefore, please do consider their value and encourage your users to explore them because, after all, a successful search is one where you get the right answer, irrespective of where it comes from.

Summary

In this opening chapter I hope that I have at least in some part laid down some markers that relate to where internet search is now, and where it has been in the past. While it's very easy to mindlessly spout out the statement that 'it's all on Google' it is not only a fallacy, but a dangerous one at that. In the rest of the book I'll spend time looking at different types of search engines that are available and I'll look at their advantages and disadvantages. I'll also focus on a few search engines that I think are of particular interest within each category and will show you how to get the most out of them. Internet searching is a fascinating and enjoyable activity (in some cases it's also a hobby as well) and I hope that you'll be as interested and intrigued about it as I am, and get sucked into the field.

CHAPTER 2

An introduction to search engines

Introduction

I'll start this chapter by asking you a question: 'How many search engines do you think that there are on the internet?' The chances are fairly high (and I know this, because I ask this question a lot) that your immediate reaction will be to provide a figure in the region of perhaps ten or a dozen. If you're wildly optimistic, you might reach for several hundred, or even a thousand. In actual fact, no one has any idea as to how many search engines are available, and there are a few reasons for this. First, there's no central database of them, so we can't get a definitive number. Secondly, as we saw in the previous chapter, the market is very volatile, with engines disappearing and others appearing on a regular basis. Thirdly, it depends on your definition of a search engine, and I'll come to that in a moment. However, that doesn't help us reach any sort of answer at all. I used to keep a listing of country-based search engines, but when it reached 5000 it was simply too much work to keep up to date. I ran several searches to see if I could track down any sort of figure but found very little. I ran searches for '400,000 search engines' and was able to increase this to '600,000', mainly from sites offering to submit your website to that number of engines. I also ran a search for the phrase 'use our search engine' and had over 800,000 results. None of these are figures that I'm prepared to trust, but I've always gone with a figure that suggests up to about 400,000 of them, and no one has contradicted me yet, so that's a figure that I'm going with, but remember, that's little more than a shot in the dark!

Did you know?
The very first search engine was called 'Archie', which hosted a collection of directory listings, and began as a university project in 1987 (https://en.wikipedia.org/wiki/Archie_search_engine).

If you find this figure just too remarkable to believe, I'd ask you to hold back on your scepticism for a few moments. 'How many search engines do you think that there are on the internet?' isn't a trick question, but it does rely on your own definition of what a search engine is. If your answer to my original question was in single digits than I'll take a stab in the dark and say that your immediate definition was something along the lines of Google, so you're thinking of Bing, DuckDuckGo and maybe Yandex here. So the question that you're actually answering in your head is 'How many search engines like Google do you think there are on the internet?' and if that was the case, you could easily justify half a dozen or so. On the other hand, if your definition of an internet search engine was along the lines of 'any search engine that's on the internet searching anything at all' then we're looking at an entirely different concept, with a totally different number attached to it. Your answer would include search engines that were limited to searching a single site, for example, or it may be an engine that was limited to searching a discrete body of data, such as the BT telephone directory. In such cases you may well find web authors using terms such as 'use our search engine', and we're into the hundreds of thousands. So – not a trick question, but perhaps one that could have been more specific and more precisely worded!

If I had said to you 'How many reference books are there?' I suspect that your answer would have been along the lines of 'Nobody knows!' Of course, that's perfectly true, but what we can do is to separate out reference works into various categories, such as encyclopaedias and dictionaries. Each of these types of reference work will exhibit their own behaviours and have their own set of defining criteria. While we still don't get an answer to our question, we can at least start to break it down into something that's rather more manageable to work with. Now, search engines can be viewed in exactly the same way – although we don't know how many there are, we can break them down into types.

Search engine criteria

We can look at various criteria that help us define what sort of search engines are available, and which engine fits into which category.

What sort of data do they index and make available to us? This may be web

Did you know?
The 'Search-Wise' search engine, at www.search-wise.net, isn't a real search engine at all, it's a prop that's used in television programmes and films when actors need to be seen running an internet search.

pages, data contained within files such as PowerPoint, tweets, social media-based information, images, sound files, videos and so on. The way in which search engines find their data is another thing to take into account; some will actively go out onto the internet to find information, retrieve it, index it and go out searching for more, while other engines are far more passive, and wait for a web author to come to them and inform them of the existence of a site. We can consider the way in which the results are displayed to us – is it in a text-based format, with one result following on from the next, or is it in a far more visual format, with thumbnails of results placed onto the screen for us?

Some search engines will have as their USP (unique selling point) the fact that they don't track users, either by way of the searches themselves or the IP address that the searcher is using to contact the engine. Yet other engines will take as their starting point an existing URL that's supplied to them by the searcher, and they will then scour the internet to find other, similar sites. There are search engines that will just search the hidden, deep or dark web (not necessarily all the same thing, as we shall discuss later), and which need special software to access them. We must also remember that there are search engines that are only used in a mobile smartphone or tablet environment.

I could go into more detail, but I think the point is clear – there are many types of search engines, all of them doing different things and returning information in different ways. They all have their own advantages and disadvantages, and in the rest of this chapter I shall look at them in a little more detail in order to give you an indication as to which type of engine you might want to use when.

Free-text search engines

Free text search engines are very easy to describe, and indeed they are the type that you're already most familiar with. You can simply search for a single word, a number of words or perhaps a phrase. You're not limited in your choice; you could search for the name of a company, a line of poetry or a song lyric, a number, someone's name, a word in a different language – just about anything. They will have a search box and you are **free** to type in any **text** that you'd like to. If this sounds fairly obvious, that's because it is. It's the format used by Google, Bing and some of the other major search engines that you'll already be familiar with.

This approach has advantages and disadvantages, as you would expect. Free-text search engines are very useful if you know exactly what it is that you're looking for, or if you are looking for a concept that can be defined in a small number of words. They are less useful if you want a broad overview of a subject, or are searching in a subject area that you don't know very well and consequently have no real idea about what are the best terms to use in your search. There are a great many search engines in this category, so if you really do think that you need to explore a few try the obvious examples of Google (www.google.com or a country variant such as www.google.co.uk), Microsoft's alternative to Google, Bing, at www.bing.com, DuckDuckGo at www.duckduckgo.com or Yandex at www.yandex.com.

The search functionality of these engines is quite varied; the key players will provide a reasonable amount of sophistication, with Yandex well out in front at the moment, though of course this is always open to change. Search engines in this category which are not so well known or used do tend to be quite limited in the way in which you can search them, to the point of only allowing you to enter some terms; the idea of Boolean operators is well beyond their capability! What you'll also find with the key players is that they will provide you with far more access to resources; they will index content within specific files and they will also give searchers options to look for news, images, videos and so on. In fact, it can be quite difficult to identify exactly what you can and cannot do with an engine, since their key demographic is not the sophisticated searcher, but the one who wants to find, not search. Ease of use is therefore far more important in that situation than the bells and whistles of Boolean operators and other advanced search functionality.

Data collection

In order to use search engines effectively it is necessary to have some background knowledge of the ways in which they work, and in particular, how they collect the information that they can then give you in the SERPS (search engine results pages). After all, if you don't know where the information comes from, you have no way of knowing if you have got all of it or not, and if you need to continue your search. Free-text search engines will make use of 'spiders', 'robots' or 'crawlers' (all the terms are interchangeable) and these are tools that spend their time exploring web page after web page. It's a simplification, but I hope an acceptable one (otherwise the explanation would drone on for page after technical page) to say that they will look at a page, include it in their index database and index it down to the word level. Once the page has been digested, as it were, the spider will follow a link to another page, do the same exact thing again and continue on. The software will take into account new sites, new pages, changes to the content on existing pages and any dead links that it discovers. The Google crawler, named 'Googlebot', has indexed over 100,000,000 gigabytes, and an unspecified number of actual web pages, but it's certainly in the trillions.

At some unspecified time in the future the crawler will return to the site to reindex it. When it does that is based mainly on how often the pages on a site are updated. After all, it's a waste of the crawler's time if it keeps revisiting pages that haven't changed in months or years. So the crawler makes a note when it last visited, and if it finds that a web page has changed since the last visit it will know that it needs to come back more frequently in the future. A quicker second visit may well also show the crawler that content has changed again and so once again, the time between visits will be reduced. For particularly important or busy pages such as a news website, crawling will take place almost all of the time to ensure that the most accurate and up-to-date information is made available. On the other hand, if the crawler finds that the page hasn't changed since the last visit it will delay revisiting, and if it leaves it even longer and the page is still the same the next visit might well be weeks, if not months. It's important to be clear at this point – when you search the internet you're not actually searching the internet, you're interrogating a search engine's index of the pages that it has found. There are two important implications here that need to be addressed. The first is that, although some engines will index trillions of pages, that's still only a small portion of the internet; somewhere between about 5% and 10%. Just because a search engine doesn't return a particular page for you doesn't mean that it doesn't exist: it means that the search engine you're using simply may not have discovered and indexed it. Consequently, if you don't find the answer that you want using one search engine, go off and try another, because that one may have indexed the exact page and information that you need. After all, you wouldn't stop looking for an answer because the first reference book you looked in didn't have the information you needed: as a matter of course you'd go onto the next one and keep going until you had success. The second implication is that in all probability you're not going to be looking at a current page in the SERPS – it will be the page that the crawler brought back some time previously. So if you've ever visited a page and you haven't found the information that you were expecting, it could well be because the web author changed the content on the page after the last crawl and the search engine doesn't know the page has been updated. Depending on the search engine that you're using, if you're in any doubt, it's worth checking to see if it offers a 'cached' version of the page, which is to say the copy of the page that it has on record. In Google you can simply click on the small half-diamond next to an address and choose to view the cache. You can see this in operation in Figures 2.1 and 2.2 on the next page.

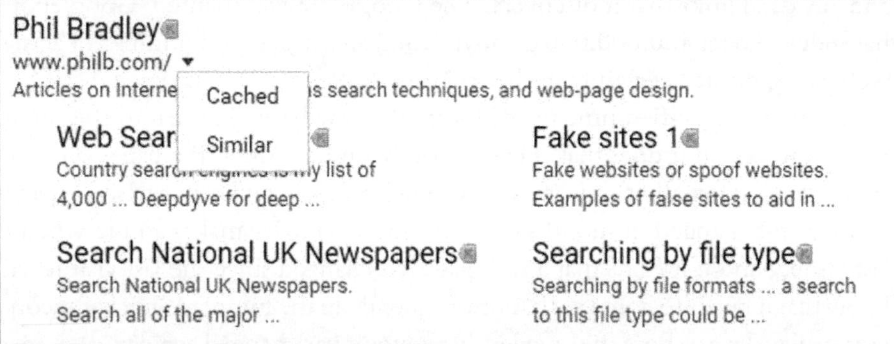

Figure 2.1 *The down arrow symbol on Google, giving you access to the link to a cached version of the page that Google holds*
Google and the Google logo are registered trademarks of Google Inc., used with permission

This is Google's cache of http://www.philb.com/. It is a snapshot of the page as it appeared on Apr 16, 2017 22:52:10 GMT. The current page could have changed in the meantime. Learn more

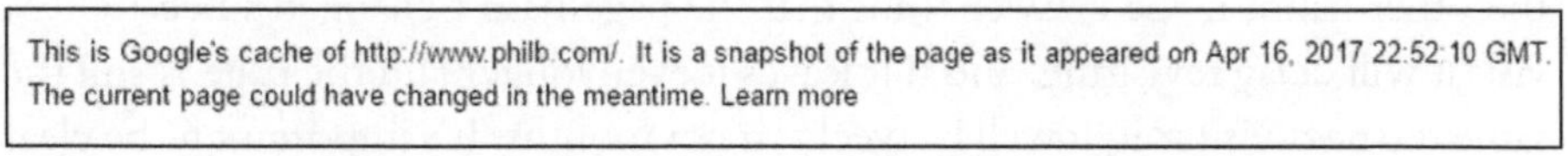

Figure 2.2 *Details of the data that Google can provide with regard to the cached version of the page; in this instance my home page was crawled yesterday*
Google and the Google logo are registered trademarks of Google Inc., used with permission

Alternatively you can simply search for *cache:<URL>* in the Google search box and go directly to that information.

Relevance ranking

So, to recap, when you search using a free-text search engine, you're actually interrogating its database of web pages. The searcher then types in their search, say 'fox red Labradors', and the software will then search through the index to find every page that includes those search terms. I ran this exact search and Google told me that there were almost 200,000 results. What that actually means is that there are 200,000 pages that include the words 'fox' and 'red' and 'Labrador' on them. The search engine then has to decide which of all of those pages are the best match for my query and so it will run through several hundred algorithms. For example, if the three words of my query are next to each other, that's regarded as a better result than one in which the words are all over the page. Whether the words are in the title of the page, the position on the page, the number of times the words are repeated, the number and quality of links pointing to the page, how quickly it loads – these are all other things that the engine will take into account. Once all of these calculations have been made the engine will return the list of results to you, hopefully in an ordered list that will give you the most relevant result at the top of the list.

This is generally referred to as 'relevance ranking' and the way in which this is done – the algorithms I mentioned – will differ from search engine to search engine. At this point we come up against another issue – since each search engine has its own way of working out why one page is more appropriate than another they will all give you different results. If you take into account the fact that they are all crawling the web finding different collections of documents it very quickly becomes obvious that the results you get can differ quite wildly from engine to engine. Once again, this shouldn't come as that much of a surprise. If I'm looking at an American encyclopaedia for example, I'd expect to find more information on the American Civil War than I would from a British one, and more on the English Civil war on a British one and less from the American counterpart.

Results will also differ for a number of other reasons as well. Some search engines will try and 'personalise' your search results based on what you have searched for previously, what you have clicked on, the adverts that you have looked at, your IP address (which tells the engine where you are physically in the real world) and the type of device that you're using to connect to the engine. So if two people do exactly the same search it should come as no surprise if the results are completely different. As a searcher it's important to remember this, because your 'third result down' is probably not going to be the same 'third result down' as the one that your enquirer gets if she tries the search herself.

Another issue that must be considered when looking at results from these engines is that it's quite easy to 'game' them. That is to say, if a skilled Search Engine Optimiser knows how a search engine ranks its results it is possible to write a page that 'ticks all of the boxes' and includes the keywords in the title, the URL, repeated several times on the page and so on. As a result it's possible to affect the search engine results themselves, and there are companies which are employed for exactly that purpose. So it's important to remember that just because a site's page is in the top ten results, it does not necessarily mean that it is a good quality and authoritative site; often it's quite the opposite.

In summary, free-text search engines are excellent if you wish to get a comprehensive set of results based on some specific keywords or phrases that

Did you know?
One of the most successful web search engines in the world is one you probably haven't heard of: Baidu, at www.baidu.com, is a Chinese search engine and, depending on figures, the fourth most popular in the world.

you're familiar with. However, it's a bad idea to become overly reliant on one specific search engine, in exactly the same way that it's not good to just go to the same reference book for every search. Try various search engines to see what they can return in the SERPS for you; you will get a better set of results in total if you do.

Index- or directory-based search engines

These search engines are becoming increasingly sidelined due to their inflexibility and small database sizes. An index-based engine (the term directory can be used instead if you prefer) works on a very different principle to that of a free-text search engine. The creators of an engine such as this will decide on their 'universe' of subject matter and will create headings and subheadings accordingly. So for example, if we take a look at the World Wide Web Virtual Library at http://vlib.org we'll see that under 'Information and Libraries' we have subsections on Advanced Browsing, Electronic Journals, Information Design, Information Quality, Knowledge Management and Published Subject Indicators. Under Information Quality we then have subsections on subjects such as Building Quality Resources, Evaluation of Information Resources, Ethics and Netiquette, and so on. The most famous example of this type of search engine was the Yahoo! Directory, which was very popular towards the end of the last century, and it was one of the really big players in the search engine market at that time. However the directory was closed at the end of 2014.

The reason that this type of engine has almost completely disappeared is the way in which data was gathered with which to populate the directory. As we have already seen with free-text search engines, they are very active in going out and finding information. An index-based engine relies on web authors discovering it, locating the correct heading and subheading for the subject matter of their website and then contacting the editor of that subheading themselves. The editor will then look at the requested entry and decide if it will be included or not. You should note here that I'm talking about websites, rather than individual pages, and this is a big disadvantage, because engines of this type can only ever be stepping stones to get you the information you want. If you are interested in the correct food to feed to a kitten, for example, you can do an immediate search on a free-text engine and get a page of results which give you exactly the information that you need. With an index-based approach you have first got to identify a website, then visit it, and then see if you can find the answer to your query – which may or may not be there. So index search engines can only ever act as a stepping stone.

On the other hand, these engines do provide a good overview of a particular subject, which can be useful if you do not know much about the subject you're searching for. Simply by looking through general and then more specific subject headings you can get ideas and suggestions as to the best way to look at the subject you're interested in. These engines are also useful because they will give you an overview of a small number of websites that are focused on a particular subject area, so it may in fact save you some time instead of forcing you to wade through page after page of results from the SERPS. Finally – although I wouldn't want to push this too far – because sites included in the database have been viewed and vetted by human editors they may possibly be of a more authoritative and accurate nature than you'll find with the results from free-text search engines. However, although these are advantages they can in no way compete with the growth of websites or social media-based user-generated content. These days you are most likely to find an index search engine in very specific subject areas, or as a country-focused search engine.

In summary, index search engines are increasingly looking very old-fashioned and worn out. There's very little value in them and you'll only really find them in very niche subject areas. By all means take a look at any that you find, but if you decide to exclude them from your searching strategies no one will think any the less of you.

Multi- and meta-search engines

These search engines are not really search engines at all, if we're being particularly pedantic about it. What these engines do is act as a go-between for the searcher and the search engine. A multi-search engine will list various engines that it works with: e.g. Trovando, at www.trovando.it, claims to work with 3351 other engines and it provides you with a search box and a list of those same engines. To run your search you simply type in your words or phrase and click on a search engine name. The multi-search engine will then pass your query directly onto the engine of choice and will display the results on the screen for you to see. You can then click on another engine and the process continues until you are satisfied with your results. A meta-search engine, on the other hand, will take the query that you have asked, pass it onto a number of search engines of its (sometimes your) choosing, get the results back, de-duplicate the results and then display the SERPS, usually in order of the web page that was found by most of the other engines and in the case of a tie, which was rated most highly in the top ten. It's then possible to simply click on one set of results after another and move back and forth between them.

These engines are useful if you want to obtain a reasonably comprehensive listing of results without have to spend an inordinate amount of time visiting search engine after search engine, re-running the search and remembering the results from the last ones that you looked at. Bearing in mind the previously explained limitations of using a single search engine, it does make sense to cover all your bases and run a search that quickly and easily searches many engines at once. Unfortunately, the advantage of these search engines – that they provide you with access to so many other engines – is also their downfall. The searcher is submitting his or her search to a number of different engines and consequently each engine needs to understand the syntax being used. Therefore searchers need to know that each engine used by the multi-search engine understands what is being asked of it. As a result, it's necessary to run searches to the lowest common denominator without using any advanced syntax to focus the search more closely. Unfortunately – and it's sad to have to say this – a lot of these engines are not kept up to date. They list search engines that no longer exist, for example, so you end up with a blank page instead of useful results. While I find Trovando useful, I counted over a dozen engines in its top listing which were no longer available. This is disappointing, and it would be remiss of me not to report it.

In summary, although these engines do have the limitations that I've just mentioned they can be an excellent way for a novice searcher to quickly experience and explore the results that they will get from using a wide variety of search engines which they may previously have been unaware of. They are also a great way to keep out of the search engine rut and remind you of the wide variety of choice available to you.

Visual search engines

The vast majority of engines will display their SERPS on the screen for you in a text-based format, allowing perhaps for the display of a few images or stills from videos. If you are lucky some search engines will give you the opportunity of previewing a result, either by displaying it for you on the screen within the search engine results themselves, or with a mouse click that gives you the opportunity of looking at a thumbnail version of the page that is being returned in the results. There may, however, be times when you want to skim through a lot of results quickly and this is where the use of a visual search engine comes into play.

Rather than a standard list on the screen you will be able to see thumbnails of all of the pages that have been returned, although the term 'thumbnail' tends to imply the images are quite small. They're actually large, certainly large enough to look at the actual text on the returned page. You can then flick between one page and the next by use of the mouse with a click-and-drag motion. These can be really helpful if you're looking for information that has a large visual component to it – for example, a search for images from the Hubble Telescope. By displaying screen shots from the results it may well become obvious very quickly as to which of them are going to be most helpful – at least from the visual aspect!

Hidden, invisible, deep and dark web search engines

Before talking about these engines in any kind of detail, let's start by defining and explaining the terms used in the heading. 'Hidden', 'invisible', and 'deep' web essentially mean the same thing, and 'dark' is something different as I'll explain.

The hidden web

Much highly specialised data is contained in databases that can only be accessed by using a password, running a search directly on a website, or taking out a paid subscription to a service. This would, for example, include the data in genealogical databases, Yellow Pages, some newspaper archives and the databases of telephone companies. All of this information is available to you (either free or for a fee), but 'hidden' from traditional search engines. Free-text search engines cannot go to these databases, run searches and index the results; even if they were allowed to, it would be an almost impossible task for them to do.

Some web authors, for whatever reason, may well choose not to allow a search engine to index their content. They can place a small text file on their site and crawlers will check to see if this is present before searching and indexing the site. The crawler may be told not to index anything at all, or it may only be allowed to index certain pages or folders and not others. You may wonder why this is the case, so let me give you a quick example. If an author is running a quiz on his or her site, and the answer is in the form of a URL to another page on the site, an enterprising player could simply ask a search engine to list all of the pages that it had found, thus destroying the quiz nature of the game.

No one knows how much information is hidden; by its very nature, if it's hidden we simply can't tell. Estimates in the early 2000s suggested the figure could be in the region of 4–500 times larger than the surface web. If you spend any time searching for an answer you'll see estimates that suggest an engine such as Google can only index 4–10% of all of the information that's available. That's a figure that I've seen reported consistently over many years, and since the surface and deep web will increase exponentially in size it's a figure that I think most of us can work with.

In order to access this information you have two basic approaches. First, do some lateral thinking and use a traditional search engine to identify a website that may well provide you with access to the data that you actually require. If you need someone's phone number you might identify that BT has a directory by running an initial search for *telephone number uk* or something similar. Then once you're at the site, look for the person that you need a number for. Alternatively, there are various engines and search resources that at the very least will identify a large number of databases for you to try. These are rather more like the stepping stone variety of search engine that I mentioned previously – the index/directory type – and exhibits a number of similar characteristics to both these and multi-search engines. Librarians used to create a lot of these guiding tools, but almost all of them have been closed or discontinued. An example is SOSIG – the Social Science Information Gateway – which aimed to provide a trusted selection of high-quality resources for students, academics, researchers and practitioners in social science, business and law. Unfortunately there is no single listing of all of these engines, so there isn't an easy or fast way of searching them, but this is where the skill of the information worker comes into play: first by identifying appropriate search engines or databases and then working out how to get the best value out of them.

The dark web

The dark web is something very different. It's a term that refers to a collection of websites that are publicly available, but which hide the addresses of the servers that run them. Consequently it's very hard to know who has created the sites and where they are. They hide their identity using an encryption tool called TOR, and in order to visit such a site the user needs to be using a TOR browser to access it. They don't all have to use it, and some will use other similar services, but the principle remains the same – a high degree of anonymity. As a result of this, a lot of the content on the dark web is dubious, morally and ethically questionable or simply illegal. The 'Silk Road' is a good example of this, and it has been used to buy and sell recreational drugs. It's unlikely that you'll need to spend much, or indeed any, time there, but if you work for a law enforcement organisation, for example, it may be useful to know how much a passport costs on the black market. I won't go into great detail (if you need to know, you will gain enough skills by reading this book to research it for yourself!), but you need a special browser, and will then need to connect to particular search engines and indexes that allow you to find the information that you need. Please, however, be aware that you will certainly find unpleasant and very disturbing material in the dark web and the Hidden Wiki at https://thehiddenwiki.org will give you a very clear indication of what you'll find. Unless you have a clear need and requirement to visit it, my advice is to stay well clear!

Multimedia search engines

One of the largest search engines in the world, which is used on a daily basis by millions of people, is also one of the most overlooked as a search engine. That's to say YouTube. 1.3 billion people use the service and almost 5 billion videos are watched every day (https://fortunelords.com/youtube-statistics). The internet is increasingly becoming a visual resource, so it's always worth considering if a video could answer a query that a user has. However, there are also many other multimedia search engines which are limited to retrieving images, sound files, podcasts and so on. Some of the previously mentioned search engines, particularly free-text ones, will provide researchers with options to search for that type of data without having to go to the inconvenience of visiting other engines. As a cynical aside, it also means that searchers will stay on their sites for longer and are consequently bombarded with even more adverts. However, it may well be worth choosing a specific engine for the specific purpose of hunting down information in a particular format, and this is especially true of copyright- and royalty-free images, for example. It's also worth mentioning that a good search engine will provide researchers with the opportunity of searching for data in different file formats such as .pdf or .ppt but, once again, there are specialised search engines that focus just on different file formats.

Social media search engines

With the dramatic increase in social media resources – blogs, microblogging platforms, social networks, photograph-sharing sites, apps and so on, we've seen an equally dramatic rise in the amount of data that is published via these resources. It's pointless to provide figures, since they will be woefully inaccurate even in the few months it will take to publish this book, so I would suggest that if you want to keep up to date, simply do a search for *internet minute* as a phrase and you'll see lots of infographics that will update you. However, if you want to get a feeling for growth towards the end of January 2017 we are looking, per minute, at 350,000 tweets, 527,000 photographs shared on Snapchat, 20,000,000 messages on WhatsApp and 2,500,000 search queries on Google. We have seen the publishing cycle go from months in the case of printed materials down to days in respect of websites, minutes when looking at blog postings and seconds with Twitter updates. Real-time searching therefore is becoming increasingly important, and traditional search engines simply cannot keep pace with the flood of user-generated content. The method used by traditional search engines when they are spidering and crawling web pages looks increasingly ponderous and old-fashioned when we need to find information that was published only seconds ago. We need to re-evaluate what we mean by 'news' and we also have to take into account authority and validity far more than ever before. 'Fake news' is becoming more and more of an issue for all of us and I deal with this in more detail in Chapter 10.

We're seeing a new breed of search engines such as Social Searcher, at www.social-searcher.com, which just focus on content found on social media sites and networks. However, to be fair, some of the traditional engines are working hard to provide access to real-time data, and Google can return results from Twitter which are only a few seconds old. However, we should perhaps consider this type of data in a rather different way; the vast majority of this will be produced by the average person in the street, and they will be expressing their own views and opinions, or may be reporting back on situations which they may not fully understand. Even so, it's still worth searching, since it may well include links to other websites, news items or other resources that will be of interest to the searcher.

Although this type of search engine may be seen, therefore, to be indexing what we might call casual or grey information it is nonetheless important that as information professionals we get to grips with search engines of this type, and start to use them.

Other search engines

Inevitably there is a miscellaneous collection of search engines and resources that don't fit into any of the above categories. There are engines that will return results in a clustered format, others which are-based on the idea of similarity, those which work within a mobile environment, some that search for people and others designed specifically for children. Some of these engines are going to be exceptionally useful in particular instances, so they also need to be looked at in some detail.

Summary

Despite the continued omnipotence of Google, it's fair to say that search is still a growing and important area. Although other engines are seemingly unable to challenge Google (I never hear new engines described as 'Google killers' any more), it's very far from being the only game in town. Indeed, the existence of other search engines that are excellent within their own niche areas keep the larger and more popular engines on their toes and provide us, the searchers, with many different resources with which to do our work.

CHAPTER 3

The world according to Google

Introduction

It may seem a ridiculous thought, but at one point in time it was possible to write a book about internet search and not include any references to Google, though you'd need to go back to the first edition of this book, written at the end of the last century, to find it. The rise of Google has been unstoppable, and it would be quite easy to just write about the search engine and the company behind it for chapter after chapter. A search on Amazon for 'Google' results in over 650,000 items for sale (up from 50,000 in 2013) and covers books, apps, videos, mobile phones, hardware and software. Google stopped being just a search engine many years ago, and is now involved in an increasing number of ventures from mobile phones to cloud computing to consumer services and more. It's the world's most dominant search engine, indexes trillions of pages and is searched billions of times every day. In August 2015 Google announced plans to reorganise all of its different interests into an overarching company called Alphabet.

Its success is mirrored by its failures, however. It has tried several times to enter the social networking environment to take on Facebook, but each of these

> **Did you know?**
> The number of searches performed by Google each year isn't known, but it's at least 2 trillion (http://searchengineland.com/google-now-handles-2-999-trillion-searches-per-year-250247).

attempts has met either with complete failure, with Google Wave and Google Buzz, or very limited success, with Google+. Google glasses failed to take off, despite all of the hype surrounding them. It's also had its fair share of failures in the software field as well, and closes down almost as many projects as reach fruition.

I've called this chapter 'The world according to Google' because it's very easy to spend your entire internet working life just using its various products and because of the way in which it tries to 'mould' its search results to you it's all too easy to limit what you do and see to these results. Consequently I'll look at the good, the bad and the ugly sides of Google in this chapter and while I'll give you plenty of reasons to use the search engine, there will be plenty of others to give you pause and reconsider. On the one hand it can provide excellent results very quickly, it's always innovative; making new resources available, and it can be extremely responsive. After the Boston Marathon bombing in 2013 it had a person search engine up and running within hours, before news agencies had really understood what was happening. On the other hand, it is dedicated to making money, and if the people at Google find a product that isn't doing that for them – however good it may be, and however many people use it (Google Reader comes to mind here, which was an excellent RSS reader) they will close it down without any hesitation, despite protests from users. We therefore have a situation where there's an excellent product but we do rely on it at our peril, because the tools come and go and the search experience can change not only from week to week but from hour to hour. In fact it's a standing joke with most internet search trainers that even if we check everything the night before on the day of the course Google will have changed something on us!

Did you know?
At least 63,000 searches are run every second on Google (http://searchengineland.com/google-now-handles-2-999-trillion-searches-per-year-250247).

The Google experience

I talk about an experience because Google has grown very far beyond the idea of a simple search engine that finds web pages for you. We can use it to search for information and find images, videos or the news. We can use it to read books, research academic articles, find out who is blogging on a particular subject and more besides. We can use it as a quick reference tool, or to translate from one language to another. It helps us run calculations, convert weights and measures, see images from streets with Streetview, store our photographs and documents on its servers and share them with other people. We can even visit the Moon or Mars!

We can use Google to chat real-time to people by voice and video and keep up to date with contacts by using the social network platform. Many people and organisations rely on Google either to bring clients to their doorstep (real or virtual) or, if they place Google adverts on their own websites, to send them a cheque every month for the revenue that they have earned by visitors clicking on them. The highest rating YouTuber, Felix Kjellberg, who is otherwise known as PewDiePie, earned US$12 million in the last year. Due to his subscriber base of over 40 million people his channel is a lucrative outlet for advertisers. While it's not entirely impossible to use the internet without also using Google it can sometimes be very hard to manage it! Moreover, the more that you use Google, either as a search engine, the Chrome browser, mobile phones or apps, the more it knows about you, and the more it can personalise the experience in ways that you'll find pleasing – because you get excellent results tailored to your interests – and scary, because you'll see adverts linked to searches that you've run, so you know that Google is keeping a very close eye on what you do and where you go.

Did you know?
95.9% of searches on mobile or tablet devices are performed by Google (www.statista.com/chart/8746/global-search-engine-market-share).

Serious researchers will use the engine for all of the reasons mentioned above and many more besides, and there's absolutely nothing wrong with that, as long as Google isn't the only resource that they consider using. One of the questions that we all need to consider when we use it is the extent to which we wish to become embroiled in the search engine. Indeed, other search engines such as DuckDuckGo have become popular because their major selling point is that they don't remember or track what you're doing in the way that Google does. In order to get the most out of the search engine I do have to say, somewhat regretfully, that the best way of getting the most out of Google is to get your own account and use it. There are many sound reasons for this, not the least of which is that if Google knows your search history it is therefore easy to give you more of what you've previously been interested in. As long as you remember this, and can log out to search, or use different engines, there's no harm done.

However, please also remember that Google will store the searches that you have run for several months, and will make this information available to anyone who legally requests it. So perhaps we should give a slight twist to the old adage 'there's no such thing as a free lunch' by saying 'there's no such thing as a free search'. I would always encourage you to regularly review your Google account and profile just so that you are happy and confident in the information that you're providing to the search giant. The easiest way to do this is to go to the

'My activity' page, which is at https://myactivity.google.com/myactivity: you will be able to see exactly how much Google has recorded about your internet life, not just with Google searches. It will show you how much time you have spent using the browser, YouTube visits and searches across the day; you'll see the websites that you have visited, the groups you have read on Facebook, if and when you visited your Gmail account, what sites you have clicked on, any games that you've played online, your location history, device information, music you may have identified with the sound search widget, YouTube 'not interested' feedback, conversations that you've had with the Google Assistant and much more besides. You can delete activity, and Google reassures you that only you can see this data, but nonetheless, it's a startling reminder of just how much of your life you spend on the internet; it really is the world according to Google! However, let's move on from that rather disquieting thought and look at the ways in which you can use Google to find the information that you need.

Google search: the basics

Given that the title of the book is, after all, 'expert internet searching', I hope that we can dispense with some of the basic search functionality quickly; I'm only including it for the sake of comprehensiveness, but it's worth reading through since it's possible that you might have missed something if you're self-taught.

The most basic search that you can do is to simply type in a word or a number of words in the search box. Google will then search through its index, find web pages that contain all of the words you have asked for, apply relevance ranking algorithms and then display the results on the screen for you. If I run a search on the two words *search* and *engines* I'll get 75,900,000 results in 0.6 seconds. The top result, ironically enough is titled 'Say goodbye to Google: 14 alternative search engines', followed by links to DuckDuckGo, Dogpile, Bing, Mojeek and StartPage. What Google has done is to look at all of the results and try and work out why these page results are better than any others. So, for example, it will see if *search* and *engines* are next to each other on the page, rather than having one word at the beginning of the page and the other one at the bottom, with no real interaction between them. Algorithms will check the position of the words – if they are in the URL, the title, the first few hundred words on the page, even down to the position in a paragraph or sentence, all will have a bearing on the position of that page in the results. There are other criteria that will be taken into account as well, such as the number of pages that link to the page in question, how quickly it loads, if it's mobile-friendly and so on. We don't know for sure how many of these algorithms are used, but the general consensus seems to be over 200. If you're interested in exploring this further one site claims to have a complete list, but I would only use it for academic interest, so take a look at the Backlink site at http://backlinko.com/google-ranking-factors.

Please do remember that the order of the words that you use will also have an effect on what Google returns to you. The earlier in the search string a word appears, the more that Google will assume it's important. So if you're running a search on say, the populations of Atlanta, New York and London, but you're especially keen on data from the capital city of Georgia it would be worth trying a search for *Atlanta population New York London* rather than anything else. You should also remember, however, that Google will find results where the words appear in any order, so if you're interested in a forested area called Comb Wood and you run your search for that, don't be surprised when Google returns results that relate to wooden combs! We'll discover how to overcome that problem shortly when we look at the phrase search option.

Boolean operators

It's worth stressing at this point that Google has just looked for the two words anywhere on the page. However, if you want to run a search that has the two words next to each other as a phrase *search engines* you need to tell Google this. It's very easy for a novice searcher to assume that's what Google has done, because it does value juxtaposition very highly, but if we place the words into a phrase with double quotes, like this: *"search engines"* we now drop to 43,000,000 results and more importantly the results themselves have changed. While we still have references to specific search engines we are getting plenty of other results that refer more generally to the topic in question. You may be tempted to use Boolean operators here, and run a search for *search AND engines*, which is a familiar search function. Other engines also use the '+' symbol to direct it to find both words, as with *+search +engines*. It's at this point that things start to get confusing, because the AND search actually does appear to work better and more accurately, giving 27,000,000 results. However, it shouldn't be necessary, since a search for two words implies the 'and' operator. The point to take from this is that the act of searching is something of a dark art, not to be relied upon for accurate and consistent results. One final point regarding Google and the '+' symbol; Google repurposed it to work with their social network, so a search for '+pepsi' would direct the user to the Pepsi Cola Google+ page, but this no longer works at all. For all intents and purposes the symbol has become invisible to Google and has no effect.

Another common Boolean operator is of course 'OR' and you can use this if you wish to find one word, term or phrase or another. You can also use the '|' symbol instead if preferred. A search for *search OR engines* returns about 12,550,000,000. If you noticed my use of the word 'about' and were also puzzled at such a rounded-off number you're right – the number of results that Google returns is only a rough estimate, not an exact one. In fact, if we reverse the order of the search terms, we don't get the same result, although we should. The figure is different: 12,560,000,000, a difference of 10,000,000 results! A search for the phrase *moon landings* gives me 428,000 results, but a search for *moon landings OR hoax* actually gives me 223,000, which is simply nonsensical, since it should be a much larger figure given that there are almost 36,000,000 results for *hoax* on its own. You could well argue that it doesn't much matter if Google gives wildly differing results because most searchers are not going to look beyond the first 10 or 20 results anyway, and if they get the answer that they are looking for, does it matter? That's a valid point, but if that's the case, is there any point in Google providing result numbers in the first place? It's a moot point, since they do – for whatever reason. So the main thing to remember as a searcher is to completely ignore the figures that Google offers, as they're worse than useless! I should also point out that the use of the Boolean operator 'NOT' can also result in inconsistent results. At the risk of namedropping, Amit Singhal, a senior vice president at Google, discussed this with me once at Google HQ London and his advice was not to get hung up on the numbers themselves; his view was as long as the results that are returned in the SERPS gave good and consistent information that's the important thing.

At this point I'm in danger of getting ahead of myself, since I have already dropped in a reference to another operator, 'NOT', or you can use the minus symbol '–' instead if you prefer. Obviously what this will do is to remove any results that include the word or phrase that you wish to have excluded. While this is a very useful function it does need to be used with care, since a search for *librarians –salary* would exclude any pages with the word 'salary' in them, irrespective of the context, meaning you may lose useful results!

So we have our three basic Boolean operators 'AND', 'OR' and 'NOT', which can be used separately or in conjunction as necessary. However, Google is poor at nested logic, so it might entirely misunderstand complex searches that use several operators. While the search engine should understand the search *movie OR cinema AND London OR Manchester*, anything more complicated than that is liable to return poor or incorrect results. If you are used to using the search functionality that comes with specialist, commercial databases you might assume that you can run the same search, but clarify your needs by writing it as *(movie OR cinema) AND (London OR Manchester)*. However, this doesn't work as far as Google is concerned; it just ignores the parentheses. Instead, try to break the search down into a number of component parts and see if you can get the results that you need that way. A good question to ask in such a case, however, is 'Is it necessary to search for 'movie' or 'cinema' anyway? Can Google realise that we're looking for the same thing?' It's a fair point to say that in this instance the two words movie and cinema can be seen as synonymous. Google used to use a synonym function with the tilde or ~ symbol. A search for *~beginner* would have given you pages that included the words 'beginner', 'beginners', 'tutorial', '101' and so on. However, that functionality was killed several years ago, and Google promised that it would include synonyms as a matter of course, so it wasn't necessary any longer. While in some instances this is true, it doesn't work as well as it used to when it was possible to specify synonym terms. Consequently, searchers need to look really closely at what Google is returning.

Phrase searching

A few moments ago I mentioned the problem of Comb Wood, rather than wooden combs. There is a simple way to overcome this problem, and that's to tell the search engine that you are looking for words in a phrase. You do this by putting the words, in the order that you want, in double quotes. Rather than asking Google to find pages with both words in any order a search for *"comb wood"* will return pages that have the words together, in that order. This is by far and away the most important single search function that you can use to find the material that you're looking for. A phrase search can be any length that you wish, but Google will automatically cut off after about 30 words. You can also include other phrases in your search as well; you're not just limited to one, such as "country park".

It's worth considering at this point that you might want to run a search to look for the answer to your question, and not the question itself. That sounds rather confusing, so let me explain in a little more detail. Imagine that you didn't know the name of the capital city of France. You could run a search for 'capital city France' and you might well get the answer that you're looking for, but you might have to wade through a few results first. However, how would the answer to your question be phrased? In all probability it would be something like 'The capital of France is' and then whatever it's called. So rather than putting in single words in the hope that Google will find what you need, a simple search for *"the capital of France is"* should pull up exactly the information that you need. This is of course a very simple example, but it does serve to illustrate the point.

I would like to say that phrase searching is nice and simple without any complications, but I'm afraid that's not possible. The search engine will sometimes decide for itself to ignore the fact that you've asked for a specific phrase and it will still attempt to find alternatives for you. For example, if you ran a search for Daniel Russell, a search research scientist at Google, it would not be surprising if Google decided to also give you results relating to a Mr Daniel Russel, an American diplomat. The obvious solution therefore is to search for *"daniel russell"* with the clear expectation that Google will simply return pages that mention that gentleman with his double l's. However, this is not the case, as Google will continue to return information on his namesake with the single l. If you really want to get around this, it's necessary to include the surname in double quotes to really hammer it home to Google that you want Russell, and not Russel. The search string then becomes *"daniel "russell""* and you should get the result that you want. I should make the point that this is quite a rare event, but one that does happen now and then, and you should keep your eyes open when looking at your results to make sure that Google hasn't decided to give you something you hadn't asked for.

Narrowing your search results

It's seldom the case that you get too few results to work with; with trillions of pages there are going to be some that match what you're after, however obscure the question. Instead, the likelihood is that you'll have millions of results, and you need to try and focus and narrow down what is appearing on the SERPS. You can obviously include more words in your search string, move from single words to a phrase, and exclude words from the results. If that doesn't work, Google has a couple of options that it makes immediately available. Under the search bar is a 'Tools' tab and if you click on that, Google provides you with the opportunity of limiting your results to 'Any country', 'Any time' and 'All results', as you can see from Figure 3.1.

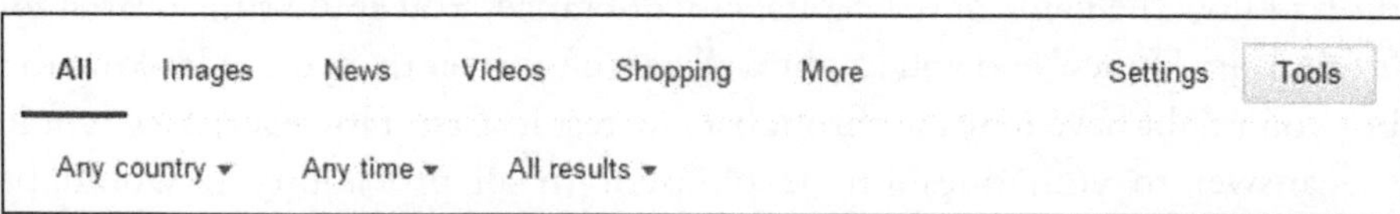

Figure 3.1 *Search options in Google*
Google and the Google logo are registered trademarks of Google Inc., used with permission

You may not see exactly the same options when clicking on 'Tools' for yourself; Figure 3.1 comes from a search using Google.co.uk and the option under 'Any country' is to simply limit to the UK. If you're using Google.com you won't see the country option available to you.

'Any time' allows you to limit results to what Google has found in the last hour, day, week, month or year. There's also an opportunity to pick a custom range of dates as well. Once you have used this option you will then have an opportunity to sort the results by relevance or by date, most recent first.

Under 'All results' there is only one alternative, and that's to search for 'Verbatim'. Those readers with long memories will recall that there used to be many more options such as 'recently visited pages', but Google has slowly been culling those over the last few years. Verbatim tells Google that it should search for exactly whatever you have asked it to find, and that it shouldn't use alternative spellings, plurals, synonyms or anything else. Of course, when running a phrase search, Google should be doing that automatically, but if you're using other words in your search you may also want just what you have asked for, without any derivatives. Referring back to the Daniel Russell example, instead of using double quotes inside double quotes you could try and limit to the Verbatim option for the same result.

Suggestions and searches related to

When you start to type in a search query, Google will come up with some suggestions for you. They're basically search predictions – possible search terms that you can use which are related to the terms that you're currently typing. Google looks at what you're typing, relevant searches that you've run in the past if you're signed into your Google account and what other people are searching for, including any trending news story. The suggestions can vary both by region and language, so a French speaker in Paris may well get very different results to an English speaker in Washington. Personalisation matters; Google wants to show you results that it thinks will be most helpful to you, so these suggestions will always come at the top of the list, if at all possible. If lots of people start to search for a particular subject, Google will notice this short-term spike in interest and will reflect that in its suggestions, for a short space of time. These predictions are generated by an algorithm without having any human intervention in the process; they're based on objective factors and reflect the range of information on the web. Consequently sometimes the suggestions may be unusual, perhaps even offensive.

Let's try an example. If I start my search with the word 'Librarians' Google will give me suggestions such as 'librarians cast' and 'season 3' for example, making the assumption that I am interested in the television show of the same name. If I continue to type, by the time I get to 'Librarians are' Google gives suggestions such as 'librarians are subversive mug' and 'librarians are awesome'. Yet again, by the time I have typed 'Librarians are u' Google is giving the less than charming 'librarians are useless' but this is tempered with the following suggestion 'librarians are the ultimate knowledge managers'. Do try it for yourself, but expect to get different results.

As mentioned, sometimes Google does give less pleasant suggestions. Simply by typing in the word 'did' the very first suggestion is 'did the holocaust happen'. This caused the search engine particular problems at the end of 2016 because the first few sites that Google linked to for that result were holocaust denial sites. So while the search suggestions can be useful, it's not worth paying too much attention to them, unless you're really struggling with your search.

At the bottom of a SERPS you may well find that Google has provided you with a list of searches that are related to the subject that you've searched for. So searches related to fox-red Labradors include their temperament, puppies for sale, breeders, information and facts and so on. You'll get these for almost any search that you run – I tried a random string of characters and I was still getting suggested searches – and so it's worth taking a look at them if you have difficulty in finding what you want.

Advanced search functionality

You'd be forgiven for not realising that Google has an advanced search function, since it's not clearly available. It used to be prominent on the home page, next to the search option, then it was available as an option from the settings in the top right hand of the page before moving to the bottom of the SERPS. It's disappeared from all of those places now, and you have to go directly to the URL www.google.com/advanced_search in order to see the options available to you. In all honesty I think calling it an advanced search page is something of a misnomer, because it really helps searchers – particularly novices – find what they need quickly and easily. It's certainly worth pointing out to anyone who is new to the search world, since it will help them get to grips with it very simply. However, I'll go through each of the options in turn, making their functionality clear.

Find pages with . . .

- **All these words.** This is a basic search, using any words that you wish, as we've already discussed.
- **This exact word or phrase.** A phrase search, and Google will put the double quotes in for you.
- **Any of these words.** A Boolean OR search
- **None of these words.** Excluding words from the search, as previously discussed
- **Numbers ranging from/to.** This is the first new search function on the page, and it's a useful one. If you were looking for something between a particular set of dates you could put the dates into the search boxes, or if you wanted simply to run the search yourself, place two full stops between the numbers of interest. So a search for the winners of the FA Cup 2000 to 2016 could use *2000..2016* as the search syntax. Alternatively, if you wished to purchase a product between $300 and $500 you could run the search as *$300..$500* – though unfortunately this doesn't work with other currencies.

Then narrow your results by . . .

- **Language.** Google does provide searchers with a wide range of language options; it recognises dozens. Simply choose from a pulldown menu to select the language of choice. The search will be run, and Google will just pull back results from French pages; that is to say, pages that are in French, rather than pages that are within a .fr domain. So it would be possible for example to return pages that are in French, but which are housed on a UK website using the *site:* function that we'll look at late. It's not a perfect set of results, but it should be acceptable for most searches.
- **Region.** This option finds pages published in a particular region. By 'region' Google means country, not region of the world, so you can limit to Oman, but not Oceania. A shortcut for this search is to use the *site:* syntax, with the top-level domain of the country that you're interested in. So a search for *librarian site:.uk* should limit results to those pages that mention the word 'librarian' and that have a URL that ends in .uk.
- **Last update.** This is the same functionality as the time option that we discussed previously.
- **Site or domain.** This is a very useful search function, which I've alluded to in the Region option. Basically it allows you to limit your

results to just those pages that include the region option (the two letter country domain such as .uk for the United Kingdom, or .fr for France), but also other sites as well. For example, if you wanted to limit your results to pages from the Wikipedia, the appropriate part of the search string would be *site:Wikipedia.org*. Alternatively, if you wanted to find pages that were produced by the British government the string would be *site:.gov.uk*, or pages from academic sites would be *site:.ac.uk.* There are an ever-increasing number of top-level domains, and it's worth exploring them. The 'original' domain names were .com, .org, .net, .edu, .gov, and .mil but these have now expanded to include .accountants, .bargains, .physio and .tattoo, to name just a few. A complete list is available from Wikipedia at https://en.wikipedia.org/wiki/List_of_Internet_top-level_domains.

- **Terms appearing.** This is another very powerful function, since you can limit your search to pages where your term appears in specific positions. For example, the title of the page, in the text on the page, in the URL of the page or in links to the page. I have always found that limiting results to pages that include 'library' in the URL has been a very effective way of giving me high-quality, accurate and authoritative results.
- **Safe search.** This is a fairly obvious function, and you can use it to filter sexually explicit content. Google does err on the side of caution here, so you may discover that some medical websites for example, or sites offering advice and support in sexual subjects, may be excluded from results. It should also be said that this does not filter out racial epithets, so it's of limited use if you want to protect young ones.
- **Filetype.** Search engine crawlers are capable of indexing the content found in various file formats, not simply web pages themselves. This can be very useful once we consider what kind of information you are likely to find in what file format. So, for example, if you need financial or statistical data, it's probably going to be in a spreadsheet format. If you're looking for explanations of research findings, or 'how-to' material, it may well be in a PowerPoint file. If you want to find a web page that looks exactly the same as the printed version an Adobe Acrobat .pdf file may be exactly what you want. So when you're searching, consider the format of the data – could this be a useful way to reduce the number of results, and can you make them more specific?
- **Usage rights.** As you will of course know, the creator of content (or perhaps their employer) owns the copyright to the material that they

produce. Simply placing this onto the internet for other people to access does not mean that they give up that copyright, and users cannot simply use material that they find without hindrance. However, there are times when material isn't in copyright – perhaps because it's been made available by a government department, copyright has lapsed due to the age of the item, or the creator has allowed other people to use it by means of a Creative Commons statement. Google tries to provide access to material that is available via licence, and there are several of them. Google recognises the following: free to use or share; free to use or share even commercially; free to use, share or modify; and free to use, share or modify even commercially. For a more in-depth discussion of these and other licences it's worth exploring the Creative Commons website at https://creativecommons.org. While this option is helpful, it's not to be relied upon, since Google may well interpret a Creative Commons licence on one item to refer to all of the content on that page, so it's really necessary to check in detail to see what can or cannot be done.

Although not included in the actual Advanced Search pulldown menus, there are other options at the end of the page. These enable you to find pages that are similar to, or link to, a URL. This option actually covers two different search functions.

The first is *related:* and this option means that Google will look at the page that you're referring to in the search string, and it will see if it can find any other similar pages. So a search for *related:facetpublishing.co.uk* will return results that are the pages of other similar publishing houses.

To see which pages link to a given URL the search function *link:* is used. So if I want to see who links to the publisher's website I can run a search for *link:facetpublishing.co.uk*. I should point out that there are other search engines specifically designed for this purpose and they all work better than the Google offering, so my advice is to use those instead, and I'm only including this for comprehensiveness.

Other search functions

Google has a wide and wonderful variety of other search functions, which are not included in the Advanced Search function page, so you either have to know them already, or be prepared to hunt them out. Alternatively, as you're wisely doing, let someone else do the work for you! So settle down and I'll continue with more search functions.

If you want to know more about a particular website, the *info:* function is a good one to explore. A search for *info:facetpublishing.co.uk* will give me a link to the site itself and four further options. I can choose to see Google's cache of the page, and I have already discussed this option in Chapter 2. I can find web pages that are similar to the page, which is just another way of getting to the *related:* function; I can view other pages from the site, which is again just another way of getting to the *site:* function; and I can find other pages that use the phrase 'facetpublishing.co.uk'. It's also worth making the point that the search functions should all be entered in lower case, rather than upper. Google will treat a search for 'Info:' differently to 'info:' – the latter being the correct way of writing the search string.

Google does have some limited functionality for searching across social media platforms. I can, for example, search for someone's Twitter handle using the @ symbol, so a search for *@Philbradley* will pull up links to my website, my Twitter account, my Twitter lists and any other references to that string of characters. Google also lets users search for hashtags, so a search for *#savelibraries* will return Tweets, images, references on web pages and across other social media platforms.

allinanchor: and **inanchor:** If a web author links to another page they may do so using words to describe the page, such as 'useful parenting site' and when you click on that link, you visit whatever the page is. The use of this function means that you'll get to see sites that people have described in a particular way. So to get results for the example that I've just used, run a search for *allinanchor: useful parenting site*. A search for *inanchor:* will run a search for the word that you have specified immediately after the function, and any other words in your search string will be treated as though they are words on the page.

allinblogtitle: and *inblogtitle:* will limit results to blog pages as appropriate. Google used to have a specific blog search option, but it's now disappeared. However, it's still possible to search for blog-based content using this function, and Google will return results from sites which are known to be blog-based, as such Blogspot or Wordpress. However, since there are many blog sites I doubt that this is going to be an all-inclusive option, so don't expect a comprehensive result if you use this.

allintext: and **intext:** *allintext:* will return pages that contain the words that you have asked for in the body of the page, and the subsidiary search function *intext:* will find pages where a term appears on the text of the page and other terms may appear elsewhere in the document, such as the title of the page or the web address.

allintitle: and **intitle:** A search using the *allintitle:* function will result in pages that contain all of the words in the title of a page. So for example a search for *allintitle:librarians books discovery* will give results such as 'Goodreads Librarians Group – Adding new books: Discovery in paperback'. A search for *intitle:librarians books discovery*, on the other hand, will return pages that include the word 'librarians' in the title of the page, and the other keywords anywhere else on the page.

allinurl: and **inurl:** Unsurprisingly we'll find with the function *allinurl:* that we just get results that contain the keywords in the URL of the page. Using the terms from the previous example with this will result in a search *allinurl:librarians books discovery* and pages returned such as 'http://books.telegraph.co.uk/Product/JoLinda-Thompson/Implementing-Web-Scale-Discovery-Services—A-Practical-Guide-for-Librarians/'. As you would expect, the search *inurl: librarians books discovery* will find URLs with the word 'librarians', but the other terms will be anywhere on the page. It's worth taking a couple of moments at this point to distinguish between page titles and URLs. URL is the abbreviation for Uniform Resource Locator, which is to say that it's the unique address for any file that's accessible on the internet. So a short URL might just be www.philb.com and a longer one might be www.philb.com/search/google/functions.html, for example. URLs reflect the way in which a site is developed and arranged, so including *inurl:library* in a search will result in pages belonging to a library service. A web page title is exactly that – the title of the page. When a web author is writing content they can include a page title – generally something that describes the content of the page. You'll see this above the URL in the results that Google returns. It's not as technically formal as the URL, but nonetheless is a really good way of focusing on content.

AROUND( ) For many years the assumption was made that Google didn't support proximity searching; that is to say, a function that limited results to term *a* and term *b* that were within a certain number of words of each other. While it wasn't a 'secret' search function it did in actual fact exist, it's just that Google didn't talk about it. You simply put a number into the parenthesis and add in your terms. The results will contain both terms within that number of words of each other. So a search for *national AROUND(4) orchestra* will give you both terms with a maximum of four words between them and a minimum of none. However, it's not a function that always works very well, and it's certainly not one that I would rely on, so it's a case of use it, but be careful!

Asterisk or * The asterisk works as a wildcard and is used to replace missing words. The searcher can't control the number of words which are replaced, so that's something of a drawback. However, it's still a useful tool; simply place the asterisk as appropriate in the search string. For example *there is a * far away* gives results which include phrases such as 'there is a green hill far away', 'there is a kind of magicness [sic] about going far away' and 'there is a city far away'.

Punctuation We've already seen that Google will take the symbols @ and # into account when searching. In the main it ignores them, but there are one or two other noticeable exceptions. You can use the percentage sign for a search on percentages; just type in *20%* for example, and you should get search results that reference those three characters, but also '20-Percent'. I mentioned that + doesn't work, and that's true, with the exception of blood types, so a search for *O+* will return valid content.

'One-trick ponies'

Google wants you to use their search engine, so as well as the ability to search the web it also provides what I call 'one-trick ponies', which is to say that it can do very specific things that aren't really that related to search *per se*, but which are nonetheless useful.

Calculator Google has an excellent calculator. You can use various symbols for different equations.

*	for multiplication
/	for division
+	for addition
–	for subtraction
% of	for per cent
=	at the end of the equation to solve it.

So for example, you could search for 75*86 as in Figure 3.2. Google will also display a very helpful calculator on the screen as well, which allows you to do far more complicated mathematics (see Figure 3.2 on the next page). This appears automatically on the screen once you run a calculation, or you could run a search for 'calculator' in the search box to bring it to the screen.

Census data A search for *population <place> or unemployment rate <place>* will return data as per the request. It's not current, however; when I tried this search I was getting data that was a couple of years old. These searches work best for locations within the USA, but I was able to get population information about my local town as well, via a link with Wikipedia.

Currency conversion This uses the format *<amount><name of currency> in <name of another currency>*. If you want to know how many Euros US$100 will buy, just search for *100 usd in eur*. It works just as well if you want to type the search out in full, thus: *100 american dollars to european euros*.

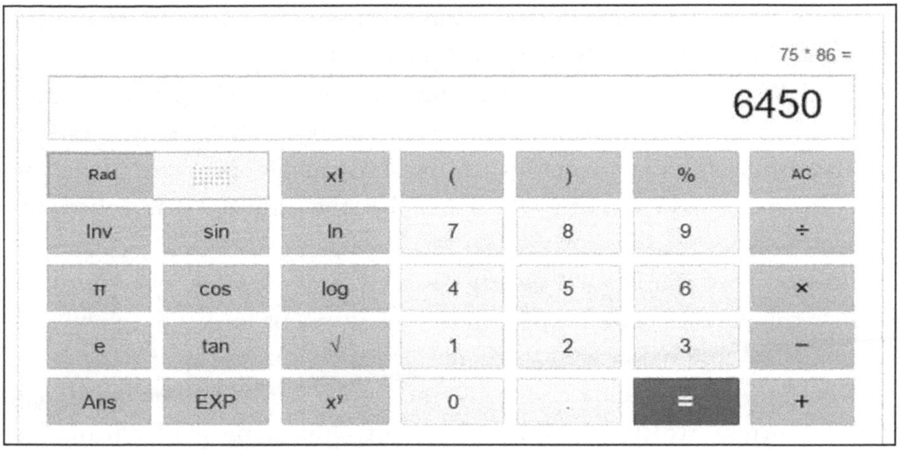

Figure 3.2 *The Google on-screen calculator*
Google and the Google logo are registered trademarks of Google Inc., used with permission

Definitions Type in *define <term>*. Google returns definitions for the term requested, a short sound file to hear the word pronounced (in an American accent) and links to translations, word origin and more definitions.

Flight status Run a search for a particular flight (e.g. *BA 123* or *United 1111*) and Google will provide details on its estimated departure, from which gate and arrival time at destination.

Movies This is great if you want to quickly find out what films are playing at cinemas in a specific location. Enter *movies <location>* and Google gives start times for the films, provides information and reviews of the local cinema and links to reviews of the films on offer as well.

Package tracking If you have the tracking number from a service such as UPS, USPS or FedEx you can enter it as a search term to see delivery and destination information. For example, if your tracking number was 1Z71EIEI013424230 just type that in and Google will find the carrier and let you track it.

Post or zip codes If you type into the search box the code that you're interested in Google will present you with a small map of the exact area.

Stock quotes You can find the current market data for any publicly traded company by typing in its ticker symbol, such as *goog* for Google. You will get the current price as well as historical data back five years or longer if it's available.

Sunrise and sunset *sunrise <location>*, *sunset <location>* will tell you at what time the sun either rises or sets, depending on your choice of function.

Time *time <place>* does exactly what you would expect; Google provides you with the current time in the location that you're interested in, and tells you how many hours in advance or behind GMT it is.

Translations The search format is *translate <word> to <language>*. A simple translation function is available directly from the search box, but you can also visit the Google translation option at https://translate.google.com. This allows users to type or paste in some text and choose the language that it should be translated into.

Unit conversion From *<quantity><name of unit> in <name of another unit>* Google can translate almost any unit of measurement for height, volume or weight. So to find out how much 10 lb is in kilograms, just type *10 lbs in kg*.

Weather As you would imagine, by entering *weather <place>* you'll get details on the current weather in the location of choice, plus information on precipitation, humidity, wind, and a week's forecast.

The knowledge graph and the carousel

Google will sometimes present searchers with an information box to the right of the search results, and it's called the 'Knowledge graph'. It was launched in May 2012 and it tries to work out how things are connected to each other. So for example a search for 'Charles I' will provide a graph with images of the monarch, a brief summary of his life, facts about his birth, death, spouse, children and parents, and a very useful section 'People also search for'. This is a really helpful tool, since all of the basic information is presented to searchers in a neat package. It works in a variety of situations; not just for individuals, but for books, companies, events and so on. You can't 'force' Google to display the knowledge graph; it chooses for itself.

The Google carousel is another function that Google chooses to display or not. It's a bar or band at the top of the search results which gives a lot of information in a very short amount of space, because you can scroll across these results from end to end, in a carousel-type fashion. You can often see it in action if you ask for a list of cast members of a film or television series, or for all of the books by a particular author. So while *agatha christie* doesn't trigger a carousel result, *agatha christie books* does. *Downtown Abbey* doesn't work, but a search for *downtown abbey cast* will display a list of many of the actors from the series. It's therefore worth remembering that if you require a list of some sort (and especially within popular culture) it may well be worth using Google for your search in the hope that the carousel kicks into play.

URL modifiers

There are a number of different things that you can do with Google directly from the URL line. You can't add these in the search box, but you can add them to the SERP's URL. So, for example, if you wanted to see all of the results for the last hour which have been added to the Google database, you would first run the search as normal and get the results. The URL at the top of the page is going to be quite long and complicated, making very little sense. However, at some point you'll find a segment that reads something like '&q=librarians' where the word 'librarians' will be replaced with the term that you searched on. Immediately after that, add onto the line some extra code, and in the case that we're looking at here, you would add *&tbs+qdr:h* and then hit enter. Google will re-run the search, and this time limit the results to pages added or updated in the last hour. You can modify this parameter in a number of different ways, so the base parameter is *&tbs+qdr:* and then add after the colon an *s* to get results from the past second, *n* for the last minute, *h* for an hour, *d* for the past day, *w* for the last week, *m* for the past month and *y* for the last year. Of course, some of these are available from the pulldown menu, but this illustrates the fact that you can exert control over the results that Google provides other than via the search box.

Putting it all together

I'm very aware that while I've listed a lot of different search functions they're still rather academic in nature, so I'd like to put some of them into practice to see how they can be used to really focus a search.

- *Librarians uk salary scale* returns 771,000 results.
- *Librarians salary scale site:uk* returns 85,000 results.
- *Librarians salary scale site:uk – "school librarian"* returns 3,990 results.

Next, choose the 'tools' option and tell Google you only want to see results added in the last year by choosing 'last year' in the 'Any time' pull down menu. At this point we lose the number of results, but we're getting appropriate material. However, many of the results are from universities, and as I've already excluded the phrase 'school librarian' it may make rather more sense to simply exclude the .ac.uk domain entirely, so my search becomes the rather more elegant *librarians salary scale –site:.ac.uk*. Rather than asking for librarians and salary and scale, let's put those last two words into a phrase search, so we have *librarians "salary scale" –site:.ac.uk*. However, just leaving our search like that won't really do the job, since we're getting a lot of results for salary scales for librarians around the rest of world, and we just want the uk. So a final tweak for our search is *librarians 'salary scale' –site:.ac.uk site:.uk*. We have our keyword 'librarians', our phrase 'salary scale', we've excluded UK academic sites, and limited the search to .uk websites.

Let's assume now that we want to find an expert in the field of automatic train protection. A simple search for *expert automatic train protection* will return lots of pages about trains, security systems, financial advice and news from the Middle East. Clearly at this point Google really has no idea what we're asking for. Let's go to the other extreme then and ask for an expert in the subject. A search for *expert in automatic train protection* returns no results at all. Taking a step back we can search for the phrase "automatic train protection" and expert, which results in less than 500 results, so we're finally getting somewhere. Many of these results include the phrase 'Ask the Nanjing 101 Expert' which is not helpful, so adding *–Nanjing* gets us down to under 400 results. Another approach is to re-examine the word 'expert', since it's rather a general term that isn't terribly helpful. By looking at some of the words included in the results the phrase 'Project engineer' appears quite often, so if we replace those for 'expert' we're now down to 121 results. We could then take a lateral approach and assume that such people are going to talk at conferences and exhibitions, so they may well put their presentations online, at somewhere like Slideshare.net, which is a site owned by LinkedIn that's used for storing presentations. Our final search string becomes *"project engineer" "automatic train protection" –nanjing site:slideshare.net* and gives us one individual. Of course, there are plenty of other approaches to a question of this type. We could assume that such individuals may well have a CV or resumé online, so it's possible to narrow our search instead by asking for pages that have the word 'resumé' or 'cv' in the title of the page, so our search then looks like *"project engineer" intitle:resume OR intitle:cv "automatic train protection"* and that returns just over 20 results. Alternatively, they may have profiles on job sites, so we could run a search for *"automatic train protection" site:linkedin.com"*. Once again, that returns several hundred results, but upon exploration of the LinkedIn website it becomes clear that there is a UK version, so it's possible to refocus the search to reflect this with a search string of *"automatic train protection" site:uk.linkedin.com*, giving us four good results. (Don't worry if your results or numbers are different to mine, and in fact that is to be expected, given the way that Google works!)

Once you start to look at the way in which websites are created, together with common words and phrases, searching can become quite fascinating. For example, lots of people will create music directories of their favourite music. If you wanted to see examples of this, run a search for *intitle:index.of mp3* and then the name of a musician or band. (While you may well be able to download and use any material you find I would advise against it, for two reasons: first, it will almost certainly be a copyright violation, and secondly an unscrupulous person may well create a virus, give it the name of a famous track and hope someone does download it and try and run it.) Alternatively, try a search for *intitle:internal use only* or to narrow even further *intitle:"internal use only"* and then add in something like *site:.gov.uk* just to see how much material is available on the web that perhaps shouldn't be! If you're feeling mischievous, replace the phrase 'internal use only' with other terms such as 'private' or 'confidential'!

If you want to find free books you could run the following search:

–inurl:htm –inurl:html intitle:"index of" "/ebooks" | "/book" chm |pdf| zip

Let's break this search down into its component parts. The first two options tell Google to ignore pages that end in .htm or .html, because we don't want regular web pages. We're interested in directories, and these are commonly referred to as 'index of', so we're running the same element of the search as we did with the music example. We then want directories which are called 'ebooks' or 'book' and I've included the double quotes to make doubly certain that Google also searches for the forward slash. Finally, I have asked Google to find common ebook formats such as chm, pdf and zip – I could have used the OR operator, but the '|' symbol did the job for me.

It would be quite easy – and fun, to continue in a similar vein for the rest of the chapter, but hopefully these few examples have given you some ideas and inspiration on searching for material.

Other Google search tools

It would be all too easy at this point to simply move on, because after all, we've discussed Google search now, haven't we? Very far from it, and indeed there are many more tools at our disposal provided by the search giant. You'll recall that once we've run a search and we have our SERPs in front of us, we have a 'Tools' option, and to the left of that there are other choices available. Specifically, Images, Shopping, Videos, News and More, but these may change depending on the search that you've run and how Google is personalised for you. I'll go through each of these in turn, in greater or lesser detail depending on the option.

Google News

There's no surprise that in order to search in Google News you can simply input the search terms that you're interested in, and Google will try and find material that matches your enquiry. Simply go to https://news.google.com and you will be presented with your own home page of news – based on your current location. There are links for top stories, locations that you have shown an interest in previously and a 'Suggested for you' collection – based on your search history. In the centre of the screen you will see an option for stories in specific locations, such as the UK, Botswana, Portugal and so on, and an option for how the news stories are to be displayed. On the right hand side of the screen are recent stories and editor's picks. Finally you can choose to personalise your news stories, and add any subjects that you want to be kept up to date on. My preferences can be seen in Figure 3.3 opposite.

Google News has an advanced search function, and you access it via the half-diamond to the left of the search button; it's actually on the extreme right inside the search box. As with the advanced search option for text, there are boxes for 'all these words', 'this exact phrase', 'at least one of these words', 'none of these words'. Specific to news are options to search for keywords occurring anywhere in the article, headline, body or URL. A filter is available to limit by time with options for recent, last hour, day, week, month, year, archives or custom date.

Searchers can limit by source, such as the BBC or the *New York Times* and by location. Alternatively if you are familiar with writing out search functions yourself you could use:

location:<place>
and/or *allintitle:*
allinbody:
allinurl:
and *orsite:*
or *source<publication name>*.

At the bottom of each news section (such as Sports or Technology) or a custom section that you've chosen for yourself there is an RSS option. In order to add the news from that section to your feed-reader of choice, simply click on the RSS icon and copy the resulting URL into your feed-reader as appropriate. If you can't see this in your results, it's probably because you're looking at a page of results when you have clicked 'News' under the search box in order to view news articles rather than looking at web pages or images for example. Simply go to the Google News page as previously given and try again.

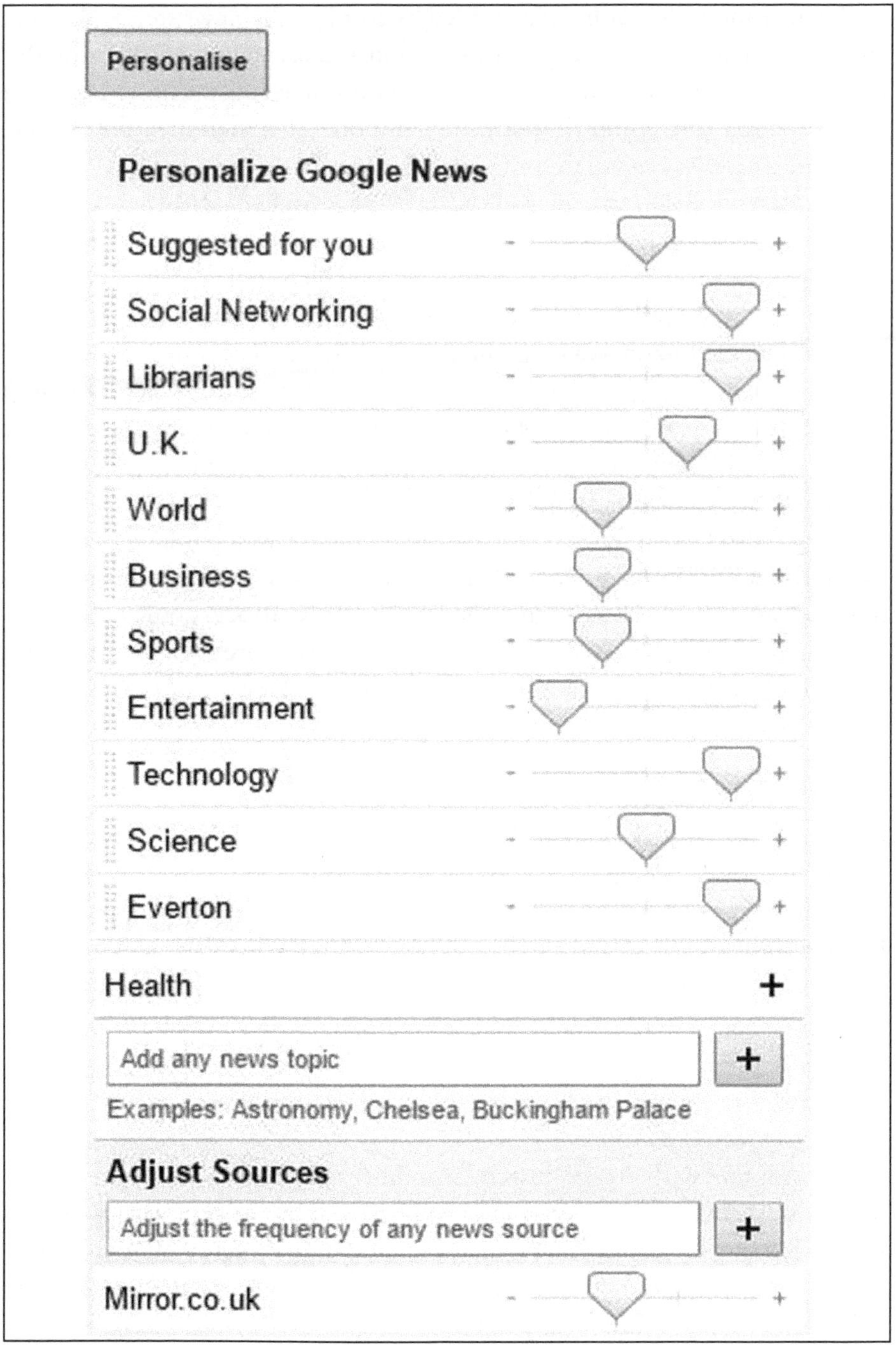

Personalise

Personalize Google News

Suggested for you

Social Networking

Librarians

U.K.

World

Business

Sports

Entertainment

Technology

Science

Everton

Health

Add any news topic

Examples: Astronomy, Chelsea, Buckingham Palace

Adjust Sources

Adjust the frequency of any news source

Mirror.co.uk

Figure 3.3 *The author's news preferences on Google News*
Google and the Google logo are registered trademarks of Google Inc., used with permission

If you're interested or indeed puzzled by some of the news stories that you see, Google explains it by saying 'the selection and placement of stories on this page were determined automatically by a computer program'. The time or date displayed (including those in the Timeline of Articles feature) reflect when an article was added to or updated in Google news.

Google will also, at its discretion, provide searchers with news or 'top stories' when running a traditional search. This has in the past caused problems, as Google has provided links to news sites which are not *bona fide* resources. For example, for searches on 'final election count' after the US Presidential election Google linked to a blog called 70 News, which claimed that Donald Trump had won the popular vote by a margin of almost 700,000, when in actual fact he lost by about 3,000,000. Google has since taken measures to ensure that fake news sites don't get any prominence in results, but it's worth keeping your eyes open just to be on the safe side.

Google also has a newspaper archive, which is not well publicised, but you can find it at https://news.google.com/newspapers. It's no longer updated, but it does contain digitised pages from hundreds of newspapers going back to the beginning of the 1800s. The majority of newspapers are local to American cities and towns, but there are a good number from Europe as well.

Google Video search

It's important to make the point that this search function isn't limited to YouTube, which is owned by Google; it will find content from a variety of different video sites, such as Pcworld.com, Steampowered.com and Udemy.com. As you would expect, simply type in the words that match what you're looking to find, and Google will return videos for you. Under the Tools setting searchers can filter on a number of settings. Results can be pulled from the web in general, or limited to your own country, duration from less than a minute to over 20 minutes long, the usual time periods, high quality, closed-captioned videos and source.

In common with image search, searchers are able to use other search functions, such as *intitle:*, *inurl:* and *site:*. These can be really powerful tools; if you are looking for information on a Microsoft product such as Word, by using *site:Microsoft.com intitle:word "how to"* you're immediately narrowing down to videos that explain functionality in the product.

Google Shopping

The shopping option displays products in a tile format, unlike the usual textual approach that you find with other Google SERPs; it's more like the way Google displays the results of an image search in fact, but there is an option to change it into a list format if preferred. Results can also be sorted by review score or price. Clicking on a link opens a larger dialogue box in the middle of the screen and clicking on that will take the searcher directly to the product on the website page. Options that can be used to reduce the number of results include location, price, category, brand and seller. More categories may be used, depending on the product being searched for, so a search for a television will include features, number of HDMI ports, width and so on. You can also save results to a shortlist to compare later.

Results come from a wide variety of stores, both online and on the high street. However, it's worth noticing that Google hides away a statement which says 'Products and offers that match your query. Google is compensated by these merchants. Payment is one of several factors used to rank these results.' Consequently searchers need to remember that there may well be other excellent products available that they're not seeing in the results because Google hasn't been paid. So as well as doing a search for the product in the Shopping option it might be worth doing another search using the traditional search option to see if alternatives are available.

Google's 'More' option

Google does have other tools and resources available, but they are not always easy to find; in fact the search engine seems to go out of its way to make it difficult to locate them. However, a few of them are available under the 'More' option at the top of the results page.

Maps

Google has an excellent maps section, available at both www.google.com/maps and /maps/ after the appropriate country-based version. Google will always try and show a map based on the IP address of the searcher, so in most instances the map which appears on the screen should be quite familiar. There's a search option in the top left-hand corner and when you start to type in keywords Google offers some suggestions. Google then offers results in a menu on the left-hand side of the screen and highlights appropriate places on the map in the rest of the screen. The menu option may include photographs, opening times (if the search is for a shop) and reviews, if appropriate. Directions are also available for car, public transport, on foot, cycling or by air.

Alternatively the searcher can look for a specific place or location by name or by post or zip code. There's an option to use 'Street View', which is a photographic panorama that the viewer can move around. It should be said, however, that the view seen may be several years old. A search for my road showed it as it existed in January 2009, that's exactly eight years ago from the time of writing. A view of Whitehall in London is dated 2012, so don't rely on Street View for accuracy! However, people can add their own views to locations, but this tends to be rather hit and miss.

There are other tools associated with the Maps option that are worth mentioning. These include Google Earth, at www.google.com/intl/en/earth, which is a product that users download onto the computer or mobile device. Depending on the location you may well find historical imagery available and information on specific places and tours; users can search for specific places, and even explore the Moon, Mars, the sky or underneath the oceans!

Google Books

The Google books project is described as 'an enhanced card catalog of the world's books'. Google has partnered with over libraries around the world to digitise books from their collections to build a searchable catalogue online. It means that users can search through millions of books written in many different languages, including books that are out of print, rare or otherwise unavailable. If the book is out of copyright and in the public domain Google makes it available for full viewing, and you can read the book from start to finish. If the book is still in copyright the tool will only display a few snippets from the book to show your search terms in context. That may well be enough to help the searcher decide if it's worth ordering through the library loans system.

By now the search functionality should be very familiar. Searchers will enter their keywords and Google will match this against the book's bibliographic record, such as the author and title, as well as its full text. Results will show the book cover if it's available, the title, author, year of publication, other editions, a quick summary that includes the words searched on, and a link to a preview. There is an advanced search option, which irritatingly isn't linked to from the SERPs, so you need to go directly to https://books.google.com/advanced_book_search. There are the normal search options of all the words, exact phrase, at least one of the words and without the words. Searchers can limit results to all books, limited preview and full view, full view only and Google e-books only, as well as choosing to search books, magazines or both. There are options to limit the search to a language, words in the title, author, publisher, subject, publication dates, ISBN and ISSN.

If you have access to a library – and I'm assuming that you probably do – this is a very useful tool for the searcher to have in their collection. When searching the internet it's all too easy to forget that other resources such as print are still in existence, and still a very useful source of information. Google books can remind us that it's worthwhile taking our heads away from the screen every now and then and looking at the shelves instead!

Associated with Google Books is the Google Ngram viewer. This search engine returns results based on the digitised versions of books between 1500 and 2008. It can search for single words, phrases and case-sensitive spellings and if found in 40 or more books they are then plotted onto a graph. The database has been populated with over 5 million books, so it's an excellent historical tool, especially useful if a linguist needs to research the use and popularity of a word or phrase over a period of time, for example. The Ngram viewer is available at https://books.google.com/ngrams.

Google Scholar

This resource is the subject of much debate as to its academic value to researchers, and while I would like to go into detail on the debate I'll limit myself to a simple explanation of Scholar, letting readers research for themselves to make up their own minds.

Scholar gives searchers a simple way to search for scholarly literature, searching through resources such as articles, theses, books, abstracts and so on. Sources include academic publishers, professional societies, universities and online repositories. Once you have found the article or piece of work that you need you can see how often it's been cited, and you can also order the document through your library service. Scholar is available at https://scholar.google.com or the appropriate country code address, such as https://scholar.google.co.uk. You can search using the usual functionality and the results are returned with title, author(s), source, abstract, number of citations, related articles and a citation in five formats (MLA, APA, Chicago, Harvard and Vancouver), and the article can be output to various databases such as EndNote, RefMan and RefWorks.

Searchers can filter results by case law, dates, and can include or exclude patents and citations. It's also possible to create an alert to send you an e-mail when new results match your search string. There's an advanced search option, available from a pulldown menu using the half-diamond in the search box. This gives access to all of the usual options; all words, phrase, OR and exclude. Searchers can also limit to words in the title as well. Extra options include returning articles authored by specific people, articles published in specific journals, and articles dated between two dates. Of course, these can be used in conjunction with each other.

The disadvantages of Google

Overall, Google is an excellent search engine. Any resource that's used billions of times a day and has had its name turned into a verb is clearly doing something right. However, we always need to remember that Google has money as its bottom line. It is not there as your friend, and everything that it does is designed to increase revenue for its shareholders. It's also worth making the point that you and I are not Google's users. The users are the people who pay the search engine to advertise their products and services based on the searches that are run. In 2016 Google's revenue amounted to US$89.5 billion, an increase of over US$20 billion on 2015 (www.statista.com/statistics/266206/googles-annual-global-revenue).

Google has something of a problem, because we all think of it as a helpful tool to find what we're looking for. However, if a searcher is looking for a new mobile phone and they run a search, see a perfect result and click on it, they haven't made Google any money. On the other hand, if they can't find exactly what they want, they may well look at the adverts that are presented to them, and click on one – making Google a few cents for the click. So Google has to walk a very fine line between making sure that we get what we need from it, and keep going back to use it, yet ensuring that we also click on adverts whenever possible. It's not in Google's interests to make search better, easier and more functional, because the more it spends time and money doing that, the better and more effective the engine becomes, the less likely the average person on the street is going to click on an advert because they can't find what they need. This helps to explain an otherwise totally irrational decision to reduce the search functionality offered to searchers year on year. In previous editions of this title I was able to wax lyrical about the use of the synonym search function, the tilde ~ sign which meant that Google would find the word that I wanted plus other similar words. Google has now removed that option; they say that it's included in the general search function, so a search for 'library' will also return 'libraries' for example. Although this is true, it doesn't work as effectively as the synonym option, and search is worse for it.

We no longer have access to limit search by visited or unvisited sites, or by reading levels, we can no longer see who is linking to a site, the choice of limiting results to web pages written to specific reading levels, a blog-specific search engine, and so on. The advanced search page has become far more difficult to find now; it used to be linked from the home page, next to the search box. Far from getting better over time, Google's search functionality is getting worse. They use the excuse that it's very expensive to run such functionality, but in my view, any company bringing in almost US$90 billion a year could afford to do it if they wanted to. The fact that they don't want to simply indicates that Google isn't actually that interested in search; for them it's simply a means to an end.

Due to the way in which Google ranks results, they are at the mercy of the people who write and create web pages. Search engine optimisers (SEOs) are employed to create pages to specifically rank highly within Google, with keywords in the URL, title element, several repetitions on the page and so on. Consequently it's quite easy to 'game' the system. Alternatively, or as well, since a lot of links to a page get it a higher ranking, unscrupulous people will create other sites and link back and forth. You'll also find that people with a specific agenda will link to sites that promote the same political or social values that they do. As a result, just because something gets a high ranking in the Google SERPs it doesn't mean that it's a 'good' or authoritative page. For example, a search for 'Martin Luther King' usually brings up a website called 'Martin Luther King Jr – a true historical examination' (it was in fifth position on my results page when I ran the search in February 2017). This page goes into great detail about his shortcomings, and has been written by an extreme right-wing political group in the USA. Searches for information on the Holocaust will often return websites that deny that it ever took place. Recently a search for the phrase 'three black teenagers' returned many results related to crime committed by such individuals, while searches for 'three white teenagers' were far more positive. This led to suggestions that Google was in some way racist, when in actual fact it was simply reflecting what other websites were saying and linking to. This is a real and continuing problem for Google, because on one hand they want to ensure that people get good-quality information that is useful to them (so they'll come back time and again), but on the other hand they don't want to censor websites. With the examples that I've given it would be easy to say that Google could remove links to racist and Holocaust denial websites, but if they do that, where do they stop?

Another area that causes problems both for Google and searchers is in the instant suggestions option. When you start typing a search query Google will attempt to predict what you are looking for and will start to display results on the screen. This can be really helpful, because it not only allows you to complete a search query more quickly but it can also help frame the question in a more satisfactory manner. However, this isn't always the case. For example, if you start a search with the word 'did', the first suggestion that Google returns is 'did the Holocaust happen'. Until recently the first results that were returned argued that it didn't. Another search relating to dinosaur extinction returned a creationist page as the first result in the instant search suggestions option. Google has now manually changed these suggestions and results, but it's certainly something to keep a note of when it comes to searching, and the instant suggestions should not be relied upon. Indeed the issue is further compounded when Google censors its own suggestions, so that it doesn't suggest as a completed search 'the average length of a penis' but instead goes with 'the average length of a pennis (sic)'. This is neither accurate nor helpful!

It could be argued that this is a problem for all search engines, but Google is a victim of its own success. Because so many people use Google it's worth SEO companies concentrating on it to the exclusion of all of the others. A search on Bing for Martin Luther King doesn't return the racist website in the top ten, for example. Tainted results should be a big concern for searchers, although of course what is 'tainted' to some people is the pure unvarnished truth to others, which simply compounds the issue.

A common phrase that you will have heard *ad infinitum* is 'It's all on Google', but of course it isn't. As we've already discussed, this is very far from the truth, but Google also censors itself, and limits what it links to, for various reasons. This may be because various government departments have asked it not to link to various pages, or there may be legal reasons why it doesn't, but Google also makes its own choices. For example, there's a site called the Internet Adult Film database at www.iafd.com and if you run a search on Google for the word *lolita* and limit it to just that site Google returns zero results. However, the same search on Bing returns over 7000 results. I hope you'll excuse the rather distasteful nature of the search, but it clearly illustrates that Google has decided not to include material in its database for its own reasons, but more importantly, it doesn't tell us this, and that's the key issue here. When searching for individuals Google does include the phrase 'Some results may have been removed under data protection law in Europe' with a link to learn more (this is as a result of the Right to be Forgotten law, see p. 147) and it has a page on the website (www.google.com/transparencyreport/removals/government) which lists the number of removal requests that it has received, from whom and regarding what – defamation, privacy, security and national security for example – so it does have a level of transparency, but you can never be sure that you're getting everything that's available. Consequently it's always worth checking with other search engines as well, to ensure that you're getting as comprehensive a result as you possibly can.

I've previously mentioned that when you run a search for a number of words Google will find pages that contain all of them, rank by relevance and then display the results on the screen. While this is usually the case, it doesn't always happen. As an example, if the searcher is looking for three terms and two of those terms rank highly, Google may well quietly drop the third term without telling you, although in some cases it will include an indication of this by displaying the ignored term as crossed out under the search result. So if you've run your search and visited the page and cannot find a term that you're expecting to see, it's not necessarily because you've done anything wrong, it's because Google has decided that it knows best and has chosen what to return to you, despite your specific request. If this happens the easiest way to overcome it is to force Google to search for all of the terms by using the *intext:* search function. You may find Google's presumptions, when it comes to search, active in other areas. A search for *teaching search skills* can also result in Google returning pages that are about teaching *re*search skills, which is an entirely different subject area. Once again it's necessary to go back and re-run the search and either include words into a phrase or use the Verbatim option to force Google to look specifically for 'search' and not 'research'.

Finally, we should say a quick word about personalisation. Google wants to personalise results for you. There are many good reasons for this; if you're particularly interested in apple the fruit and search for it on a regular basis you're not going to want to see references to the company or the record label. Over time Google learns what you click on and where you go so that it can tailor results more to your liking. It also means that it's able to serve up advertisements to you that you're more likely to click on as well, of course. Now, you cannot stop Google doing this. Even if you do not have an account and Google has no way of knowing who 'you' are, it will work on your location as defined by the IP address of the computer that you're using. This is all well and good when you do want apple the fruit, but when you are looking for any other type of apple, Google isn't going to return results that you'll find particularly helpful. In fact, it's worse than this, because Google will make assumptions about what you are going to want and like in the future – based on what you've searched for and clicked on in the past. So for example if Google knows that you like a particular news channel it's going to return results that are either pro- or anti-gun control. As a result it's very easy to end up in a filter bubble; only seeing material that reaffirms your beliefs.

Of course there are ways to mitigate this behaviour. Don't log into your Google account when you search is probably the most obvious suggestion to make. If Google doesn't know who you are, it cannot associate previous searches and actions with current ones, though as already mentioned, it will still have your IP address to work on. As we'll see in a later chapter on multi-search engines, you can search Google by using a third-party search engine, and that way Google is even more removed from the searcher and their previous search history.

Summary

Google is without a doubt the premier search engine, and I cannot see this changing at any time in the future. It does an excellent job of retrieving good-quality search results quickly and easily for the searcher, so it's not a surprise that all other engines trail in its wake. However, it's not perfect and there are plenty of occasions and reasons why you might not want to use it. Fortunately there are plenty of good-quality alternatives available to searchers, and we'll look at those in the next chapter.

CHAPTER 4

Other free-text search engines

Introduction

If I asked you which reference book you used in your work, you'd probably think that you'd misheard me, because of course you probably use quite a lot of them. Similarly if I asked which professional journal your library subscribed to, you'd think that was an odd question as well. However, in my work as a trainer people often think that just using one search engine is a perfectly acceptable way to work, and a common question that I'm asked is 'What's the "best" search engine?'

Did you know?
The average person conducts 3.4 searches every day (http://kingkong.com.au/15-secret-facts-google-search-doesnt-want-know).

There is no best search engine, as there is no best reference book or professional journal. We match the appropriate tool to the question that we've been asked, and if we don't get the answer we need, we just simply move onto the next resource until we have been able to come to a conclusion. Search engines are exactly the same. Google is a great search engine, there's no doubt about that, but as we've seen it does have its drawbacks. Consequently it's a good idea to have various alternatives ready to hand if you can't find what you need, or you simply want an alternative viewpoint on your query. This chapter will look at some of those engines, and in common with the approach that I used with Google I'll look at how they can be used, any interesting new search functions and of course, a critical look at their weaknesses.

Bing

Bing is the Microsoft alternative to Google. Microsoft has had a very chequered career with the internet and has tried several previous incarnations of search to try and compete with Google. This is the only one that's really had any success, and it doesn't look as though it's liable to change or be morphed into anything else by Microsoft at the moment. Much of the functionality is the same as Google's offerings and the data collection method is the same; that is to say, spidering websites, copying the contents of pages back to home base and then indexing them.

Like Google, Bing allows you to create an account and log in before you start to search. Searchers can then see their previous searches, irrespective of the machine that they're using. It's worth setting preferences once logged in, to ensure that you have a consistent experience with the search engine. Settings include moderating content with safe search, location, search suggestions turned on or off, choosing how many results to see on a page, and country and region. This last option is quite important, because once you select your country/region this will not change based on your location. So if you set it to the UK and you travel to India, you'll still be present with UK-based material. You can choose the search language, limit the SERPs to pages written in specific languages and you can choose how the home page is displayed. Finally you can tell Microsoft how you want your privacy and security handled as well. You can tell Bing about any particular interests you have in order to personalise the service, and to receive suggested topics and stories. Bing will track these interests for you and will show related news and updates on the Bing homepage. Moreover, because Bing is tightly integrated into other Microsoft products, these interests can carry across to Cortana (Microsoft's voice-controlled virtual assistant) and mobile phones using Windows Phone software. In order for this all to work though, you do need to have a Microsoft account.

You can also save material and view it later, on any device, such as video and images. You can view your search history, which is of course very useful if you want to return to a search that you ran last week, and can't quite remember what syntax you used. Of course, you can do the same thing with Google's 'My Activity' but Bing allows you access to this material with a couple of mouse clicks. You can also search your search history and limit to web, images, videos or news, as well as choosing particular dates, so it's a nice, fast and very effective way to return to your recent, or perhaps distant past to check out your search activity.

At the bottom of the home page there are a number of tiles related to current news and these can be scrolled across, rather like the Google carousel option. Clicking on a tile opens a page of results that link to the story, as well as providing searchers with related search options. If you have an interest in national or international news, this is a useful function to keep you fully up to date with what is happening in the world of business, sports, entertainment, world and national news.

Did you know?
The average search query contains about three words (www.writemysite.co.uk/from-search-behaviour-st-patricks-day-content-marketing-trends/2017/03/17).

Bing's search functionality

For anyone searching with Google, Bing will offer no unpleasant surprises. When you start to type in your search terms Bing will offer appropriate suggestions (depending on your settings), even down to concluding a search for 'did' with 'the Holocaust happen'. The SERPs is quite unremarkable; it provides a set of images at the top of the results if appropriate, a small box to the right giving factual information, adverts underneath and a list of web pages. The web pages display the title of the page, the URL and a summary of the content focused on the search terms used. There is also an option next to the URL to see Bing's cached version of the page. Finally, at the bottom of the results is a list of related searches, usually about eight in total.

Searchers are presented with a menu of filter options under the search box. First of all there is an indication of the number of results (which I would put as much trust into as I would with those offered by Google), a date option for the last 24 hours, week, month or custom range, a language option and an option to limit results to your country settings. Depending on the search that's being run Bing may also give basic dictionary definitions as well. So a search for 'dog' will give several definitions, the word pronounced aloud through your speakers, the word used as a verb, word origin and related forms. The equivalent knowledge graph will also link to appropriate Wikipedia entries, other facts and figures, related people and an option for 'People also search for'.

By default all searches are AND – based, that is to say the search will return results that include all of the terms that have been searched for. Bing also understands and utilises the other basic Boolean operators OR and NOT. Bing does have an order of precedence which, unlike Google's, is clearly laid out. So AND has a higher precedence than OR. Therefore a search for 'movie star OR television celebrity' will be viewed as a search for movie and star, or television and celebrity, and not movie and star or television and celebrity. Symbols can be used instead of words, so cat AND dog can be written as cat & dog, cat NOT dog can be written as cat – dog and cat OR dog can be written as cat | dog. The phrase option is the same as that used by Google, which is to say double quotes. You'll also find that *site:*, *define*, *filetype:*, *inanchor:*, *inbody:* and *intitle:* all work in exactly the same way. There are a few different syntaxes though, such as '*url:<a url>*' which works in the same way as Google's *info:* option.

Bing does, however, have some different options which are unavailable if you're searching with Google. If you're looking for a search term, and you also want to find pages that include specific file types (rather than including the search term within a filetype) users can search for *<term> contains:<filetype>*, so a search for *library contains:ppt* should limit to pages that include the search term and links to PowerPoint files. Bing provides a search function to enable searchers to find pages that contain RSS or Atom feeds, which can then be added into a feed-reader. Consequently a search for *site:www.nytimes hasfeed:books* will give results from the *New York Times* website that have feeds that contain the term 'books'.

Bing has a *near* operator, similar to Google's *AROUND(x)* function, and it works in the same way – to limit the distance between terms to that chosen by the searcher. A search for *library near:5 London* should return results where both words are within five words of each other. It does work, but in my experience not always with the greatest level of accuracy, so is not to be relied upon.

A language operator does exist, and it's simply *language:* and then a two-letter abbreviation for the language you're interested in, so Russian is *ru*, German is *de*, and so on. Unfortunately, it doesn't work very well. A search for *librarians language:ru* should just return pages which are about librarians and for which the language is Russian. While this is generally the case – most of the results are in Russian – there are still a reasonable number in English, but these pages do tend to have some link to the language of interest; part of the page may be in Russian, or there's a link to a Russian language PDF, for example. So it's not an entirely satisfactory search function, but is reasonable.

Finally, Bing does not have an advanced search options page at all. This is disappointing, since it used to, but Microsoft has dispensed with it now. So to that extent it's not as user-friendly as Google, and searchers need to have a better grasp and understanding of search engine functionality to get the best out of it.

Bing Image search

It will come as no surprise to see that Bing's image search functionality is almost exactly the same as Google's. You run your search, either by running a web-based search and then clicking on Images from the top menu, or you go straight to the image search page at www.bing.com/images. Bing presents searchers with various search options related to your search term, so when I looked for *fox red Labradors* I got options to view *silver Labrador retrievers*, *Labradoodle* and so on. When users cursor over an image they have options to save it (obviously it's necessary to be logged in to do this), a link to search for 'more like this', the size of the image in pixels and what format the image is.

Clicking on an image to see it in full size displays it in the centre of the screen with arrows right and left to move from one image to the next. The dialog box shows details of the page that the image is found on, tags used to define the image and a summary of the image. Other options allow users to view the image on its own page, add it to Microsoft's 'OneNote' resource, pin it to Pinterest, or run all of the images as a slideshow. I can also see how many pages Bing has indexed that contain the exact image that is being viewed, options to see different sizes of the image and links to related images as well.

Bing has an option to filter image results, and once again, it's very similar to that provided by Google. Searchers can limit to specific or general sizes, specific colours, colour only or black and white only, type of image, including photograph, clipart, line drawing, animated gif or transparent. Other options include layout, that is to say square, wide or tall, faces, heads and shoulders, dates, or specific Creative Commons licences. Finally, Bing does have a safesearch filter, which works reasonably well; a search for 'blue tits' returns appropriate avian imagery and nothing else! However, as with all filters, it cannot be relied upon 100%, so 'viewer discretion is advised' might be an appropriate phrase at this point.

Bing Videos

Bing's video offering is very similar to that which they use for images. Searchers can either run a search and then click on the 'videos' option, or go directly to www.bing.com/videos/. Bing will offer various search options at the top of the screen allowing for the possibility of a tighter more accurate search. Below that are a series of filters, which I'll come back to, and underneath those are the videos themselves, presented in a tile-based format. Each video tile is overlaid with its title, and below it is a useful collection of facts about it. The source (such as YouTube for example), length, number of views, format, upload date and creator. With the majority of videos simply placing the cursor over the video will make it play in a preview mode. If the video is very short you may get to view the entire thing, but if it's longer, a shortened version will play. This can't be guaranteed, since some videos don't have a preview option though.

An important point to make here is that you can of course turn safe search on or off, or leave it as 'moderate', which is the default. However, this is a simple toggle on the page that anyone can do. It's therefore an excellent way to get around any filtering systems that might be in place, as you may well find that because the video is being viewed within Bing it escapes any filtering software on your machine or network. This is both an advantage and a disadvantage, of course, but is something to be aware of.

As previously mentioned, there are various ways of narrowing down and filtering the search results. These are length (short, medium or long), date (past 24 hours, week, month or year), resolution, source (based on the results that have been returned, so these will differ every time), and price (free or paid). If searchers are logged into Bing they can also save videos to view later.

In comparison to Google's video offering I think that Bing's version is far superior. It's more informative, easier to see on the screen and the mouse-over is very helpful.

Bing News

Bing pulls its news from a variety of different authoritative news sources such as the *New York Times*, the BBC, the *Washington Post* and other national news sources. Searchers can either run a search and choose the news option, or go directly to the appropriate URL, which is www.bing.com/news. News stories are pulled together into various news groupings such as Top Stories, World, UK, Business, Politics and so on. Stories are placed on the page in a tile-based format, consistent with their image and video results, with real-time news in a bar on the right-hand side of the screen. Each story has a headline, matching image, URL and/or summary, an indication of source and a keyword summary which can in turn be clicked on to run a new search.

A search will pull results from all of the resources available, irrespective of source or country. However, using the *site:* option it's easy to limit those results to particular country and you can also use the same function to narrow results to a particular source. So a search for *librarians* will give the searcher a global set of results, *librarians site:.uk* will restrict to British newspapers and magazines, while *librarians site:.tvguide.co.uk* will restrict even further.

DuckDuckGo

DuckDuckGo (DDG), named after a child's game, focuses on protecting the privacy of the searcher, so it doesn't profile its users and makes a point of showing all users the same results for a particular search term. This makes it particularly useful if you're working with a client over the phone, for example, and they are running a search at the same time as you are, following your instructions. Your 'third result down' comment will work, since their third result down will be the same as yours, unlike Google, which we've previously discussed. DuckDuckGo pulls its SERPs from key sites such as Wikipedia and partnerships with other search engines such as Bing and its own web crawler. It also doesn't include results from what are often referred to as 'content mills', which are websites that produce large amounts of poor-quality content in order to make money from advertising.

DDG has a very simple SERP, with an emphasis on the title of the page, a brief summary that includes search terms, and the page URL. A mouse over the result gives searchers the opportunity to view more pages from the site in question; it's essentially just adding a *site:* function to the existing search terms. For some search terms DDG adds a carousel function, similar to that offered by Google, particularly when the engine isn't sure of what the searcher wants. So a search for *Charles II* will give results for the English king, but above those will be opportunities to search for Charles II of Navarre, Spain, Naples, Lorraine and so on. DDG will provide as many possible answers as it can find and will also arrange them into categories to make it easier to find.

In common with Google, DDG may at times also produce an instant answers option showing summary information, an image and basic facts and figures such as dates of birth/death, spouse and related topics. As with Google, it's not possible to 'force' an instant answer, but searches for individuals, places, events and so on will produce one. There are over 1100 instant answers available and DDG provides an overview list of them at https://duck.co/ia.

DDG only provides a very small number of filters, unlike Google and Bing. Searches can be limited to results from one country from a pulldown menu, or a period of time – past day, week, month. The results are on an infinite scroll, so as soon as you move to the bottom of the page a second page of results displays and so on; there's no moving to page 2 and onwards in the way that Google requires.

DuckDuckGo Images

DDG obviously has an image search function, but in comparison with some of the other search engines in this category it's really quite poor. Images are displayed and a mouse-over reveals the size of the image. Clicking on it displays it in the middle of the screen in a dialogue box with links to the page that it comes from. The only option is to limit to one of three sizes, small, medium or large. DDG does have a safesearch option which can be toggled on or off, but even if the option has been turned off, it doesn't present extreme imagery, though obviously it's worth checking, just to be on the safe side.

DuckDuckGo Videos

DDG also employs an automatic filter on videos, which are displayed in a tile-type format above traditional web-based results. The tile includes a screen shot of the video, title, source and the number of views that it's had. Clicking on the link allows it to be viewed either at DDG or on the originating site. DDG does warn users that YouTube does not allow people to view videos anonymously, and as such 'watching YouTube videos here [on DDG] will be tracked by YouTube/Google'.

DuckDuckGo News

The news functionality is similarly limited to a collection of tiled links above the main web-based results. The news stories include title, summary, source and date of the story.

DuckDuckGo advanced search syntax

Although there isn't an option to go directly to an advanced search page, DDG does support some advanced search functionality. We've already seen that it will automatically include *site:* if requested. In common with other engines searchers can use *inbody:*, or *b:* for short, to make sure that the keyword appears in the body of the page. To make sure that the keyword appears in the title of the page use *intitle:* or *t:*, and to ensure that the results contain files of a particular type searchers can use *filetype:* or *f:* with the appropriate extension.

Unlike Google, DDG will not try to autocorrect your query terms, and as you'd expect, will attempt to AND them. The OR operator will only function between adjacent words, so a search for 'movie star OR actor' means that DDG will look for pages that include 'movie' and either 'star' or 'actor'. If this isn't what is required, double quotes to define a phrase will ensure DDG searches appropriately. In the previous example a search for *"movie star" OR actor* will return pages with the phrase 'movie star' or the word 'actor'. In a chain of ORs the middle groups of words are automatically quoted. Consequently a search for *hubble telescope OR mars venus OR jupiter* will be read as a search for:

Hubble and telescope
OR mars and venus
OR Jupiter.

If this isn't what you want or expect to happen DDG allows searchers to group ORs together. So *mars OR Jupiter AND images OR pictures* will run a search for:

Mars or Jupiter
and either images or pictures.

The Boolean operators are applied in the order of OR before AND. So a search for *hubble telescope OR NASA and research exploration OR planets* is the equivalent to a search for:

hubble and telescope
OR NASA and research exploration
OR planets.

This means searches will include hubble and either telescope or NASA, and one of either research exploration and planets. Searchers can also use OR in conjunction with other search syntax, so a search for *"American President" site:bbc.co.uk OR site:cnn.com* will return results for that phrase as it's found on either website.

DDG allows searchers to boost different regions. There's a setting on the settings page that allows users to choose to emphasise a particular region, or alternatively choose the region option that's available above the results. For a one-off search the region can be changed by adding the search parameter *r:region code* to the search, such as *r:fr* for France. This boosts the results from that region, rather than excluding results from other places in the way that the *site:* option does. DDG provides a very comprehensive list of the parameters that you can use, at https://duckduckgo.com/params. This is worth checking, since it allows you to edit the URL on the SERP (as we saw with changing the time search parameter with Google in Chapter 3) to add in country codes, safe searches, open instant answers, set privacy options, colour settings and interface settings.

DuckDuckGo 'bangs'

So far DDG looks like a perfectly normal, ordinary search engine without anything in particular – other than the privacy aspect – to really recommend it. However, perhaps the most useful feature of the engine is the 'bang' functionality. A 'bang' is a search function that makes use of the exclamation mark plus a short code immediately after it which tells DDG to execute a specific search. So, for example, if I wanted just to retrieve answers from Wikipedia my search would be *!w <keywords>*, where the *!w* is the 'bang' that the searcher uses to tell DDG exactly what to do and where to look. The bangs are a superb shortcut to get you directly to the information that you want quickly. There are currently over 9000 different bangs, and more are added on a regular basis.

That's quite a daunting figure, so DDG provides a little search engine at https://duckduckgo.com/bang which can be used to find bangs that are of interest. A search for *BBC* brings back 15 different results, all bangs that will do different things. A search for *!bbcsport everton* in the DDG home page search box will take the searcher directly to the BBC website and execute the search for the better of the two Merseyside football teams. Alternatively a search for *!bbc elections* will result in the user going directly to the BBC website and running that specific keyword search.

DDG also provides searchers with a category approach to finding bangs. Below the search box previously mentioned eight categories are available, such as Entertainment, Research, Shopping and Tech. The Research category has over 20 sub-categories, such as Academic, Government, Health, Reference and Travel. Clicking on any of those options will take the user into an alphabetical listing of available bangs. I would thoroughly recommend spending some time exploring these, because the bangs will not only save you a lot of time, but they'll highlight resources that you probably were not even aware of. The Research>Reference category starts with *!airframes* for aircraft registration and ends with *!zanran*, allowing the user to search the Zanran search engine directly.

If in the unlikely event that you don't find a bang search that matches your needs you can always create one for yourself: to add a new one, or to update an existing one, go to https://duckduckgo.com/newbang.

Other reasons to use DuckDuckGo

Although the bang option is a very good reason to prefer DDG over some of the other search engines that we'll be looking at, there are also a number of other very clever tricks that the engine does which none of the others do, or don't do as well. Some of these come from the collection of instant answers, and others are simply things that have been coded into the search engine.

Social media profiles DDG allows you to check out someone's social media profile without leaving the SERP. A search for @philbradley, for example, provides a brief overview of information associated with that account – photograph, name, general location, website and Twitter biography. If you needed to search for someone's Google+ biography simply add G+ before their name.

Expanding shortened URLs You'll be familiar with shortened URLs; there are lots of tools around which will take a long URL and provide you with a much shorter version. You simply type in the short version to your browser, the browser checks with the originating site, finds the expanded link and then takes you directly there. However, until that happens you have no real way of ensuring that you'll go to the site you expect. Of course, the person putting the short version together might give you a hint, so that the Bit.ly link of http://bit.ly/philsocmed216 will in all probability take you to some sort of social media page of information created by someone called Phil – but you don't actually know. However, if you run a search for expand http://bit.ly/philsocmed216 DDG will produce a result that shows you the expanded URL, in this case www.dropbox.com/s/ccbrtiajohzcrqc/SocmedintroJan2016.pptdl=0. Alternatively, if you have a long URL and you want to shorten it, simply type or cut and paste it into the search box and precede it with 'shorten'. DDG will use the is.gd service to provide you with a smaller version, in this case https://is.gd/xWvxMJ.

Generate passwords If you need some help in generating strong passwords DDG can do this for you. Run a search for *password 8* to get an average-strength password that's eight letters long, such as 6iLBUjwg. For a stronger password simply add 'strong' into the search, so you'll get *password strong 8* and in my example DDG suggested JUHU7&U! If you're not happy with any of those, DDG can produce a collection of four words that you could use together. Search for *random passphrase* and in my example DDG returned 'launch link technological comprehensive'. According to the website 'How secure is my password' (https://howsecureismypassword.net) this would take a computer about 24 quattuordecillion years to crack. I'm not sure quite how long that is, but I'm guessing it's going to be pretty safe!

Changing case I have no idea why DDG does this next trick, since it has nothing to do with search, but it's very helpful. If you run a search for *titlecase lucy in the sky with diamonds* DDG will capitalise the first letter of every word –

and in this case will also provide a list of the lyrics that go with it as well. Alternatively, if you want everything in upper-case letters, just run a search for *uppercase* and then the words you want in capitals. As you'd expect, *lowercase* does the opposite.

Site down check If you're having trouble getting through to a site it's possible that it's currently down, or unavailable. Alternatively, it could simply be that there's a local problem that's stopping you accessing a site. Running a search for *is <name of the site> down* will provide a response pulled from the Is It Up? website at https://isitup.org.

Finding rhymes and anagrams DDG can find lists of words that rhyme with a keyword that you provide. A search for *rhymes with bradley* returns results of 'badly, gladly, sadly and madly'. Another word-based option is to find anagrams by simply running a search for *anagram <word>* and the engine will give you a list of them if it can find them.

Calendar If you need to see a calendar for a previous year, DDG can display that directly on the results page for you. Simply search for *calendar july 1863* to get a calendar for that month and year displayed for you. Do note, though, that it has to be in that order, as a search for *calendar 1863 july* will simply run a straightforward web page search for those terms.

Colours *Color codes* as a search phrase will display a listing of different colours and their values; useful if you're a coder or a web page designer.

Create a QR code I know everyone seems to hate QR codes, but they do have a value now and then. Simply type '*qr*' before a URL and get a QR code for that site.

Yandex

Yandex is one of the largest internet companies in Europe, operating Russia's most popular search engine and its most visited website. According to LiveInternet, as of April 2015 it generated 58.6% of all search traffic in Russia. It also operates in Ukraine, Kazakhstan, Belarus and Turkey. It was first developed back in 1990, the website was launched in 1997, and it became profitable in 2003. Yandex has over 5000 employees and offices in Russia, Ukraine, Belarus, USA, Turkey, Switzerland and Germany. It says that its mission is 'to answer any question internet users may have'. Yandex features parallel search, which in their words 'presents on a single page the results from both our main web index and our specialised information resources, including news, shopping, blogs, images and videos'. Yandex has a refreshingly different approach to search from that of Google. It says that the 'happiness of the user' is of crucial importance, and the happier the users, the more a business model will follow. The search makes its money from contextual advertising and annual turnover exceeds US$1 billion. That doesn't put it into the same category as Google of course, but I'm more interested in what it can do as a search engine than inspecting the balance sheet.

Did you know?
The United Arab Emirates has the highest internet penetration, accessed by 99% of citizens (https://thenextweb.com/insights/ 2017/01/24/digital-trends-2017-report-internet).

Search functionality

As you would expect, Yandex comes with the usual search box, with search options along the top for images, video, mail, maps, metrica and the Yandex browser. The mail option allows users to get access to their e-mail accounts as provided by Yandex. 'Metrica' is a tool to monitor an apps performance, and the browser link takes you to a page where you can download their browser, oddly enough. So the menu isn't just for search, it links to other company options, which to be honest I don't find terribly helpful – they would be better served by having those items at the bottom of the page, in common with most other search engines. Finally, in the search bar is a keyboard icon, which when clicked presents users with an onscreen keyboard. I'm somewhat bemused by that, but then I saw that you could change the language to a number of others, so if you wanted to search more easily in Cyrillic for example, you'd be able to.

Search is straightforward – simply start to type in your keywords and Yandex will supply suggestions, which you can obviously accept or continue typing. The results are in the usual format of title, URL and summary. The site favicon is also displayed to the left of the title. You can also click on the half-diamond to see the cached version, more from the site or to complain about the site. Video results are also shown, with an indication as to the numbers of results, and a link to see other videos. You can also see a few appropriate images, and click the link to view more of them. At the bottom of the page is an option to try the search on both Google and Bing, which is interesting. All very straightforward, with nothing particularly exciting, though it's worth mentioning that Yandex didn't take into account my location when I was searching, unlike Google. I'm in two minds as to the value of this, but on the whole, I prefer a straightforward feed, rather than a personalised one.

An advanced search function is offered. This is to the top right of the results.

You can choose a location, a specific site, an exact match for the search, language (Russian or English with seven more options), file type (web, Microsoft Office, Open Office) and date (last 24 hours, past two weeks, past month or from/to). You can also change and save search settings. These are standard or advanced descriptions, opening results in a new tab or the same window, results language, safe search and correct searches or offer search suggestions.

At first glance, that looks like all that you can do. However, if you persevere, more options present themselves. You can link words together using the '&' function, so '*librarian & school & London*' will result in a query that finds all of the words in the same sentence, rather than anywhere on the page. You can do an exact match either by using the already mentioned advanced search function or by using the double quotes option, so that's fairly standard. You can run a search to find words within a certain number of other words, so '*school /+3 librarian*' finds the word 'librarian' located up to three words after the word 'school'. Interestingly you can also run a search such as '*school /-3 librarian*', which will limit results to pages that contain the word 'librarian' up to three words before 'school'. It's possible to be even more precise than this, however. By running a search such as '*school && /3 librarian*' you can limit the search to pages that contain the two words within three words of each other in the same sentence. This is very helpful in avoiding false hits. If that's not complex enough, you can run a search for either option and it's in the form of '*school /(-1 +3) librarian*', to find results where librarian is either one word before school or up to three words afterwards. This really allows for some very precise searching, far superior to anything that Google is capable of.

Yandex will also exclude words for you, by using the minus symbol, so '*school –librarian*' will remove pages that contain 'librarian', but it also offers you the chance to change your mind, and you can cancel the operation, just searching for both words instead. However, we don't need to stop there. Instead of using the minus symbol, you can use the tilde symbol, so '*school ~~ librarian*' (double tilde) will give you the same result as '*school –librarian*'. On the other hand, if you run a search for '*school ~ librarian*' (single tilde), results with the word 'librarian' will be excluded only if the two words are in the same phrase. You do have to leave a space after the ~, rather than run it straight onto the keyword. (Rather confusingly, Yandex requires there to be no space after the minus symbol, but there has to be a space after the tilde symbol.)

The OR operator works as you would expect, with '*school OR librarian*' giving results with web pages that contain either or both terms. If you want to be absolutely precise you can restrict Yandex from searching for alternatives by using the exclamation mark. For example, searching for '*dog*' will also return terms such as 'doggy', but searching for '*!dog*' just gives you exactly that term. What's really helpful is that this function allows you to limit results by capitalisation, so '*librarian*' will find you any page with the term, but '*!Librarian*' should return pages that only have the word with its initial capital letter.

Limiting by language is fairly obvious – if you don't want to use the advanced search function, to limit to French, for instance, simply add in 'lang:fr' to the search. There are only a few options available, so 'ru' stands for Russian, 'uk' for Ukrainian, 'be' for Belorussian, 'en' for English, 'fr' for French and 'de' for German.

You can search for pages with a specific title, and the functionality is '*title[School Librarian]*' or you can also use '*title:school librarian*'. This version gives you variants on the terms though, so you'll get results that contain 'school library'. In order to get exactly what you want, you would need to run a search for '*title:school !Librarian*'.

As well as title searches you can search for fragments of a URL such as '*inurl:school*'. As you'd expect you can also search through a specific site with the function '*site:philb.com*'. It's also easy to search for a specific type of site, with the '*domain:*' option, so '*librarian domain:.gov.uk*' will limit the search to pages from the UK government that contain the word librarian.

The asterisk works in searches and will be replaced by any other word, such as '*"national orchestra"*'. Please note, however, that you must include the double quotes, or the search will not work – you'll just get results for 'national orchestra'.

Multimedia searching

Images I like the way that Yandex does image searching; it provides a variety of different filters, such as size, (large, medium, small or specific size), recently added images, a wallpaper option, orientation, type (photo, with white background, pictures and drawings or people), colour, specific file type (jpeg, png, gif) or images on a specific site. You can also get Yandex to search based on an image that you provide, either that you upload or that you point it towards on the web. When you have run a search the images appear on the left-hand side of the screen, with the right-hand side being reserved for a larger-sized version of the image result that's been highlighted. You can then use that to search for similar images, or the same image in different sizes. Finally, you can share the image directly onto Facebook, Pinterest or Twitter.

Video Video searching provides various different options as well. You can search by duration (any, less than 10 minutes, 10–65 minutes or more than 65 minutes), HD format, recent videos, or sort by relevance or date. One thing that I particularly like is the fact that you can choose a particular video and it will run directly on the search results page – you don't have to go off to the originating site such as YouTube.

Map There is a map search function, and this is the only thing that I found to be really quite poor. I found the actual map very colourless and devoid of detail, unless you really zoom in. You can search nearby restaurants, cafés, museums and hotels, but this function simply didn't work at all; it was a total failure.

Other free-text search engines

If you're looking for a direct competitor to, or alternative for Google, I think that in all probability you'll have found it with one of the three options that I've looked at so far. However, it would be remiss of me to stop at this point, since there are plenty of other free-text search engines available, and it's worthwhile taking a look at some of them.

StartPage

StartPage, at www.startpage.com, takes its results from Google, which offers you the search functionality and results format that you're already used to. The obvious question is 'Why would I use StartPage when I can just use Google?'; it's because StartPage offers a level of privacy which isn't offered by Google. It has a number of useful features that may make it an attractive alternative. There is a proxy service, and this lets users browse websites without passing on any private or personally identifiable information. In the normal course of events when you click on a link and visit a page listed in the SERPs the website you visit may be able to see and record your IP address, place cookies onto your browser and possibly even read those put there by other websites. It can observe and record everything that you do on the site; the pages you visit and the links you click on. If you are involved in competitor intelligence this is obviously the very last thing that you want to happen! However, because of the StartPage proxy service it can go to the website page that you're interested in, retrieve the page and display it for you. This means that the website doesn't know who you are (just that StartPage requested a copy of the page) and it can't see or store any cookies on your computer. The disadvantage is that because it's a two-stage process – StartPage getting the content, arranging it and then passing it onto the searcher – it can take slightly longer for pages to load, and some features that require javascript may not work correctly.

StartPage also has a URL generator which allows you to save your search engine preferences. Normally this would be done by a cookie that resides on your computer, but instead StartPage can provide you with a specific URL that lists all of your preferences there, instead of in the cookie. Finally, StartPage supports Secure Socket Layer (SSL) connections, which creates a secure connection between your machine and the engine's servers. When you see the part of the URL that is 'https://' rather than just 'http://' you can be assured that all of the searches that you make cannot be intercepted by anyone else.

As previously mentioned, StartPage pulls results from Google, so you shouldn't experience any problems using it. There is an advanced search page at www.startpage.com/uk/advanced-search.htm which is very similar to that provided by Google, with the same kind of parameters such as language, file type, domain, date and so on. The SERP is also very familiar, with the title of the page displayed in the results along with the URL and a brief summary. However, there are options to allow searchers to view the proxy version of the page (as previously discussed) and there's an option to view the page with the search term(s) highlighted to make it easier and quicker to scan the page. The only search filter available on the SERP is the opportunity to limit results in a time frame of the last 24 hours, week, month or year.

Image searching is very basic, with pictures and a mouse-over giving size details. Clicking on the link will display a dialogue box with title information, a link to the originating page and opportunities to visit the page, visit the page anonymously or to view the image (always anonymously). Filters are available for adult language or adult video results.

Video search provides a tiled list of results with a thumbnail, title, number of views and length of video. Clicking on a tile will provide a dialogue box which also contains details of who produced the video and when it was uploaded.

Metro5

Metro5 is another straightforward search engine, at http://metro5.com, which only offers web and news searches. It displays the top 50 results that it finds in a text format, but its unique point is that you can rate a site by clicking on a link to indicate if you like or dislike it, and why. The ranking is confirmed by tweeting it for everyone else to see. This makes it particularly useful, since you could quickly and easily create a tweet with hashtags for others to follow, so would be particularly useful at a conference. You could of course do this manually, but it's a nice, easy and effective way of doing it. Metro5 supports the usual Boolean operators, phrase searching, filetype searches, site, feed and intitle searches.

Oscobo

Oscobo, at https://oscobo.co.uk, is a UK-based company that also prides itself on privacy when it comes to searching. It doesn't track any information, so the SERPs are based solely on the words that the searcher uses and nothing else. Oscobo offers search functionality across the web, videos, images and news. Results are very straightforward, with title, URL and summary, but it does include a thumbnail of the returned page whenever possible. Unfortunately it doesn't have an advanced search function, or a list of functionality, so it's difficult to know exactly what searchers can do with it. The site function worked, but *intitle:* didn't, so I'm afraid it's a bit of a hit and miss approach.

The video option gives results in the same format as the web-based search, with title, URL, summary and thumbnail, but there's the addition of the date it was uploaded. Image search is quite poor, with a collection of images and a click on them taking the searcher directly to the originating web page. News options are limited to title, URL, summary and, depending on the search, a collection of the latest tweets from Twitter.

Oscobo is worth using if you want to keep your anonymity and prefer to use a British-based search engine, although of course the results are global in nature.

Other examples

In this chapter I have tried to pull out interesting examples of free-text search engines, and indicate why they are different and what their unique selling point is. Of course, there are many others available, and there isn't the space to go into detail on all of them. Consequently I've decided to simply list a few other alternatives. There's nothing wrong with any of them, and indeed you may find one that you absolutely love to use, so they are worth exploring at least once or twice.

- AOL search, http://search.aol.com/aol/webhome
- Draze, www.draze.com
- Entire web, www.entireweb.com
- Exalead, www.exalead.co.uk/search

- HotBot, www.hotbot.com
- Lycos, http://search20.lycos.com
- Surfcanyon, www.surfcanyon.com
- Yahoo!, https://search.Yahoo!.com.

What to look for when exploring a new free-text search engine

Of course, in between my writing this edition and your reading it, it's quite likely that other free-text search engines will have emerged onto the search engine scene. Consequently I thought it might be useful if I provided a quick overview of some of the things that I check when assessing a new find, so that you can do it as well; hopefully it will save you time and effort.

Before doing any type of search at all I'll look for an 'about us' or 'FAQ' page to see if I can learn anything more about the engine; who produced it, where it's located, something of its history and so on. If I can't find anything I'll do a quick web search on the name to see if there's anything already out there which mentions it. That information should give me a good start, and hopefully an indication of the unique selling point of the engine, with reasons why I should use it.

I'll then run some sample searches that I have used before. I have a variety of these, both professional and personal in nature, so that I can compare the results from major engines like Google and Yandex with the new pretenders. Obviously the results are going to be different, so it's worth choosing one or two sites that you know are really good; where are they found on the SERPs? Hopefully they will be somewhere within the top ten, and if they're not, that's not a good sign. I'll also run a search to see if any fake or dubious sites are returned, which helps me understand if there's any quality control.

It's worth looking for a sort of 'advanced search' option, but these days that's quite rare, though if I do find one, that's a good sign. I'll then see if there are any hidden supported search functions, such as *site:*, *filetype:*, *intitle:* and so on.

Comparing the results against Google and Bing is always worth doing. Not all search engines spider the web themselves – some, such as AOL Search, will take their results from other providers (in the case of this example, Bing) and they may or may not be particularly upfront about it. However, a quick comparison of results should make it fairly clear.

Finally I'll look to see what other search options are available; does the engine also search images, videos, news or social media-based content? Putting all of this together doesn't take too long and gives me a fairly clear idea as to the value of the engine and if it's worth remembering in the long term and mentioning to colleagues.

Summary

Free-text search engines are really the 'bread and butter' of the expert searcher; we generally know what we're looking for, which key words or phrases to search on and how to quickly evaluate the results. Some of the engines are more complicated or functional than others, and while they don't tend towards the complexity of traditional commercial database search engines they do the job reasonably well. Hopefully I have demonstrated that there are several very good alternatives to Google which are worth exploring. Being realistic, most people are always going to turn to Google first, since that's where most people have always gone, and it does usually return acceptable results. However, for more in-depth searching it's not always the best solution, so having a familiarity with others is never going to do any harm.

CHAPTER 5

» Directory, clustering and similarity search engines

Introduction

In the 1990s this class of search engine was extremely popular, and Yahoo! was leading the charge. It's hard to believe that at one point Yahoo! was worth over US$100 billion (www.youtube.com/watch?v=5DpspOXs1rM) and it was a huge brand, closely associated with search and its search directory. It acted as a portal to the internet when there really wasn't very much organisation at all. Websites were springing up at the rate of thousands per day and early engines such as AltaVista simply couldn't keep up with this flood. Rather than try and seek out all of these websites Yahoo! and others like them took a different approach – web authors came to them, looked through their search directory hierarchy and found an appropriate niche for their site. This would then be submitted and once approved, the website would be included in the directory. The portal approach used directory search to encourage people to visit and to stay on the website. Coupled with news, video and messaging services it was hoped that a compelling offer would ensure that consumers wouldn't look anywhere else.

However, this failed to take into account the fact that people wanted to search more quickly and effectively, and by tying advertisements to the type of searches that people were running Google was able to take an increasingly larger share of the marketplace. The growth of Facebook, Twitter and YouTube meant that people were also getting their news from various different places, and communication tools such as Messenger and WhatsApp further depreciated the value of the portal approach. Finally, because of the sheer amount of growth of websites, and importantly the increase in technology,

Did you know?
There are over 123,780,000 registered .com domain names (https://hostingfacts.com/internet-facts-stats-2016).

speed of spidering websites and fall in storage costs meant that free-text engines were able to index far more, and more effectively, than directory-based engines. As users deserted the sinking ship of Yahoo! and similar sites, advertising revenue decreased and it simply wasn't possible to change course and go from a directory-based to a free-text approach, although Yahoo! did attempt that with their 'Yahoo!-Microsoft Search Alliance' in December 2009. In late December 2014 Yahoo! closed its Directory offering, 20 years after it began.

Now, the purpose of this introduction isn't to be overly critical either of Yahoo! or the premise of directory-based search engines, but it's important to understand their role within search, which is increasingly sidelined. With Google, search and advertisements work hand in hand; with directory-based search engines the strength lies in the value of the portal and its overall offerings, but unfortunately these offerings are increasingly under attack by other tools and resources, particularly social media. Directory engines do have a part to play in internet search, but it's an increasingly niche one.

Directory-based search engines

I've discussed the generalities of directory-based search engines in Chapter 2, so let's move straight on and take a look at some that are available.

The WWW Virtual Library

In an internet where everything is always assumed to be brand-new and straight out of the box, the Virtual Library, at http://vlib.org, is the oldest of all the tools and resources we'll be looking at in the book. It was started by Sir Tim Berners-Lee in 1991 at CERN in Geneva. It's run by a collection of volunteers and they compile pages of key links for different subject areas. Each volunteer or maintainer is responsible for their own content, although they all follow a set of guidelines.

There are 16 major subject areas or headings, and these are:

1 Agriculture
2 Arts
3 Business and economics
4 Communications and media
5 Computing and computer science
6 Education
7 Engineering

8 Humanities and humanistic studies
9 Information and libraries
10 International affairs
11 Law
12 Natural sciences and mathematics
13 Recreation
14 Regional studies
15 Social and behavioural sciences
16 Society.

Each of these subject areas is broken down appropriately to its subject coverage. 'Information and libraries', for example has subheadings on advanced browsing, electronic journals, information design, information quality, knowledge management and published subjects. Each of these subheadings contains more information and links to different websites. 'Advanced browsing' leads to six subheadings, including 'The future', which in turn leads to areas such as 'Anonymity and privacy', together with 'see also' subject links. There is a 'quick search' function on the home page and this is replicated on every other page in the directory.

Without wishing to be negative or critical of the resource, particularly because of its place in internet history, it's of very limited use. Some sections have not been updated in several years, and it has the air of a rather neglected old house which is slowly falling to rack and ruin. It still does have some use, if searchers are not clear on exactly what they want, because the construction of the directory does point people towards subject areas they may not have previously been familiar with.

DMOZ

DMOZ, at www.dmoz.org, called itself 'the largest, most comprehensive human-edited directory of the web'. It was originally created in 1998 and by 2015 was listing almost four million websites in over 1 million categories and was owned by AOL. Unfortunately, however, in March of 2017 it was closed by AOL. I'm not in the habit of including search engines that have closed, but since this one has been around for so long, it's quite likely that readers will wonder why I haven't included a reference to it in this chapter, so if you're one of those people, I'm sorry to have to break it to you!

However, there are other examples of this type of search engine which provide different functions and features, so it's worth exploring some of them in a little detail.

Findelio

The Findelio search engine, at www.findelio.com, is a very basic-looking search engine, with a list of headings and subheadings, a search box and an alphabetical list of categories. It provides a collection of regional quick links for a small number of countries (mainly US and European), as well as a sponsor listing of the day. It's been active since 2005, so it certainly has longevity on its side. Rather than having editors who actively go out and find websites to add to categories, Findelio requires web authors to submit sites directly to them, which they will then assess for inclusion in the directory. Consequently the collection of links is self-selected and you can't expect anything to be even remotely comprehensive. However, if you don't like the Virtual Library or DMOZ, this is a fair alternative to try.

Gigablast

Gigablast, at www.gigablast.com, acts as both a free-text search engine and a directory-based search engine, so searchers get two for the price of one. A free-text search will provide a list of web pages as you would expect, but it also links to different categories as well. A search for *librarians* results in over 100,000 results, and links to several categories in Reference, Regional and Science for example, as well as a specific subheading 'Library and information science'. This in turn took me to a list of almost 200 weblogs, which was an excellent collection. This really helps illustrate the value of a directory search engine – I could, of course, go to a free-text engine and run a search for *librarian weblog* or even *librarian weblog list* but in a matter of seconds, by following the hierarchical structure provided by Gigablast, I was presented with a good listing with virtually no work on my part.

1Websdirectory

This engine, at www.1websdirectory.com, started life in 2009 and currently has over 600 categories over a listing of more than 10,000 websites. As with Findelio, authors submit to them for inclusion. It has a regional web directory which is rather more extensive than that of Findelio, and covers regions as well as individual countries.

Alternative directory search engines

➡ Azoos, www.azoos.com

- Beaucoup, www.beaucoup.com
- Galaxy, www.galaxy.com
- Info service, http://info-s.com
- Re-quest, www.re-quest.net
- Smart Links, www.smartlinks.org
- Sunsteam, www.sunsteam.com.

Clustering search engines

Although a slightly different category, clustering search engines are similar enough to be considered alongside index and directory engines. A clustering search engine looks and acts like a free-text engine, collecting and indexing web pages in the same way, providing searchers with a search box and the ability to look for whatever they want, but the difference comes with the SERPs. As well as the traditional collection of web pages, a clustering engine will take a certain number of results (around about 100 usually) and cluster them into an on-the-fly directory.

Carrot²

Carrot², at http://search.carrot2.org/stable/search, describes itself as an open-source search results clustering engine. Simply run a free-text search as normal from the search box and view the results. To the left side of the results is a list of folders which can be expanded. A search for *Australia* results in folders for Tourism, Photographs, Maps, Reviews and so on. Clicking on a folder will open thc results into the main body of the screen and it's then possible to search for more information similar to that which is being shown on the screen.

The search engine has three different ways of showing the relationship between subjects. The first, as already mentioned, is by grouping web page results into specific folders, which is a very traditional view and one that everyone can get to grips with quickly. It also displays results in a circular format, which is far more in-depth. It shows results grouped together in a circle, as shown in Figure 5.1 on the next page.

The more results that reflect a subject the larger the slice of the circle they own, and conversely, the fewer results, the smaller the part of the circle. Finally there is a 'foam tree', which displays results in a hexagonal manner, and clicking on any of those displays the appropriate results on the right-hand side of the screen.

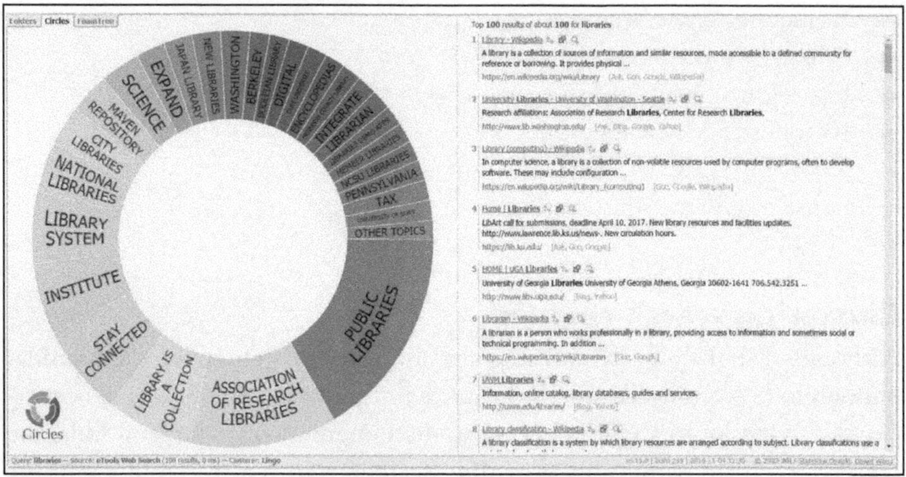

Figure 5.1 *The circles category of 'Librarian' as defined by Carrot²*
Reproduced with permission from https://carrotsearch.com/

Yippy

A similar engine to Carrot² is Yippy, at www.yippy.com, although it provides a rather larger clustered collection. While Carrot² stops clustering at 100 results, Yippy goes further, and in the case of the same example search for *Australia* it collated data from over 800 results into about 30 categories, with more precision. Furthermore, although it doesn't have the circles or foam tree approach it allows results to be reordered by topic (the default), source, sites and time. It's therefore very easy to gain a good overall understanding of a subject; if I want to see which news resources have been making reference to Australia I get a very clear indication with a simple mouse click. Of course I can go to Google or another news search engine and run a similar search, but the listing of results isn't as clear or as precise as I get with Yippy.

Similarity search engines

While directory search engines have fallen out of favour another type of engine has developed over the last few years and while they are still relatively small in number engines of this type provide an excellent service to answer a very particular need. We've already seen something of the type with the Google *related:* search function in Chapter 3; Google can look at a particular web page and essentially interrogate it to find out what it's about, and then find other similar pages. It used to be a far more powerful tool than it is at the moment, and there are engines that have been designed to do the same thing. They require the searcher to input a suggested website or page and then the engine creates a list on the fly to match the subject coverage. The idea of similarity search engines is relatively new, although of course the concept of 'if you like x you'll also like y' is an age-old idea.

One of the first places that people were introduced to this concept on the internet (as opposed to in their library by a friendly librarian) was on the bookselling website Amazon. Due to the sheer number of people looking at, and then buying, products it became very easy for the company to suggest to their users that if they bought a particular book or record it would be quite likely that they would like something similar, since hundreds or even thousands of people who bought the same item bought particular other items. Of course, since this can be done for books and music, there's no reason that it can't be done for websites as well.

There are a number of ways in which this can be achieved. By taking the keywords from one site (from the title, URL, headings and so on) it's possible to map these across to other websites that use similar words in similar positions.

Did you know?
There are over 1,175,000,000 websites (www.internetlivestats.com).

Alternatively, a similarity search engine is able to anonymously track usage and if they discover that a lot of people visit website B after visiting website A it's very easy to create a link. The value of these engines shouldn't be underestimated, as they are a tremendously useful way of researching a particular subject. I find myself drawn to them on a regular basis, especially when I need to create lists of alternative products, software packages, websites, tools and resources, for example. They are an extremely fast and effective way to produce a 'top ten' listing of websites or other resources – though of course the researcher will need to spend time on each identified site to check that the similarity does in fact exist. However, having a list of resources already created for you is a great way to save time.

Similarpages

The Similarpages website (www.similarpages.com) has a very good reputation for finding comparable pages and will often return up to 300 different suggestions. Users can simply type in a keyword or a website URL into the search bar in order to see what the engine can suggest. A search for *cilip* returned a list of results that included the Carnegie Greenaway site, the

Authors' Licensing and Collecting Society and Information and Libraries Scotland. A search for *cilip.org.uk* returned a list of 257 alternative sites, including the Museums, Libraries and Archives Council, the American Library Association and the Canadian Library Association websites.

Similarpages returns a good collection of results from organisational websites to academic sites and personal websites. Searchers are then able to choose the site that interests them, or narrow down the search further. For example, having done the *cilip.org.uk* search and having seen that there's a similar organisation in the USA, the searcher could ask Similarpages to find other sites like the ALA to narrow down their search. Of course, this isn't going to be a comprehensive list of results – but then that's never going to happen anyway. SimilarPages has an index of about 3.2 billion pages and 200 million hosts, so there's a reasonable chance that searchers should find what they need!

Finally, the search engine has released a browser add-on for Firefox which allows you to enrich a Google results page with its lists and give you an opportunity to find other more interesting sites. When browsing web pages, users of the add-on can right click anywhere on the page and a contextual menu will appear, offering to locate alternatives to the site currently being viewed. Unfortunately it's not yet been made available for other browsers.

Similarsitesearch

It's a very rare and unusual search engine that doesn't have competition in the marketplace, so it's no surprise to see other similar similar site search engines. (At this point my word processor isn't happy with such repetition, but it was hard to resist). Similarsitesearch (www.similarsitesearch.com) does exactly the same job as its close neighbour. Simply enter a website address into the search box and the engine will work its magic and return a list of results for you. I ran the same *cilip.org.uk* search again, and got significantly fewer results – 50 instead of 257 – but the information given was far richer. You'll find an overview of the site with its name, popularity, a rating (if available), a site category and site topics. Simliarsitesearch explains that it looked at the CILIP website and combined terms such as research, reference, library, libraries, resources, information and information literacy and found other sites with a similar set of topics, and added in factors such as language, country, user suggestions and popularity.

Users can rate sites from 'I hated it' to 'I loved it' and there's also an option to give a thumbs up or down for the question 'Similar or not?' The engine also gives a 'tag cloud' for the site in question and provides a list of related searches as well. Search results can be filtered by language and country, and there's also an option to 'search with topics'; the engine provides a list of key topics that are pertinent to the website in question (for my example of www.cilip.org.uk key topics were library, information, libraries and professional).

When searching for keywords rather than a specific URL it's possible to include some search functionality, although the obvious option of 'phrase searching' isn't available; the double quotes get stripped from the search. However, it's possible to limit the search using the *site:* function (although with Similarsitesearch it's just *site* without the colon), and you can also search for a specific site and keywords. The option to exclude words using the minus symbol is also supported. Interestingly, and rather unusually these days, the use of the '+' symbol is also supported to force a keyword, so a search for *library +London* ensures that 'London' is boosted in importance in the results.

SimilarWeb

The SimilarWeb search engine (www.similarweb.com) is another that requires a specific URL to make it work. This engine is more interested in providing users with information about the specific site requested, rather than any other kind of search. It starts with an overview of a site, such as its global and country ranking. It also uses a category rank as well, so that the CILIP example is found in the 'Reference>Libraries and Museums in the World' category and this can be further limited to a specific country. SimilarWeb provides an estimate of traffic to the site for the last five months, average visit duration, pages visited per visit, traffic by country, traffic sources (such as referrals, mail, search and so on), top referring sites, top destination sites, organic and paid keywords, website content including subdomains, audience interests, a topics word cloud and a small list of similar sites.

As a search engine, SimilarWeb is of limited value in finding out information about a subject, but as a way of exploring a specific site it's quite invaluable. If you're trying to check the authority and validity of a website, this tool is an excellent first step to use. The only drawback with it is that users are limited to seeing a small number of results, since it's a priced product.

Other similarity search engines

There are a variety of other tools that are worth including in this section, which perhaps might be better termed as 'discovery' engines, but they are still going to be of value in some specific situations.

Alternative To This is a slightly different take on the idea of alternatives. The website at www.alternative.to will, as the name suggests, find alternatives for you. However in this instance it's not looking for alternative websites, but alternatives to devices, singers, trainers and so on. For example, if I ask for an alternative to the iPad it suggests various other tablet-based devices with the option of adding in comments and voting the alternatives up and down. It's a useful tool if you get enquiries about gadgets, cars and so on. One of my favourite jokes in the search engine field (and let's be honest, they are few and far between) is that if you ask Alternative To for alternatives to librarians it replies with 'It appears that we have no alternatives for this right now'.

Bookseer Another in the discovery field for books is Book Seer, at http://bookseer.com, and this asks a very simple question; 'Greetings, I've just finished reading ___ by ___. What should I read next?' Simply fill in the blanks and Bookseer will attempt to find matches for you, based on Amazon recommendations. It also provides links to your local library as well, which is a nice touch.

TasteKid Another example of tools that provide you with similar material is the Tastekid website, at www.tastekid.com, which is a site that specifically focuses on music, movies, shows, books, authors and games. Simply type in something that you're interested in, such as a television programme, and it will come up with alternatives. For the series *Game of Thrones* it suggested *Vikings*, *Spartacus*, *The Borgias* and the book *A Song Of Ice And Fire*, for example. I then asked for alternatives to the author of the series of books the television series is built on, George R. R. Martin, and had over 20 suggestions for other authors, all of which looked very good choices indeed. As well as providing suggestions users can click on them and see information about their choice which they can then share across social media, and indicate their likes and dislikes.

Other discovery tools

At this point I'm in danger of veering rather too far into the area of general discovery tools, so I'll draw a halt at this point. However, I can assure you that there are plenty of others out there, and if you were so inclined you could use a similar site tool to find other similar sites, but perhaps that's getting slightly too esoteric! A few other places to visit however, if you still want to explore are:

- FindSimilarSites, www.findsimilarsites.com
- Itcher, http://itcher.com
- Riffle, www.rifflebooks.com
- Similar To, www.similarto.us
- SitesLike, http://siteslike.com
- SimilarSites, www.similarsites.com
- Spotibot, www.spotibot.com
- Whichbook, www.openingthebook.com/whichbook
- Your Next Film, www.yournextfilm.com
- Your Next Game, www.yournextgame.com.

Summary

Index- or directory-based search engines have been one of the victims of the growth of the internet, specifically Google and social media. They no longer have the same 'pull' that they once did almost two decades ago, and are increasingly being sidelined. However, they are still useful to the expert searcher in that they allow us to view subjects in different ways, they suggest terms and phrases that we might not have considered using in a search, and they provide simple and quick lists of sites that we may wish to explore in more detail. They're certainly not comprehensive, but they were never intended to be, and each type of engine has its own Achilles heel. While it's unlikely that any of the engines mentioned in this chapter will become your 'go-to' engine of choice, they still retain value and do an excellent job in a niche area.

CHAPTER 6

» Multi- and meta-search engines

Introduction

We don't know how many search engines are available on the internet, but we can be certain that there are plenty more than we're aware of. As you have already seen, and will continue to see in the course of reading this book, there are plenty of options available to a searcher. Given that they all have their own advantages and disadvantages there's little point in just sticking to one. However, to go from one search engine to another and then another is going to be time-consuming and confusing, so while we might all agree that it's probably not best practice to just go to just one engine, it's understandable.

However, there's a type of search engine that helps us to overcome that problem, though if I'm being strictly accurate it's one type of engine with two variations: multi-search and meta-search. A multi-search engine can perhaps best be described as a search engine that doesn't actually run searches itself, but provides searchers with the ability to search a number of other engines from a portal or launch pad page. A meta-search engine, on the other hand, will take a query, pass it onto other search engines on behalf of the searcher, take the results that are returned, de-duplicate them and provide a single list of results.

There are many advantages to using this type of search engine. They can save users a lot of time, since results are generally returned more quickly with a single mouse click instead of the searcher typing in one search engine address after another, visiting, and then re-running the same search. Secondly, they're a good way to really highlight which results all the search engines think are the best, rather than relying on one engine to do that job for you. Thirdly, they're an excellent reminder to searchers that there's more to life than Google, and it's a good way to introduce them to others. Finally, because the searcher is interrogating a search engine via a third party, the engine can't personalise results, since it doesn't know who they are for.

Did you know?
It's estimated that 50 million brake horsepower worth of electrical power is required to keep the internet running (www.lifewire.com/ surprising-facts-about-the-web-3862898).

Now, of course, if these search engines are so good why don't we use them all of the time? There are several reasons for this, not least because a search on them can only be quite basic. If my search string contains a function such as *site:.uk* an engine like Google will understand perfectly what is being asked of it, and will respond accordingly. However, if the same search is then sent to an engine that doesn't use the *site* function it's simply going to look for pages that contain the string of characters s-i-t-e-:-.-u-k which will give entirely the wrong set of results. Of course, most search engines will understand the basics such as phrase searching and Boolean operators, but it's not always going to be the case. Consequently you can really only run very basic searches with one of these engines. Moreover, some engines have very specific functionality, such as instant answers or a Knowledge Graph, news or video searching, and these features are not necessarily going to be available when using a multi-search engine. Meta-search engines also pride themselves on how quickly they can get answers back to you, so if one search engine is being slow in providing responses they're not going to hang around – they will simply present results from those engines that have responded quickly, leaving the searcher with a less than comprehensive set of replies, which is exactly what they wanted in the first place from such an engine! Finally, many of these engines are, sadly, not well maintained. You should expect to find options to search engines that don't exist any longer, or the software used to interrogate a particular engine hasn't been kept up to date so it can't pull results back for you. Results, therefore, can be less than accurate and you can sometimes waste more time than you save. However, there are plenty that do work well and those are the ones I'll focus on.

Multi-search engines

There is of course no one 'best' search engine in this (or indeed any other) category, and most of them will do exactly the same job. Preference really comes down to the search engines that are offered for intermediate searching, what can be searched, such as news, images or video, and how the results are displayed on the screen. This very much comes down to individual choice, so you're advised to try all of these out to see which ones work best for you.

Fefoo

Fefoo (http://fefoo.com) is a very neat search engine. It has a very sparse home page which provides access to search functionality for the web, social media, videos, music, torrents (large files that are combined to create a film or piece of music, for example) and people. A pulldown menu also provides searchers with the ability to search e-books, blogs, health resources and more. A second pulldown menu provides searchers with the ability to search Google, Bing, DuckDuckGo and several others. Searchers simply choose what they want to search for, type in their search terms, choose their engine and just search. The searcher is then taken directly to their search engine of choice to see the answers. When they have finished viewing them they can return to Fefoo and re-run the search or try something different. Moving on to search in the Social category FeFoo provides access to more than a dozen different engines, while Video, Music, Torrents and People do exactly the same thing. So from a starting point of one search engine there are links to many others. Unfortunately several of them are no longer active and so you will get an error message, but a toolbar appears at the top of the screen allowing you to quickly choose other engines instead. Fefoo is a small and neat engine with an elegant way of displaying options which are mostly hidden away and it's more powerful than it might at first appear.

Gooframe

Gooframe, at www.gooframe.com, limits itself to providing results from two search engines, Google and Wolfram|Alpha, (the latter is described in more detail in Chapter 12, but briefly it's an engine that provides facts and figures, rather than links to different websites) and these are displayed on the same screen side by side, although this may require scrolling to the right or resizing the screen in order to see everything easily. This is a useful engine, in that Google gives users a listing of websites to visit, while the Wolfram|Alpha element of the search provides facts and figures about the subject. Consequently a search for a subject such as *Jupiter* will really pay dividends very quickly. Searchers can get information on the size of the planet, its consistency, distance from Earth and so on but also see web pages that go into more detail about it.

Myallsearch

Myallsearch (www.myallsearch.com) has, in common with Fefoo, a very unprepossessing home page – a straightforward search box with options to search for images, videos and news. However, once you run a search the options available to you start to open up. In web search mode there's the opportunity to search eight different search engines. Simply type in your search, choose the engine that interests you and click on it. However, in comparison to Fefoo, the results are framed on the page, which means you stay on the Myallsearch site and can simply move from set of results to set of results by clicking on different search engines. It's a nice and elegant approach, and makes it really easy to skim from one set of SERPs to another.

Users can, as already mentioned, search through various different categories, and a pulldown menu adds more: blogs, downloads and torrents. Each of these options loads a different set of search engine possibilities for the searcher to choose from. In total there are almost 40 different engines available, which is a nice wide selection.

Qrobe

Qrobe (which is pronounced Krobe) is located at http://qrobe.it. It has a very simple search interface and searches the web using both Google and Bing. However, it also has some interesting powersearch commands, which are similar to the options provided in the Bang search function at DuckDuckGo. Consequently a search for the term flowers on Google image search can be run using the function *flowers /gi*, while on Bing the search would be *flowers /bi* instead. Various other options allow for searches to take place on resources such as YouTube, Netflix, the Internet Movie Database and Wikipedia. There is also an option to limit results to a specific country as well.

Qwant

Qwant, at www.qwant.com, takes a different approach to multi-searching because it searches across the web, news resources and social information from Twitter. This is a very useful engine if you require a really broad approach to help answer your query, as it's providing traditional search (of websites) with news-related items for current information and social-based information that combines the two. The results are shown in an easy-to-view three-column approach. Qwant also allows searchers to find images, videos, shopping-based content, music and 'boards' which are curated by end-users.

SearchBoth

SearchBoth, at http://us.searchboth.net, provides users with the option of comparing results from two different engines – there is a choice of Google, Yahoo!, Bing, Ask, Dogpile, Metacrawler, and Websearch. It also offers search categories such as images, video, shopping and news. It's a very straightforward engine, but the chance to compare so many engines is good, and would be an excellent way to indicate to a novice searcher that not all engines are created equal – certainly not when it comes to their results. The only drawback that I found was that because screens are limited in size SearchBoth emphasises one set of results over the other by giving it the major portion of the screen. Placing your mouse over the other set of results then shows that as the main part of the screen, and this can take a bit of getting used to initially and is a bit tiring on the eyes!

Sputtr

Sputtr, at www.sputtr.com (and I have no idea how to pronounce it), is quite daunting at first glance, since the home page is full of icons for a large range of different tools – not all of them search engines. There are options for variants of Google, Delicious, the Internet Movie Database, Amazon and eBay, for example; 36 in total. However, if you set up an account with the service you can customise the icons on the page. Otherwise, simply type in the search that is required, and click on an icon. Sputtr will open a new browser tab, taking the searcher directly to the site, and the search will run automatically. Simply close the tab and return to the search window to run more searches. This is quite simple and elegant, but it does mean that there is rather too much tabbing back and forth, particular if a comparison of results is what's needed.

Soovle

Soovle, at www.soovle.com, has yet another take on multi-search. It uses seven search engines – Amazon, Answers, Bing, Google, Wikipedia, Yahoo! and YouTube – and they are all circling the search box. As soon as you start to type in a search term, Soovle will present a list of options from each of the engines. For example, I started to type in 'do' and was presented with options as diverse as 'Donald Trump', 'dodge charger', 'dominos', and 'dog toys'. Once I'd typed out my query (*dog*, just in case you were wondering) I could click on any of 70 different options (ten per engine). Because it was easy to see which results came from which engine it was a simple option to choose to view videos of dogs that

I could watch, or dog collars over at Amazon that I could buy. Soovle is a refreshingly different engine and fun to use. You can see the interface in Figure 6.1.

Figure 6.1 *The Soovle results page.*
Reproduced with permission from http://soovle.com/

TurboScout

This search engine has a long history, going back to 2004, and you can find it at www.turboscout.com. Its tagline, which I think is perfect for all of the engines in this category is 'access all search engines without retyping'. Users can get access to over 20 different engines in the 'web' category, although as mentioned earlier, the list has not been kept up to date, and so some of the search engines don't work, or redirect to others. Other search options include images, reference, news, audio and video.

Trovando

Trovando, at www.trovando.it, uses the tagline 'search different', and it's a long-time survivor in the search engine world, having started life back in 2005. It provides access to over 3000 search engines across ten different categories – web, images, reference, tags, news, price, blogs, audio/video, torrents, URLs. It also has a personalisable custom search engine where users can add engines from a choice of over 3300, and save the customisation with a browser bookmarklet, without any registration. Trovando uses a very traditional multi-search engine approach, with a search box and list of engines underneath, which changes depending on what search category is being used. Choose keywords, run the search and choose the engine to get results from. Trovando will display the results in a framed window, while still retaining all of the search options at the top of the screen. Consequently users can simply click on the results and move swiftly from one set of results to the next.

Meta-search engines

There are a decreasing number of these engines available now, since they're technically more difficult to program.

Did you know?
The first registered domain was symbolics.com (www.buzzfeed.com/katienotopoulos/50-surprising-facts-about-the-internet).

Dogpile

Dogpile, at www.dogpile.com, is one those search engines that has been around for so long it can certainly be considered a veteran of internet search. It provides access to web, image, video, news, local and white page results, and uses 'all the best results from leading search engines including Google and Yahoo!' to create its results page. The results are arranged by relevance, and each result provides basic details, including which of the three engines found the result. Dogpile also suggests other relevant searches as well. It does have an advanced search function, but this is limited to the Boolean operators, language and domain searching.

eTools

eTools, at www.etools.ch, simultaneously searches major Swiss and international search engines, then merges the results and shows them in their own relevance rank-sorted format. Results are displayed with title, summary and then URL, with a list of source search engines that returned a particular result. Users can check the status of the website and get a preview of the web page prior to visiting it. eTools also displays results by topic, domain and source, giving searchers other ways of slicing the results that have been returned. Results can further be filtered by country and language.

There is an advanced search function, which allows users to focus on country and language (as already mentioned) but also the number of results from different search engines (the more results requested the more comprehensive the result but the longer it takes), the number of results displayed on the page and all the search engines available, just the fastest or the searcher's custom preference. eTools provides users with a list of the engines available, which given the amount of secrecy some others use is quite refreshing, and users can tell the engine which of them to use or disable, and how important the results are. Consequently users can take considerable control over the results process, which again is refreshing and novel.

Info.com

The Info site, at www.info.com, claims to get 'the best results from the world's leading search engines', although annoyingly it doesn't say quite what those are. Options are available to search the web, jobs, images, news and video. It does offer an advanced search option of sorts, with an adult content blocker and the ability to limit results by country and/or language. Results are displayed in traditional format, with a related searches option and an 'are you looking for?' option to narrow your search results further, which is a nice touch. It's a very straightforward search engine, with nothing particularly exciting, but it does do a good job.

iZito

iZito, at www.izito.com, doesn't provide users with a listing of the engines that it uses but simply explains by saying 'iZito searches multiple types of information from multiple sources to generate optimal results'. Results appear on the SERP in a traditional manner of title, URL and summary. Depending on the search users may see an option for related searches and 'Answers', which are instant answers to the question asked. An image search has filters for size and colours, video searches are run on YouTube, which offers the usual YouTube features as discussed in Chapter 11. News results come from global resources, and there's also a 'wiki' option that provides content from Wikipedia.

Alternative options

- Addict-o-matic, http://addictomatic.com
- Be Nosey, http://benosey.com
- Monster Crawler, www.monstercrawler.com
- SearchDazzle, www.searchdazzle.com
- WebCrawler, www.webcrawler.com
- Yometa, www.yometa.com
- Zapmeta, www.zapmeta.com.

Summary

Multi- and meta-search engines fulfil a very specific role, which is to say that when you need a comprehensive set of search results you can use one to quickly flip from one set of results to another. Alternatively, if you're looking for the 'best' result, any site that is found in the top ten of various different engines is surely going to be worth a few moments of your time. They do have their drawbacks as previously mentioned – poorly maintained and limited to simple search syntax – but other than that, they're another useful tool to have in the expert searcher's armoury.

CHAPTER 7

Social media search engines

Introduction

Before we can start to talk about search engines that cover social media we really need to take a step back and work out exactly what 'social media' is. It's a term that gets bandied about quite happily, and most people have a rough idea as to what it means, but let's explore it in a little more detail. If I visit Google and ask the question 'What is social media?' I get the response 'websites and applications that enable users to create and share content or to participate in social networking'. Wikipedia says that 'social media are computer-mediated technologies that allow the creating and sharing of information, ideas, career interests and other forms of expression via virtual communities and networks'. That's a helpful start, so let's break it down a little further into a bullet-point format:

- content that is user-generated
- content that is shared with other people
- actively communicating and interacting with people in virtual communities
- online social networks.

We're all familiar with popular networks such as Facebook, Twitter, Instagram and Pinterest, but social media networks are far larger in scope and size than just those. For the expert searcher it's necessary to be able to identify appropriate networks and learn how to search them. Before we get to that point, however,

Did you know?
Facebook users spend three times more time watching live videos than traditional ones (http://newsroom.fb.com/news/2016/03/news-feed-fyi-taking-into-account-live-video-when-ranking-feed).

there are a few other things to take into account. First of all, the amount of user-generated data is immense, and growing at an exponential rate. In fact, it's growing so quickly there's hardly any point in providing you with facts and figures, since they will be out of date before I've finished writing this chapter, let alone by the time you read this book. However, in the previous edition of the book, published in 2013, I said that 50 hours' worth of video was uploaded to YouTube every minute. This figure is now closer to 500. I said that 150,000 tweets were added every minute to Twitter, and this number is now closer to 400,000. On Facebook every minute over 500,000 comments are posted, 300,000 statuses are updated and 136,000 photographs are added. If you want to find out what the current statistics are just run a quick search for *social media statistics 2017* (or any other year) or if you're interested in a particular platform, try something like *tweets per minute 2017* or *facebook status updates 2017*.

So, the sheer amount of data available on social media is an issue. Another big problem, which I'll talk about in much more detail in Chapter 10, relates to how much of that information is false, fake, biased or otherwise just plain wrong. Just because you are able to find information on Twitter, do not take it as the gospel truth; double- and triple-check it before you do anything else with it. On the other hand, currency of information is astonishing. I learn most of my news via Twitter and Facebook; as soon as something in the world happens, someone will tweet or post about it, and this is generally minutes, if not hours, before traditional news media will do so. This is partly because news outlets need to double-check stories to make sure that they are accurate; on social media this isn't such an issue – at least for the person publishing.

Did you know?
38% of British consumers cite social media interaction as their reason for visiting a retailer's website (https://hostingfacts.com/internet-facts-stats-2016).

Another issue to take into account with social media is that it's very often individuals, rather than companies or organisations, who are posting and tweeting. Therefore we need to take into account the integrity of the person's tweets and posts, which is a double-edged sword. If I find an expert in a particular area it really doesn't matter to me if they work for a university, for a government department or from their own back bedroom. If they are an expert, that's all I care about. The problem, of course, is trying to identify that they are the expert that they appear to be. Therefore it's necessary to do far more work to check them; what other social media accounts they have, how many people follow them, how active they are and so on. If the tweet is from or on behalf of an organisation it's a much easier matter to check the credentials of that organisation.

Traditional search engines do not provide searchers with the information that they need when it comes to this form of data, and this has led to the rise of the social media search engine, which concentrates on providing access to this flood of data. You could ask 'If they can do it, why can't traditional engines do the same thing?' and it's a good question. To be fair, however, traditional engines tend to focus on what they know and understand and are not geared up to searching for and indexing the volume of content or the speed of its production. Let's start by looking at a few general social media engines before concentrating on those which specialise on particular platforms.

General social media engines

Did you know?
75% of male internet users are on Facebook, in comparison to 83% of female internet users (www.wordstream.com/blog/ws/2017/01/05/social-media-marketing-statistics).

Socialmention*

Socialmention* (www.socialmention.com – as an aside, please don't look at the bottom of the page for the asterisk reference; it's part of the name of the engine!) describes itself as:

> a social media search and analysis platform that aggregates user generated content from across the universe into a single stream of information. It allows you to easily track and measure what people are saying about you, your company, a new product, or any topic across the web's social media landscape in real-time. Social Mention monitors 100+ social media properties directly including: Twitter, Facebook, FriendFeed, YouTube, Digg, Google etc. (www.socialmention.com/about)

Socialmention* was one of the earliest social media search engines and was established back in 2008, but really only came to prominence in late 2009. It's a particularly useful tool for searchers who need to get some general indication of the way that people are currently feeling about a particular subject, but the ability to create RSS feeds and e-mail alerts is also very valuable and an easy way to keep on top of a fast-moving subject area.

Searchers can either search across all categories in one search or can choose from blogs, microblogs, bookmarks, images, or videos. Data is pulled from a variety of resources for each of these sections, but such is the fast-moving world of social media there is little point in trying to list these in detail; suffice to say they include sites such as Twitter, YouTube, Diigo, Flickr, Netvibes, Wordpress, Blogger and Facebook. Figure 7.1 shows the results page for a search on *cilip*.

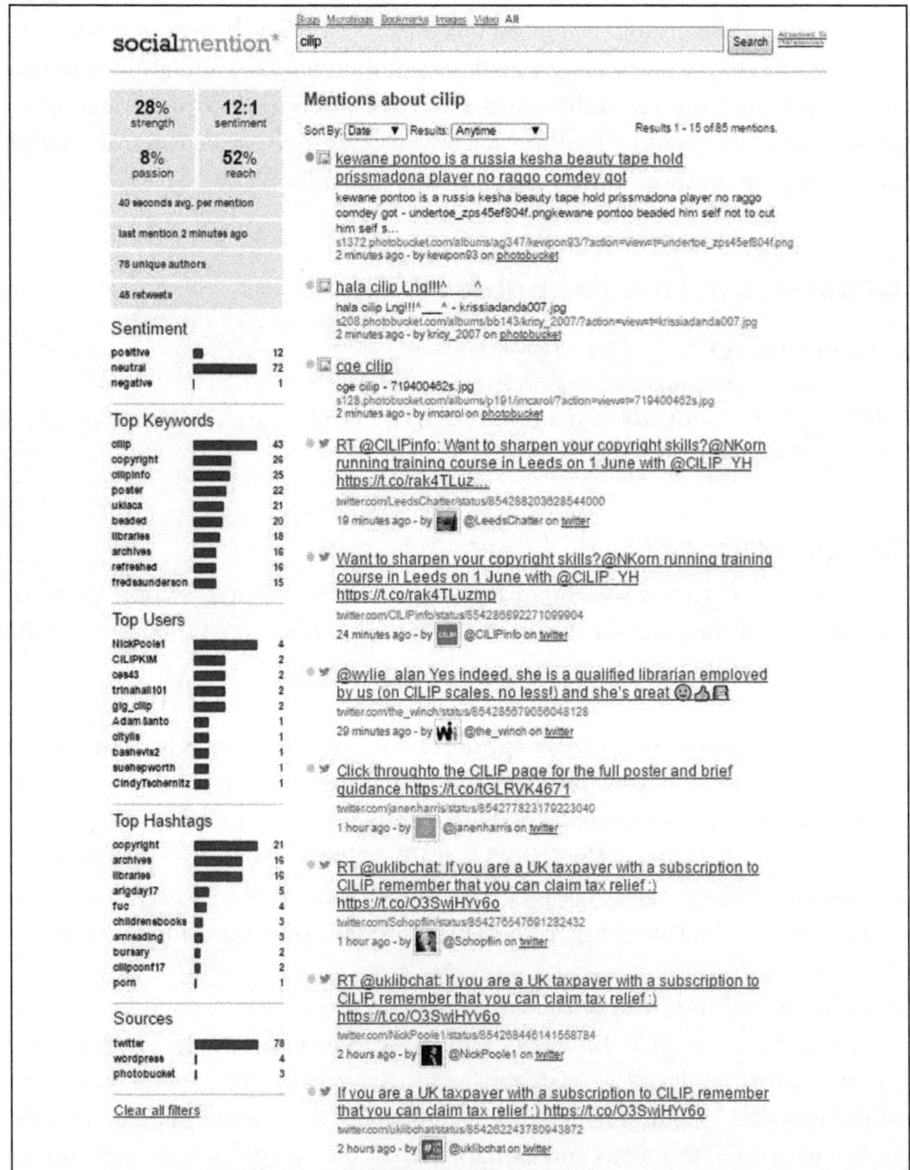

Figure 7.1 *Search results from the Socialmention* search engine*
Reproduced with permission from Socialmention*

As you can see, the searcher is presented with a rich variety of information. The central element of the screen is results drawn from appropriate resources, and these can be arranged by date (as illustrated) or by source. They can also be time-limited by the last hour, last 12 hours, day, week or month. Searchers can also create an RSS feed for the search or an e-mail alert, or the data can be exported as a CSV or Excel File.

On the left-hand side of the results page, the engine provides searchers with a unique set of data. The first element is a square of four criteria – strength, sentiment, passion and reach. Strength is the likelihood that the subject or brand is being discussed in social media. This gives searchers a better 'feel' for the extent to which the subject that interests them is currently in the news. This is worked out using a simple calculation – the number of mentions in a 24-hour period divided by total possible mentions. Sentiment is the ratio of positive to negative mentions. Passion is the measure of the likelihood of individuals repeatedly talking about the brand or subject. Finally, Reach is a measure of what they call the range of influence. That is to say, the number of unique authors referencing your brand, divided by the total number of mentions.

Below this cube the searcher can see the average number of mentions per hour, the last time the subject was mentioned, unique authors, and the number of retweets. Next, one can see more information, based on sentiment, top keywords (very useful if searchers need to go into more depth for a subject), top users (useful to identify key experts in an area), top hashtags and key sources.

Socialmention* has an advanced search function, which allows users to limit by words, phrases, excluded terms, sources, time periods, results per page, language and sort by. Users can also limit results to specific geographic locations, and they can also choose not to show results from specified users. A useful function provided by the engine is a 'Trends' section, which shows the top 24 trending topics, aggregated from numerous sources.

Did you know?
Almost 84% of UK internet users are on Facebook (http://gs.statcounter.com/social-media-stats/all/united-kingdom).

Social Searcher

This search engine, found at www.social-searcher.com, describes itself as a 'free social media search engine'. Users can search Twitter, Google+, Facebook, YouTube, Instagram, Tumblr, Reddit, Flickr, Dailymotion and Vimeo for any publicly posted content without having to log into any of the platforms. Social

Searcher was created in 2010 and has been developing and adding new functionality since then.

> **Did you know?**
> Facebook's original name was 'Thefacebook' (www.buzzfeed.com/katienotopoulos/50-surprising-facts-about-the-internet).

Search results appear in a tiled format, with details on the poster, the tweet or post, any linked URLs, the ability to share the result, and the ability to link to the original post. Results can be displayed on the SERPs in a traditional text format, or in columns. This can be really useful if you're particularly interested in seeing the results from one specific platform as you can scroll across the screen, find the appropriate column and then scroll down the screen. At the bottom of the SERP is a scrolling bar of different social media platforms and the searcher can click on any that interest them to see results from it. It's a very fast and effective approach to take.

Results can be sorted by date or popularity, both of which are very sensible ways to approach social media – by currency and by the amount that a posting has been liked (although it's worth making the point that just because something is popular doesn't make it accurate or correct). Results can further be filtered by sentiment, which is to say positive, negative or neutral (based on semantic investigation of the words used in postings), by post type, such as link, photograph, status or video, and by particular network. Traditional search functionality doesn't of course work here, since we are not looking at words in a URL or a title, for example. There's no need for a *site:* option either, since that's inbuilt into the search engine results. There is, however, an opportunity to limit results by language.

Results can be exported in a comma-separated values (csv) file, which allows the data to be saved in a table format, and Social Searcher also allows users to create e-mail alerts for searches that they want to be kept up to date with. There is a very useful 'analytics' section to the results as well. They are broken down into several different aspects, such as general, sentiment, users, links, types and keywords. It's very easy to see when most posts on a subject are created by day of the week and by hour. There are links to hashtags, popular posts, a listing of key networks, popular and active users (both further divided by social media platform), popular links, popular videos and 1, 2 and 3 keywords.

Social Searcher also has a 'Google social search' dashboard that's available to users at www.social-searcher.com/google-social-search. Basically this is a sort of multi-search engine that allows searchers to search top social networks such as

Facebook, Twitter, Google+, Instagram, LinkedIn and Pinterest by using the Google search engine. Consequently, this allows searchers to use phrase searching, exclusions and the OR operator when constructing a search.

Did you know?
Facebook has over 1.55 billion active users (www.digitalinformationworld.com/2016/12/infographic-the-internet-in-numbers.html).

Mamuna

The Mamuna engine, at http://mamuna.com, is rather different, because it's not searching for posts or tweets, but instead is focused on finding social media platforms. Of course, we're all well aware of the major ones, but there are plenty of others. A search for *books*, for example, returns dozens of results, listing websites, forums and social media platforms for the discussion of books. Search results are in a tile-based format, and can be ordered by name, rating, critics rating, popularity and submission date. The information provided is the name of the platform or group, a summary, keywords and related reviews. Results can be filtered in a number of ways, such as blogs, social networks, tools or platforms and virtual worlds.

Buzzsumo

This search engine, found at https://app.buzzsumo.com, lets users find the most shared content for any topic or domain. A keyword search results in a tabular display, with the popular links for the subject on the left with the option of being able to view backlinks, sharers and to share it as well. The important section, however, is towards the right-hand side of the screen, with an indication of how popular the link has been on various social networks such as Facebook, LinkedIn and Twitter, together with a total number of shares. It's a very useful tool if a searcher isn't quite sure of where to start looking for information; it can be a real time-waster to start searching on LinkedIn for example only to find there's very little there, and only to later discover that there are lots of posts and engagements over on Pinterest. Buzzsumo ensures that isn't going to happen, as a quick topic search should highlight activity across networks and make it much easier to focus on one or two in particular.

The search engine offers various filters, such as date, in-depth articles, language, country, domains, and content type. Results can also be exported and alerts created. Other search options provided by Buzzsumo include trending topics, backlinks, content analysis and a Facebook analyser, although some of these are limited to a paid, professional account.

Other social media search engines

- Addict-o-matic, http://addictomatic.com
- Lanyrd, http://lanyrd.com
- Metro5, http://metro5.com
- Qwant, www.qwant.com
- SocialSearch, http://socialsearch.thingweb.com
- Tagboard, https://tagboard.com
- Whos Talkin, http://www.whostalkin.com

Searching Twitter

Twitter is a key resource when it comes to social news and information, with thousands of tweets per second, news updates, information on conferences and so on. In a relatively short period of time it has become one of the key resources that a searcher will use in order to find out exactly what is going on in the world at any given moment in time. While some search engines include tweets in the data that they return this isn't always the case, and there are a number of specialist search engines that are worth considering when trying to keep up to date with the firehose of information.

Twitter Search

Twitter provides users with both a basic and an advanced (refine) search function. The location of the search option depends on the interface that you're using to access Twitter, and the version of Twitter that you're using, since they are prone to change the look and feel of the service on a regular basis. The best suggestion here is to simply look around the page until you find the search box! The advanced search option is available directly from the page at https://twitter.com/search-advanced.

The search options are generally not particularly exciting and you could probably predict most of them without ever looking at the page yourself. All the words, exact phrase, any words, none of the words, a specific hashtag and language are all standard. There is, however, an option of searching for people, which could be very useful if a searcher is trying to find an expert in a particular area for example, or trying to track a particular individual down, since the options available are searching From an account, To an account or Mentioning an account. There is a geographical option to search Near a particular place, an option to limit from one date to another and finally a miscellaneous 'Other' section, which makes use of the positive and negative emoticons of J and L as well as a question mark. A major disadvantage of Twitter's own search options used to be that it was quite limited when it came to a time-based search; searchers were usually limited to about a week's worth of content. However, this is no longer the case, and you can go back weeks and months when running a search.

The SERPs are in a column, tile-based format, with the tweet itself, who created it, who and how many people retweeted it (copying it onto their own followers), any associated images, details on the number of likes it has had and the opportunity to copy the tweet, share or embed it, and other basic 'share' options that are common across social media platforms. The SERPS are in a tabbed format, with the top tweets displayed first, followed by other options, in order. 'Latest tweets' are obviously the most recent tweets displayed chronologically. 'People' is a collection of Twitter accounts that relate to the subject being searched for, with options to follow them, and information on who they are followed by. The 'Photos' tab displays images attached to tweets with sensitive content hidden by default, 'Videos' displays tweets that link to and contain videos, 'News' shows tweets from news organisations such as *The Guardian*, the *Irish Times* and the *New York Times*. Finally, the 'Periscopes' option links to videos that have been created by the Periscope app and shared onto Twitter.

Other Twitter search engines

Backtweets (http://backtweets.com) is an engine that is designed to allow users to check links to specific sites or pages. Simply type in a URL that is of interest and Backtweets will find links regardless of their form – shortened links, URLs with or without the www prefix and so on. It's a great tool to check to see what people are saying about a particular company, site, web page or person.

Hashtags can be found at http://hashtags.org. It allows you to search for specific hashtags, such as #librarian or #cilip and shows you a trend by timeline, with user, message and when it was posted.

Snapbird (http://snapbird.org) allows searchers to sign into the service and identify themselves so that they can then search their friends' tweets, direct messages and users' favourites. This can be tremendously useful if you can recall seeing something on Twitter, with the likelihood that it was one of your own contacts who tweeted it, or to check something that you can recall having tweeted, but are having difficulties finding again.

Twiangulate (http://twiangulate.com/search) is designed to allow searchers to compare two accounts. Simply add the accounts that are of interest and Twiangulate will return a list of people who follow both accounts, or who are followed by both accounts. The engine will also provide details on the 'reach' of a particular user, which is to say, if their top followers retweeted that person's tweet to all of their followers, how many would in theory see it. The engine can also check through a person's followers to see how many of them use a particular named keyword in their biographies. It's an excellent tool to use in order to research a particular individual, and to check how authoritative they are, and how they are viewed by people in the 'twitterverse'.

Some other Twitter search engines are:

- Filta, https://filta.io
- Followerwonk, https://moz.com/followerwonk/bio
- Twazzup, http://new.twazzup.com
- Twipho, https://twipho.net
- Tweet Binder, www.tweetbinder.com.

Hashtags

A subject that often causes problems and consternation among searchers is the hashtag. The hashtag symbol '#' has been in active use since 2007 and it is designed to highlight what is basically an uncontrolled controlled vocabulary. Users create hashtags simply by placing the symbol immediately before the keyword that they think is appropriate, such as '#CILIP'. This allows people to quickly search for tweets or posts that contain the hashtag, even if they are not following the person or people writing about it. Consequently, if people are interested in the Oscar awards ceremony they can simply search for *#oscars* and find all of the tweets people have made. Hashtags have to be a continuous series of characters, so *#oscarsceremony* is acceptable, while *#oscars ceremony* is not.

Hashtags develop over time, although that 'time' may only be a few minutes or an hour. Initially if there is a news story, breaking event or natural occurrence people will use lots of different hashtags that they make up for themselves, but users decide which ones to use and which to drop, so it doesn't take too long before a general consensus is reached. At other times people will decide on a particular hashtag for an event, and so the Internet Librarian

International Conference will use the hashtag #ili2017 and that will be found on the website and in the literature that's made available to potential delegates. Visitors to the conference will be encouraged to use the hashtag when they tweet about it, and others who want to keep up to date with what is happening will use the tag to identify appropriate tweets.

It's worth saying that no one decides what hashtags can or cannot be used, and no one can insist that they are used for any particular purpose, which has the advantage of freedom of use and currency. However it can lead to 'hashtag spam', when people notice a particular tag is trending so they will use it themselves to attempt to sell or highlight something totally different.

When it comes to searching for hashtag tweets and posts there is a certain amount of serendipity involved. Is there an obvious acronym that could be used perhaps? Or the name of a person, place or event? Run some searches and see what tags are being used, and then search on those to try and narrow down which one(s) are most prevalent. Find an appropriate website, and see if a particular tag has been mentioned as the one that a person or group has decided to use. Alternatively, use one of the few engines that are available to try and focus in on the subject that interests you.

Hashtags (http://hashtags.org) allows you to search for specific hashtags, such as #librarian or #cilip, and shows you a trend by timeline, with user, message and when it was posted.

Hashtagify, at http://hashtagify.me, is an engine that allows searchers to search for a particular tag and will then display similar or associated hashtags. So some of the top ten hashtags related to the tag '#iamalibrarian' are '#medlibs', '#librarylife', '#factsmatter' and so on. Hashtagify will also list recent media search results that use the tag, usually, but not exclusively, Twitter. It's then possible to dig deeper into the tags, to find out their popularity, weekly and monthly trend. So '#factsmatter' has a popularity of 45.8 in comparison to '#iamalibrarian' and has a correlation of 17.2% with the aforementioned tag. It's then possible to see who the top six influencers are for the tag, popularity trend, hashtag comparisons, a hashtag 'wall' displaying recent posts and from which social media platform, and the ability to track tags on the Instagram platform – although some of these require a free or commercial account.

Hashatit, at www.hashatit.com, is a fairly basic engine; simply run a search for a particular hashtag and Hashatit will provide a tiled list of results. There is a filter to limit results to specific social media networks such as Twitter, Facebook, Instagram or Pinterest. Results can be embedded or shared as a link.

Keyhole (http://keyhole.co) is a commercial product, but does have a free option. It provides information on the use of a hashtag; popularity over the preceding week, top posts, related topics, most influential and most recent users. It also lists top websites linked to the hashtag, location of tweets, share of posts, sentiment, top sources and demographics. It also has some advanced search functionality, such as the use of the *OR* operator, and the ability to search on Twitter and/or Instagram.

#Tagdef If you see a hashtag and you're not sure what it means – and a lot of them are very obscure, made up by shortened words and acronyms, you might want to take a look at #Tagdef, at https://tagdef.com. Just type in the hashtag that interests you, and see if it's been defined. #Tagdef will also provide links to other hashtags that are related to the one that's of interest to you. Conversely, if you have a hashtag, you can use the site to enter your own definition, which may help others.

Google Finally, of course, you can actually use Google to search for hashtags. Simply enter the tag (with the # symbol) and either run a general search or use the *site:* command to limit to one specific network to see what results you get.

Searching Facebook

Facebook is unsurprisingly the poster child for social media, and I'm sure that I don't need to add in the URL, as virtually everyone who is reading this book will have an account, but if you're the exception it's www.facebook.com The amount of information on Facebook is quite breathtaking; over 2 trillion posts can be searched, there are 2.5 million advertisers, 50 million small businesses own pages on the site, and there are over 1 billion users who visit monthly. I'm not going to bother with more statistics, since they are going to be woefully out of date, so I'll simply paraphrase Douglas Adams' *The Hitchhiker's Guide to the Galaxy* with a twist; 'Facebook is big. Really big. You just won't believe how vastly, hugely, mindboggling big it is.'

Facebook has its own search engine, at the top of every page on the site. Results are split into various categories; top results, groups, latest, people, photos, videos, shop, pages, places, groups, apps and events. These can be filtered further to limit to content posted by anyone, yourself, friends, groups, friends and groups, locations and date posted. This is useful as far as it goes, of course, but it's still quite limited. Facebook doesn't support things like the Boolean NOT operator for example, and there's no such thing as URLs or title elements available either. So other than very basic search concepts there's not a great deal which can be done. However, all is not lost, because there are search engines that can search Facebook directly. Of course, we have Google, so it's possible to do a search with the *site:facebook.com* option in the search string, but there are two specialist engines.

Search is Back

This is based on the concept that Facebook was exploring a few years ago of the graph search option, whereby it was possible to search for various concepts, such as men who had an interest in Everton Football Club and who lived in Exeter. Unfortunately, Facebook decided against developing this search concept and decided instead to limit users to the already mentioned basic search functionality. However, Search is Back, found at https://searchisback.com, has explored these search options in more detail. The search interface is shown in Figure 7.2.

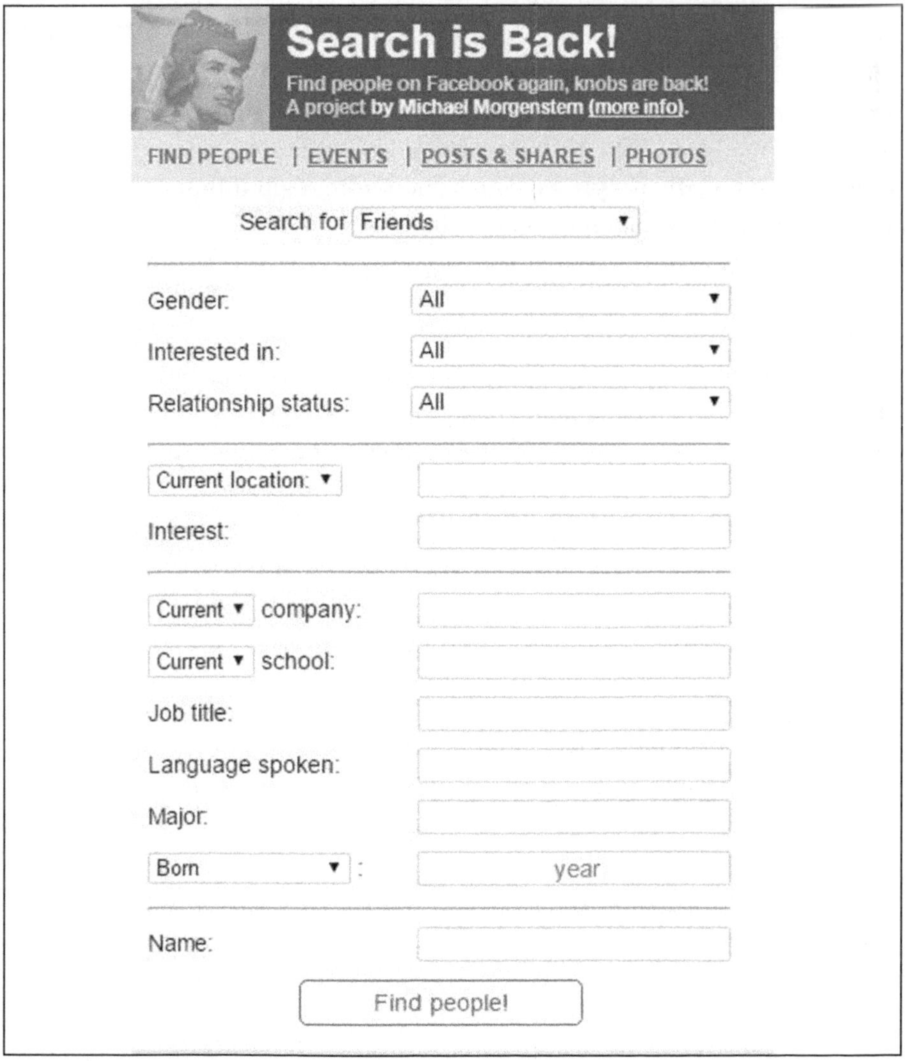

Search is Back!

Find people on Facebook again, knobs are back!
A project by Michael Morgenstern (more info).

FIND PEOPLE | EVENTS | POSTS & SHARES | PHOTOS

Search for Friends

Gender: All

Interested in: All

Relationship status: All

Current location:

Interest:

Current company:

Current school:

Job title:

Language spoken:

Major:

Born: year

Name:

Find people!

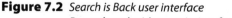

Figure 7.2 *Search is Back user interface*
Reproduced with permission from searchisback.com

Users can search for friends, all people or non-friends, or populate their own list of people to search on or about. The first search filters allow people to limit searches to a specific gender and interests, but can then add in location and interests. Former or current schools and employers can be added into the mix, as well as job titles, languages and so on. It's therefore a fairly effective people finder, and excellent if it's necessary to locate particular people or those who share similar interests – perfect for recruiters!

As you will see from Figure 7.2, there are also tabs for events, posts and shares and photos. As you might expect, the search options available for those are appropriate to the subject, so with events it is possible to search for locations, dates and event titles, as well as who is invited. With posts and shares searchers have the option to search on posts by anyone, or friends, and the text in a post. Finally, with the photographs option there are filters to limit results to locations, specific people who took the photograph if they uploaded it or were tagged in it, commented on it or liked it.

IntelTechniques

A rather more in-depth search engine that can be used for Facebook is IntelTechniques, at https://inteltechniques.com/OSINT/facebook.html. This allows users to find a specific Facebook profile and then interrogate Facebook to find information such as: the places the person has visited, liked, checked in and recently visited; photographs of, by or liked by the individual in question; videos of, by or liked by the person; and their employer(s), co-workers, friends, followers and relatives. It's also possible to target multiple profiles to compare, for example, places that two people have been to. While this all sounds very creepy, it only works with publicly available information, so that if people keep their accounts private and locked down, only very limited information will be available.

The search engine also allows searchers to find individuals who fit a particular profile. So, for example, it will identify people who have worked for a specific employer, who were born in a certain year, and have lived in a particular place. Again, this is very useful for recruitment companies; if the task was to locate people who live in Cairo, speak French, have acted as a customer service representative and who currently work for a telecoms company, this can be achieved in a matter of seconds using this tool. However, once again, it can only work with publicly available information, and anything that has been marked as private by the Facebook user cannot be found or used.

Summary

While the search engine market is volatile, this is particularly the case when looking at social media. More engines have disappeared from this particular niche than in any other, and some of them only last a few months before we get the dreaded 404 error message, meaning the site has closed. If you find a new social media engine, my advice is therefore to make the most use of it that you possibly can for as long as you possibly can, because in all likelihood it will not last a year.

That's all very depressing, so let's try and end this chapter on a more positive note; there are still plenty of good engines that do return good information that users would otherwise find difficult, if not impossible to discover anywhere else. Consequently, if you're looking for current (a minute ago or less) news, you need opinions, first-hand witnesses, or experts in a particular area then try some of the engines that are listed in this chapter before trying the old faithfuls.

CHAPTER 8

Visual and image search engines

Introduction

In Chapter 5 we saw that clustering search engines such as Carrot[2] were able to display results in a non-linear form, by the use of folders and grouping like results together. There are various advantages to this approach, such as preventing searchers from thinking that the first result is in some way 'the best'. A logical next step on from this category is to be able to see the websites themselves directly in the search results, rather than having to click on a link to go to them. The tile approach is also becoming more popular, based on the increased use of mobile devices. This chapter will look at search engines that use this approach to display results. However, that's only one side of the visual search coin – rather than seeing search results portrayed in a visual format you might actually just want to search for images themselves (which of course has a very visual component in the way that results are displayed) and this chapter will also look at some image search options in detail.

A visual search engine will display results by showing searchers the actual web pages themselves that are returned from the search that's been run. Some engines (particularly free-text) may include a thumbnail of a screenshot, but that's more to simply help identify a site, rather than offering any practical use. However, those in the visual search engines category (and it should be admitted that it's a very small category) do rather more than that – the results are the web pages themselves. Searchers can flick from one screen to the next and get a very good indication of what's on the web pages from the SERPs, without going directly to the sites in question. There are a number of advantages to this approach; users can view a page safe in the knowledge that no one at the website will know that they are looking at it, which is helpful when it comes to competitive intelligence. Secondly, if the search contains a largely visual component – say for example that a user wanted to see images produced by the Hubble telescope – then it's going to be a matter of seconds to see if the sites returned from the search will be image-heavy or primarily textual in nature. Also, if a searcher is working with a child, for example, a site with lots of images may be rather more desirable than one that's mainly text.

Some visual search engines

Dothop

Dothop, at http://dothop.com/home, used to be known as RedZ, but since the last edition of this book has changed its name, although it works in exactly the same way. Users will run a search and Dothop provides a list of results in an arc of images, as can be seen in Figure 8.1.

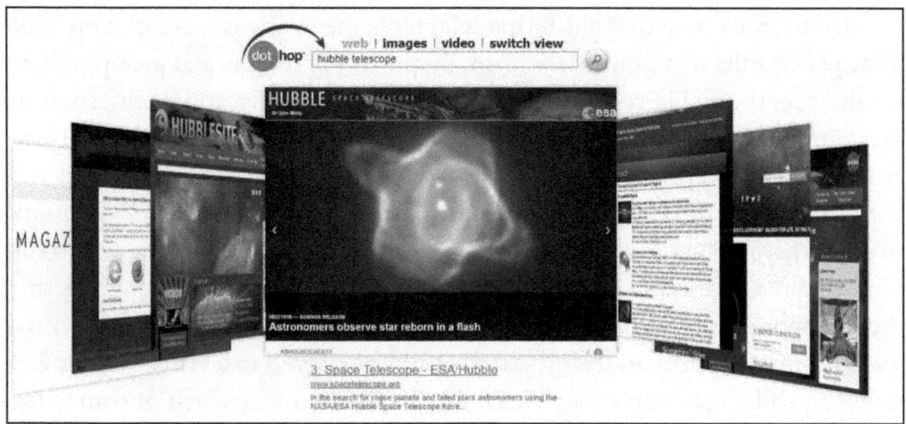

Figure 8.1 *The SERPs from Dothop*
Reproduced with thanks to Dothop

Simply by moving the mouse across the screen the arc of results moves from right to left and back again. Under the central image Dothop provides basic information about the page; title, the URL and a brief summary. This is a very quick and effective way of moving quickly through a large number of results. At the top of the screen Dothop provides a number of different options; searchers can look for images or videos. Finally, there's an option to 'switch view', which means that viewers can move from the arc display to a tiled display, which has the added advantage that results can be clicked and dragged to a 'bookmark' section of the page for safe storage while searching – a really nice approach that makes it easy to go back and look at key results again quickly and easily.

Dothop does have some basic search functionality, so users can limit by excluding terms using the minus symbol and the *site:* function works, as does *intitle:*. Annoyingly, however, Dothop does not provide any indication as to exactly what functionality it has made available, and there isn't an advanced search function option either, so it's necessary to just try and guess available functionality, which is less than helpful.

Spacetime3D

The Spacetime3D search engine, at www.spacetime3d.com, is very similar in concept to Dothop in that it provides searchers with an arc of images, and these can then be flicked through by clicking and dragging with the mouse. Results are pulled from Google, with a maximum of 30 pages to scroll through. Spacetime3D is rather more effective when it comes to images, however – although searchers are limited to a total of 19 results, they load quickly and are much larger than the thumbnails provided with engines such as Google. Spacetime also offers results from Wikipedia and YouTube in the same format. It does, however, require the use of Adobe Flash, which is not widely used these days, and so may prove to be something of an obstacle if searchers have to seek permission to download and install that software.

Cluuz

When you first look at Cluuz (www.cluuz.com) with its jigsaw piece logo you'd be forgiven for not assuming that it's a visual search engine. It appears to produce fairly straightforward textual results, but once you start to look at the SERP in a little more detail you'll notice that it provides a word cloud, which is to say a collection of words and links that relate to the search that you've just run. There's also a collection of top linked entities to the subject and a series of spoked links, as can be seen in Figure 8.2 on the next page.

The links are sensibly sorted out – so from the image you can see that CILIP groups are found on the right-hand side of the 'wheel' while all of the university links are in the top left-hand quadrant. Clicking on the link allows users to discover more about the site in question. This isn't so much a search engine that finds specific web pages that match your search query, but more of a search engine to identify and explore websites. Consequently it's useful if you are exploring a subject area of which you have limited knowledge, or if you were conducting a reference interview with a member of the library and were using this as a basis for discussion.

Cluuz also has an advanced search function and a preferences option. Results

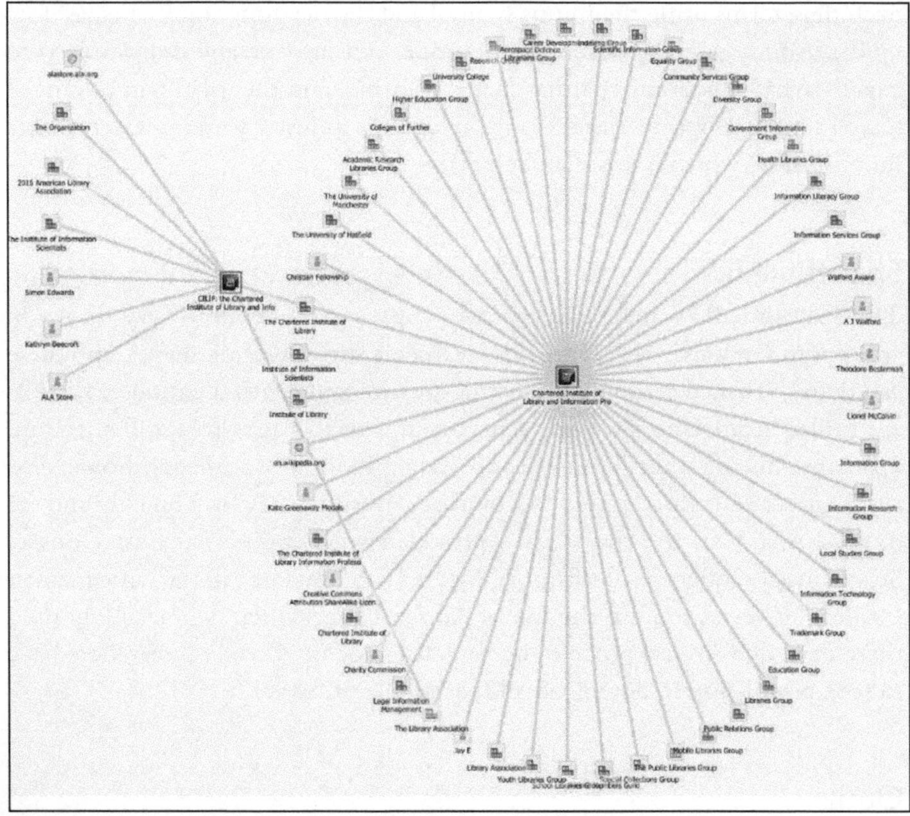

Figure 8.2 *A set of visual results from Cluuz for the search term CILIP* © Cluuz

can include or exclude people, companies, organisations, phone numbers, e-mails, addresses, domains, dates or geography, so it's a good tool to quickly and easily narrow down a set of results in combination with the visual element.

Major Image search engines

Many search engines – certainly all of the major ones – offer access to images as part of their search offering, as we've already seen in some cases. However, there are plenty of search engines that focus their efforts on finding images, rather than websites or pages. In this section I'll cover some of the major tools that you may want to use when it comes to searching for images. I've also included Google Image search in this category, since it's such an effective engine I wanted to be able to give it proper prominence, but please remember that I've also discussed image search in descriptions of other search engines in their appropriate chapters.

Google Image search

Did you know?
Google image searches result in 3% of all total search clicks (http://kingkong.com.au/15-secret-facts-google-search-doesnt-want-know).

In Google, once you have run a search you can simply click on the 'Images' option to see images that relate to the subject(s) that you're searching for. Alternatively, if you want to go directly to the appropriate URL you need to point your browser at www.google.com/imghp, which is where we'll start. The first point to make is that you can search for an image by using an image. In the search box to the right you will see a camera icon (see Figure 8.3)

Figure 8.3 *The Google image search interface*
Google and the Google logo are registered trademarks of Google Inc., used with permission

If you click on the camera Google will give you the opportunity to search by image using the image URL. In order to get the URL of the image that you're interested in, just right-click on the image on the web and choose 'Copy Image Address'. Go back to the search box and paste in the URL and click search. Google will then see if it can find other versions of the image, links to other sizes for it and a 'best guess' for the image, which will be some descriptive terms Google thinks appropriate. You will also have other visually similar images displayed in the results as well.

If you have an image on your computer that you want to use in a search, perhaps to see if it has been used elsewhere for example then click on the 'Upload an image' option, find it on your computer and upload it for Google to work on. An alternative approach, depending on your browser and how it is configured, is to just do a right mouse click on an image you see on a webpage and choose the 'Search Google for image' option. This is an extremely useful search tool to have in your armoury. If you have any doubts over the veracity of an image, a quick check will soon tell you if it's been used before and on what website(s). If you don't know what a particular item is, take a photograph of it, upload it to Google image search and you may be lucky enough to find other images of similar objects. If you are asked to friend someone on Facebook, do a quick search for their profile photograph and see if it's a stock image rather than a real picture of them.

When you run a search for a term Google will – obviously – return images that hopefully closely match what you have asked for. The images that are returned are also subject to various algorithms; if your search term is in the name of the image file, such as *.librarian.gif* that will ensure the image ranks highly. If the search term is in an alternative text tag, or the term is physically close to an image on a page, these will also rank highly as well. Google will present some options at the top of the search results, depending on the search that you have run. It may be a collection of words on coloured backgrounds, or it may actually be images themselves, with various options. A search for *librarian* gives us further search options, for 'female', 'male', 'cartoon', 'technology' and 'book', for example. The search term *dog* will give us 'clipart', 'drawing', 'cute', 'and cat' and so on. If you look for images of the actor Jonny Lee Miller the options that are returned will reflect his life and work, so you'll have options to narrow the search down by 'movies', 'Angelina Jolie', 'Tattoos', and 'Trainspotting'. Clicking on an image creates a large dialogue box in the centre of the screen with the image on the left and options on the right to visit the page the image was pulled from, view the image, save it, share it and view related images.

As with searches for words or phrases there is a Tools option available, focused on elements of images. It's possible to limit results by size, colour, type (face, photo, clipart, line drawing or animated), time, usage rights (the same concerns apply here as they do with the Creative Commons option in a text search) and show sizes. Google has an excellent collection of options for image searching, and it's relatively easy to narrow down your results to a small number of high-quality images. However, what's not clear is that you can also use many of the same search functions that we've already looked at with text searching with images. So for example, if I wanted to get a collection of images of librarians' faces from the UK with a largely blue element in the picture I could start my search with *librarian site:.uk* and then under Tools choose the colour blue, and under any type choose 'face'. It doesn't always give perfect matches, but it may well help on those occasions when you get asked for 'the book about dinosaurs with the blue cover'.

Did you know?
Chrome is the most popular browser in the world, with 52% of market share, followed by Safari, with 14% (http://gs.statcounter.com/browser-market-share).

Flickr

Flickr (www.flickr.com) is a resource that is designed to allow its users to upload, tag and share the images that they have created. They can be added to different groups and notes can be added to them, and they can also be made available to other users via the Creative Commons options. Flickr has over 10 billion images and the vast majority of these can be searched; users do, however, have the option of restricting access to specific images if they so wish. On average over 1 million images are shared daily and there are over 2 million different 'groups' on Flickr. A group is created by an individual or number of people to focus on a specific subject – it may be Welsh castles, American Civil War re-enactments, or simply 'things that are blue' for example.

Search is very straightforward – simply type in the term(s) that are appropriate; there is a limited use of search operators, so it's usually best to be as simple and straightforward as possible when choosing terms. Results are displayed with a number of different options – they can be sorted by relevance, currency or 'interesting' (Flickr uses various arcane methods to work out what makes a photograph interesting, often based on the amount of activity it inspires in users). Photographs can be viewed in small or medium size, or with details, such as title, views, comments, notes, locations and tags. Flickr also provides access to photographs based on groups, specific photographers and tag clusters. A search term such as *librarian* will return over 193,000 images, links to the 'Libraries and librarians' and 'Libraries from around the world' groups, the Food Librarian photographer, and the option of searching on tag clusters such as library, books and libraries and librarians.

Searches can also be done to directly identify groups that Flickr users have created to share their images and to discuss them, and you can also search for specific individuals in order to see the photographs that they have publicly shared. There is an advanced search option which allows users to restrict their searches to tags or full text of the image description, and search can also exclude terms as well. Searching can be limited in a variety of ways, depending on whether you have an account to Flickr (which is free) or if you're searching without one. Searches can be limited to safe search, and this is something that I would generally advise; safe search is automatically turned on by default if searchers are not searching via their own account, and while there is a lot of adult material on Flickr it is generally well contained behind a Flickr firewall. Once you have your own account, however, you may accidentally find material that is objectionable. Content can also be searched by content type – photographs, videos, screenshots and screencasts and illustration and animation. It's also possible to further break down the first option to just photographs or just videos. Flickr includes a date search function, with photographs taken or posted before or after specific dates. One really powerful search option is that of Creative Commons, to limit the search to licensed content. This is a tremendously valuable option, as it is possible to find images that you can reuse without seeking specific permission. There are six different licence filters; all Creative Commons, commercial use allowed, modifications allowed, commercial use and modifications allowed, no known copyright restrictions and US government works. If you need images for a PowerPoint presentation or to include in a report, and don't want to have to spend time seeking permission to include them, this is a fast and effective approach.

Flickr also allows searchers to limit results to those which are primarily one of 15 different colours, black and white, with a shallow depth of field, minimalist or patterned. The advanced search option includes filters for orientation, size, date taken, photographs or videos, and search terms created as Flickr tags, or words included in the description of the image.

Flickr-related search engines

Flickr is an extremely popular site and a number of other search engines have been created to provide access to the wealth of data that is contained on it. While the actual images are exactly the same, the interfaces and search options will differ. Behold, at http://behold.cc, emphasises Creative Commons search options. Tag Galaxy (http://taggalaxy.de) pulls images from Flickr and creates a 'galaxy' concept, with a central sun (the original search term) with planets of related terms around it. Clicking on a 'planet' calls images from Flickr which then cover the surface of the 'planet'. While it is rather a novelty, it is a quick and effective way to scroll around a lot of images very quickly in an enjoyable way.

Pinterest

Did you know?
Over 50 billion images have been 'pinned' to Pinterest (www.omnicoreagency.com/pinterest-statistics).

Pinterest, at www.pinterest.com, was founded in 2010 and has quickly become one of the major players in the social media scene. It has 150 million active monthly users, over 50 billion images (or 'pins'), over 1 billion boards, and over 14 million articles are pinned every day. The idea behind Pinterest is very simple – if you see an image that you want to keep while you're looking around the internet you can 'pin' it, which is to say, you can add it to your own collection (assuming you have a free account), and you can place the image into any of the 'boards' (basically folders) that you have created. These boards can be kept private or shared with other people or made available publicly. If you want to see my collection it's available at https://uk.pinterest.com/philipbradley and you're free to take a look at all of the images that I have pinned. It's obviously a very useful service, since it keeps all of the images (or indeed videos, since they are also supported) that you like in one place. As a searcher, it's an excellent tool for a number of reasons.

People tend to pin images which are of good quality; there's no point in saving an image of a landmark, for example, which is out of focus or poorly presented. Consequently, unlike Google, which will give searchers anything it finds, without a concern for picture quality, in most instances a search on Pinterest will result in higher-quality images.

If you find a particular individual who has an interest in a subject, or is an expert in their field, it's quite likely that they will also have their own Pinterest account. Once you locate the person in question you can then follow them, or any of the particular boards that they have created, and Pinterest can inform you when there are updates. So with my account, for example, it won't come as much surprise to you to know that I have boards on internet search, infographics, books and library posters. By identifying and locating the individual you can then see their images and save them for yourself into your own collections.

Pinterest allows people to contribute to a board that has been created by someone else. There are plenty of examples of boards that have been created by librarians, for example, such as 'Award winning books', 'Books for boys to enjoy' and 'Troubled teens'. School librarians can pin their own images to the boards and share them, while at the same time making them available for other people to see. Consequently, searchers can find an appropriate board and check to see who the members of it are, and if they are experts or authorities in their own fields, and then use the information and images that have been pinned.

Searching Pinterest is very straightforward. At the top of each page is a search box, and searchers simply type in whatever they're looking for. Pinterest isn't particularly strong on complex search strings, so keep it simple if at all possible.

Did you know?
More than 14 million articles are pinned to Pinterest every day (www.omnicoreagency.com/pinterest-statistics).

Pinterest will quite often provide searchers with suggestions as you type, so with my search term *library* I was presented with options for 'library', 'library room', 'library architecture', specific people or organisations such as Sussex County Libraries, and boards such as 'library/books pictures' and 'The librarian's list'. Once the keyword has been chosen and the search run, Pinterest may provide some further options to focus and narrow the set of results (this can't be relied upon, though it tends to work with broader, rather than narrower, search terms) and users can simply click on the one that interests them. Pinterest refers to this as 'guided search'. My library search provided filters such as home, room, logo, displays, design, public, old, art, and office. Results can also be narrowed by limiting results to 'your pins', 'people' and 'boards' rather than the more general 'all pins'. Once an image has been found, it can be clicked on to view in more detail. Pinterest provides details of it, such as the image title, who pinned it, where it came from, and a brief summary, with the option to like or send it to other people, to add it to the user's own board and the chance to visit the website the image was pulled from. Finally there is an option to view other similar, related images based on shape, design and colour.

An alternative search method is to use the category approach. This isn't readily visible on opening screens, so point your browser towards https://uk.pinterest.com/categories (or your local country version if you have one available), and Pinterest will display the 36 categories users can browse, from 'popular', 'animals and pets' and 'art' to 'weddings' and 'women's fashion'. Once you choose a category Pinterest breaks it down further into subheadings (just like a directory search engine) and then even further, displaying the guided search options again. So for example, clicking on 'Illustrations and posters' offers general images, with the chance to narrow to 'posters', then to 'advertising posters', then 'retro posters' and so on.

It's worth pointing out that the image may be within copyright, so don't assume that just because something has been pinned and found on Pinterest that it can be used for any purpose. Unless it's clear that the image is in the public domain or has a Creative Commons licence attached to it, users should visit the originating page and research further.

Reverse image searching

As mentioned with Google, it's possible to upload an image, or to provide an image URL in order to use that as the basis of a search. There are lots of good reasons for doing this – while a picture speaks a thousand words, if you don't know what any of those words are going to be, it's not terribly helpful.

However, by uploading an image of a plant, for example, or perhaps a photograph of a picture, you may quickly obtain the thousand words to provide you with the information that you need. Reverse image searching is also useful when it comes to identifying fake news and social media accounts. For example, I was approached on Facebook by a company offering to contact the American government for the 'money that they owed me'. It was an obvious scam, but there was an image of an official-looking person on the Facebook profile page; a quick reverse image search showed me that this was a US Senator, who I am sure would have taken a dim view of knowing that his image was being used by a scammer! If you see a news item – say a group of protestors – it's easy to quickly research the image to see if they were actually protesting about that subject on that day, or if the image had been re-used from years before by a lazy reporter who just found an appropriate-looking image to use.

If you're a keen photographer, you might want to make sure that people were not using your images without your knowledge – or as importantly, payment! By doing reverse image searches on your own images you can quickly see if this is the case.

Reverse image searching can also help you identify people, places or products. Upload an image of a place that you like the look of, and you will in all probability find out exactly where it is. If you see an image of a person and don't know who they are, reverse image searching will often tell you. Finally, if you see a product that you want to know more about you may be able to identify the manufacturer and the website that sells it.

Tineye

TinEye, at www.tineye.com, is a reverse search engine that has been designed for exactly this purpose. Upload an image, drag and drop, or provide a URL and the search engine can begin its work. It searches almost 18 billion images in less than 2 seconds to provide the searcher with results based on best matches, most-changed (in terms of colour, aspect, inclusion in other images and parts of an image) and size. To that extent, it's a far more useful engine than Google's reverse search, the 'most-changed' being an extremely powerful way of identifying how images have been used.

RevIMG

RevIMG search engine, at www.revimg.net, finds images according to its matching algorithm, based on shape, dimensions and colours likelihood. The resulting links are listed by matching percentage. The unique selling point of this engine is that search results can be limited to various predefined collection type sets. This provides a neat and effective shortcut that other engines are missing. The engine also uses 'search depth', so 'small depths' provides a small set of results, limited to identical or near identical images; 'large depths' provides a larger set of results, but it takes longer to complete a search. It's also possible to keep results that match the original image to more than a specific threshold, so images that are below the threshold, and are therefore quite different, will be excluded from the search.

Imageraider

Imageraider (www.imageraider.com) has been primarily designed for use by photographers who need to check to see if their images have been stolen and used on other websites without consent. Simply upload an image (or download it first of all, then upload it) to their server and Imageraider will check to see if other copies of the image are available on the internet. Users can choose to see a list of (up to 20) websites that carry the image, view results from all the sources Imageraider used (Google, Bing and Yandex) or just Google, or filter results based on specific text and domains.

Pinterest

Pinterest has already been mentioned as a tool that links to similar images, but it is possible to go further with it. Choose an image (and it has to be one that you've pinned, so it's necessary to have an account to do this) and focus on a particular part of the image. Pinterest will then attempt to find other images that match it, so it's quite easy to take a large image, and choose say, a particular piece of furniture and get Pinterest to find other pictures of the said item.

Creative Commons image searching

I'm often asked to suggest search engines that people can use in order to find images that they are able to use without payment and/or which are free from copyright issues. As we have already seen, Flickr is an excellent source for this kind of material, but there are plenty of other search engines that can be used.

CCSearch

The Creative Commons search engine, at https://ccsearch.creativecommons.org, is an excellent tool to use. Simply start by entering your search query, and deciding if you want to find something that can be used for commercial purposes and/or to modify, adapt or build upon. The CCSearch engine will then act as a multi-search engine by checking collections such as 500px and Flickr for photographs, and museums and library sites for cultural works. In total almost 10 million images are available for searching. The search engine is unfortunately quite poor, and can't cope with complex search terms using lots of keywords, so keep it simple with short phrases. Results are displayed in a tile format, and once an image has been clicked on it will expand into the screen and provide information on the title, creator, the licence and originating website. There's also an option to copy the credit for the image as text or HTML (to add it to a web page). Users can also favourite images, save them to a list and add tags to them. At the time of writing (spring 2017) the search engine is still in a beta format, so there may well be changes to it by the time you visit yourself.

Wikimedia Commons

This resource, found at https://commons.wikimedia.org/wiki/Main_Page, is a collection of over 37 million freely usable media files and people are encouraged to add their own to it. Search is available for images, sounds and video and by free-text search, topic (nature, society, culture, science or engineering), location, type, author, licence and source. A general search will take the enquirer to a specific category, and they can then drill down into subcategories as necessary. So a search for *posters*, for example, links to posters by subject, then to an option for 'sporting event posters' and then into six other subcategories and so on. Once the enquirer has found the appropriate image and displayed it on the screen they can also see the full title, creator, licence and file history. There is also a wealth of information about the allowable uses of the image by other people.

LibreStock

LibreStock, at https://librestock.com, is a free multi-search engine that will check through almost 50 different websites to find images that you can use. I quote from the site:

> I know it's hard to understand complex legal licenses so let me break it down for you. all the photos indexed on LibreStock are licensed under the Creative Commons Zero (CC0) license. this means you can use these pictures freely for any legal purpose. (https://librestock.com/about)

That's great – so what about the images themselves? My search for *books* came back with over 570 images from a variety of sites. A lot of the images, however, were nothing to do with books, including the one with a woman sitting on some steps looking at a penguin (don't ask me, because I don't know!). There were zero results for *librarian* but everything else I searched for I got something back. There's no specific listing of all the sites that the engine pulls data from, but when you cursor over each image you'll see the source site and tags for each image.

The images are of excellent quality – sharp and of a good size. Lots of variety, black-and-white and colour, and I had the feeling that the vast majority came from professional photographers. Most of the photographs did provide information on who the photographer was – even though you're not obliged to include that information, I know that a lot of people would want to do so.

My main disappointment (indeed my only disappointment) was that it's a fairly small collection, coming in at about 62,000 images. However, it's easy enough to search through, and if you don't find what you want you can easily move onto another site. So if you're looking for excellent imagery, high-quality and entirely free for you to do anything you want to with it, this is certainly a site worth looking at.

New York Public Library digital collections

This collection, at https://digitalcollections.nypl.org, is a treasure trove of images. Maps, posters, ancient texts, drawings and manuscripts – over 600,000 images, without use restrictions. Each image comes complete with information about it; artist, date created, genre, download options, library locations, notes, rights statement and so on. You can expand the image to view it more clearly, print directly from the browser window, or rotate it. You can even turn it into a 3D image in some cases.

Search options are excellent. You can browse by items, collections and divisions and also do a keyword search. Then you can filter by topic, name, collection, place, genre and so on. When you've found the image you want you can download it, order an original scan or an art print, and you can share the image across Twitter, Facebook or Pinterest. Whatever your interest, I can pretty much guarantee you'll find something of interest to you. I did try a search for 'Everton' (my favourite football team) and I got back a fair number of images, mainly cigarette cards of players from the 1930s, which I really wasn't expecting, given the American origins of the collection.

Other image search engines

Readers will be familiar by now with my lament that search engines are closing their doors wherever you look, but in the area of image searching the exact opposite is the case. There are dozens of engines that provide free images, although they often do so as a loss leader to their paid resources, but nonetheless, if you find the image that you want for free, you can use it!

General image search engines

- Picjumbo (https://picjumbo.com) is a nice resource but only has a small number of images (600 or so), though they are of excellent quality.
- Unsplash (https://unsplash.com/) is excellent – my search for *books* returned a lot of results (277) and they were really interesting pictures.
- Stockvault was another good site, at www.stockvault.net, and again I got a fair number of results for books, but the images were rather more boring, to be honest.
- Negative Space, at www.negativespace.co, gave me a few book images, but I hadn't seen them anywhere else, so was happy with that.
- Kaboompics, (http://kaboompics.com) has a great name and some superb photographs.
- Stocksnap (https://stocksnap.io) has some really excellent images, and my books search gave me 145 really good-quality and interesting images.
- Splitshire (www.splitshire.com) had no books pictures (but it did have some really fantastic images, so it's worth a look).
- Life of Pix (www.lifeofpix.com) has some really good, very high-quality and good-resolution images. Only a couple of books pictures, but certainly worth exploring the database.
- Pexels is a multi-search engine at www.pexels.com, with access to almost 4000 images and more added every week.
- ISORepublic (http://isorepublic.com) has free stock photos for creatives. Lots of excellent images.
- Free Refe (http://getrefe.com/downloads/category/free) is a good collection of high-quality images.

Specialist image search engines

This section is by way of a miscellany; there are so many different types of images that fulfil so many different functions that many simply refuse to go into a specific category. So I apologise for the random nature of this final collection of engines, but as you read through them I hope you'll understand why!

The IconArchive, at www.iconarchive.com, and **IconFinder**, at www.iconfinder.com, are two excellent engines that will assist users in finding appropriate icons to use on web pages, in presentations or in a printed format. Between the two they list over 2 million icons in various categories.

The **Vintage Ad browser**, at www.vintageadbrowser.com, is a fascinating engine which has over 100,000 vintage advertisements to explore, with categories ranging from Airlines to Xmas. This is a sister site of the **CoverBrowser** site, at www.coverbrowser.com, which has over 450,000 covers of comics, books and DVD covers.

Twicsy (http://twicsy.com) is often referred to as the 'Twitter pics engine'. Millions of images are posted onto Twitter every day and Twicsy is one of the ways of searching for them; it has access to over a billion images. Simply pop in your preferred search term, and see what it comes up with. It's a fairly random collection, as you might expect, and results often have little to do with the term you input, so it's not brilliant. You get results from the past hour, past day and so on. Please be aware that images which are NSFW (Not Safe For Work – see Summary on the next page) do often turn up as well. It has a particular value in that it highlights images that are related to trending words, phrases or hashtags in Twitter at any particular moment in time. So if you need to grab some images quickly about a big sporting event, volcano or politician, Twicsy is certainly worth having on your list.

It's worth spending a few words to talk about **Instagram**, which is a photograph-sharing resource that's owned by Facebook, and you can see it at www.instagram.com. It's primarily a social media tool, but it can be searched for images, hashtags and people. A search for *library* listed a large number of results for libraries that have Instagram accounts, such as the British Library and the Library of Congress. By clicking on a link to an account you can view the images that they have uploaded and shared. You can make comments on

Did you know?

Tweets with images receive 150% more retweets than tweets without images (https://blog.bufferapp.com/the-power-of-twitters-new-expanded-images-and-how-to-make-the-most-of-it).

the images that you see and can also choose to follow particular accounts if you're a registered user yourself. The search results that you see are based on several factors, such as the people that you follow, your connections and what you have previously 'liked' for yourself.

The **Folger Shakespeare Library** digital image collection at http://luna.folger.edu/luna/servlet/FOLGERCM1~6~6 includes over 80,000 images, including books, theatre memorabilia, manuscripts and art. Users can show multiple images side by side, zoom in and out, view cataloguing information when available, export thumbnails, and construct persistent URLs linking back to items or searches. It's an amazing collection, and has been made available under a CC licence so that you can use them as long as you share.

Summary

For the image searcher, the world is currently very rosy indeed. The internet is becoming a very visual place as ever-increasing numbers of images are uploaded and shared across social media. Whatever you need a picture of, it's a virtual certainty that it's out there, simply waiting to be found. There are obvious caveats though; always check and double-check that the image that you want to use is either in the public domain or has a Creative Commons licence attached to it, and if in doubt, either don't use it, or seek permission first. Another point that it's unfortunately necessary to make is that, when searching for images, however innocent your search happens to be, you'll find Not Safe For Work (NSFW) images. These will run the gamut of mildly rude through to explicitly hard-core pornography. Even if you turn on any safe search filters, some material will always get through. As a result, if you're training, or working with an end-user, apologise in advance, or if you can, try your searches out first. This is particularly true in my case, since I am the owner of a name that is shared with an American gay porn star, and I have learned through painful experience not to use my own name as an example when running image searches!

CHAPTER 9

People-based resources

Introduction

Whatever else the internet is or isn't about, people come pretty much at the top of the list. If we're not e-mailing them, we're searching for them, and if we're not doing that, we're talking with them on social media. In this chapter we'll be taking a look at finding people, and also using the tools and resources produced by people. In other chapters I have alluded to the importance of the individual, so let's really bring that point into the open right now. In 'the old days' we would run a search, find a website, visit it and get the information we required and then move on. Now of course those sites were run by people (often entire teams of web editors), but in the last few years we've seen a significant change in the way that we use the net. With the increase in social media and user-generated content the role of individual content creators becomes more important every day. For example, if I'm interested in what's being said at a conference that I am unable to attend, I'll go to Twitter, find an appropriate hashtag and then follow along with what is being said, thanks to the helpful tweets from attendees. I don't actually care that much if the tweeter comes from a university or a blue chip company, I'm interested in what they have to say and to report. It doesn't matter to me if the person reporting on a protest in a local city is young or old, black or white, Muslim or Christian, as long as I can trust the information that they are providing me with. Now of course, people do have their own agendas, biases and opinions and this is going to affect what and how they report information, so I need to ensure that I can trust the person who is reporting on the content. We'll discuss the whole issue of fake news in Chapter 10, so for the time being we'll assume that people are being honest and open with their tweets and status updates, though we still need to research them if they're not immediate friends or colleagues.

There are different approaches that can be used to try and identify specific

Did you know?
North Korea is the world's least connected country, with less than 1% of the population having access – about 16,000 people (https://thenextweb.com/insights/2017/01/24/digital-trends-2017-report-internet).

people. The first is obviously to use standard search engines in the hope that the person that you are looking for is active on the internet and is referenced on web pages. You can use specific e-mail search engines that will attempt to identify them, try a 'people finder' to look for individuals, or try a small number of social media tools that will try and find where specific names are used. Then, of course, there are the times that you want to find someone and you have absolutely no idea who they are, because you're just looking for an expert in a particular subject area. It then becomes necessary to consider where and how such people will be identifying themselves on the internet, and identify key tools to track them down.

Standard search engines

The first place to start when looking for an individual is with the traditional search engines such as Google and Bing. There's no magic to this type of search – just type in the person's name and see what transpires. I'll use my name as the example here – not particularly out of an attempt at ego boosting, but simply because it would be unfair to put any friends or colleagues under the spotlight! A Google search for Phil Bradley returned 21,200,000 hits, and 321,000 when searched as the phrase *"phil Bradley"*. Bing provided me with 1,300,000 and 60,600 results – a considerably smaller set to work from. Both engines, however, gave similar information – websites, blogs, Twitter accounts, Flickr feeds, LinkedIn accounts and so on. It is interesting to note the sheer amount of social-based data that turns up in searches, in comparison to even a couple of years ago.

Of course, a search like this is not very effective – a quick tour of the results shows me that my namesakes include a porn star, a country and western singer, a basket weaver, a baseball star and so on. The search also ignores the fact that in some places on the web people will refer to Philip or even Phillip, and then there are also the times when middle initials are included as well. It's possible to use the asterisk in a Google search which will result in something such as *Phil * Bradley* or even *"Phil * Bradley"*, which will result in a different set of results again. Now, while this search may well catch instances of my name where it is included as Phil W. Bradley or even Phil W. H. Bradley (I know, I know, my mother had a thing for middle names), it's not going to catch Philip Bradley, and it will also give me results such as Phil and Mary Bradley. In order to search comprehensively then, the search starts to become rather unwieldy quite quickly. One possible option that is worth considering is the use of the @ symbol – Google has recently started to index this, so if you have an idea about the type of e-mail account someone has, it might be worth trying a search for *philipbradley@gmail.com*. However, this itself has complications, because the e-mail address of philbradley at gmail.com has also been taken, and it is a very polite and patient gentleman who owns it and he kindly forwards e-mail to me on a regular basis, and I have been known to forward mail onto him as well. So the wise searcher will view the results that are returned from a search of this nature to see the context within which they are being used. The @ symbol can also be used in a search such as *@philbradley* to try and catch other social media references. The other obvious search element to add in is something that will hopefully be unique to the person you're after, so *"phil Bradley" librarian* should cut out most of the false drops. Alternatively, add in a further qualifier such as *home page* or limit to a particular type of site, such as academic or government, if you know the area in which your target works.

As previously mentioned in the chapter on Google, the search engine has a habit of thinking that it knows best, so I would remind readers that a search for *Daniel Russell* may return results for Daniel Russel, missing a second 'l'. To overcome this, either try a search using the verbatim option, or enclose the offending name in double quotes thus: *Daniel "Russell"* to really make sure that the search engine does as it is told.

You may have heard about the 'right to be forgotten', which has arisen out of the various country acts (such as the UK Rehabilitation of Offenders Act), which ensure that people have a right to privacy, particularly when it comes to internet searches. For example, if someone runs a search on a particular individual when using a search engine they may see a reference to a trivial crime that the person committed many years previously, and it's argued that it is unfair on them that this is constantly being surfaced on the internet. In 2012 the European Commission agreed the European Data Protection Regulation, which includes specific protection on the right to be forgotten. In order to exercise this right an individual has to make representations to search engines directly and complete a form. Search engines can then – if the request is approved – 'delink' references to individuals from search results. The information about the speeding offence (for example) may still be held in various places on the net, such as newspaper articles, but the engines do not return those links in the SERPs. This is by necessity a very brief overview of the current situation, but there is a more authoritative factsheet at http://ec.europa.eu/justice/data-protection/files/factsheets/factsheet_data_protection_en.pdf which explains it in more detail. Suffice to say that when looking for an individual you are not guaranteed to find out everything about them from a search, and indeed Google reminds you of this – at the bottom of the SERPs there is a line 'Some results may have been removed under data protection law in Europe'. Both Google and Bing in particular also provide more information, and it's worth reading their explanations in more depth at www.google.com/policies/faq and http://help.bing.microsoft.com/#apex/18/en-GB/10013/-1/en-GB respectively.

Google has made some major changes in the way that it identifies individuals, and this may make life a little bit easier when it comes to finding the particular person that you are looking for. The search engine has integrated its social network Google+ into search results. I've made no reference to the Google+ network elsewhere in the book because quite frankly it's not a social media platform that's widely used and has little, if any, reference to most of us in our day-to-day searching. However, if you are really having difficulties finding an individual it may be worth taking a look at the site, at https://plus.google.com, and running a search for an individual in the search box at the top of the screen. You may also occasionally still see references to articles that people have shared via Google+ towards the bottom of the page of results, as seen in Figure 9.1.

Did you know?
The physicist Russel Seitz has estimated the billions of 'data in motion' moving electrons on the internet weigh about 50 grams in total, the weight of a single strawberry (www.lifewire.com/surprising-facts-about-the-web-3862898).

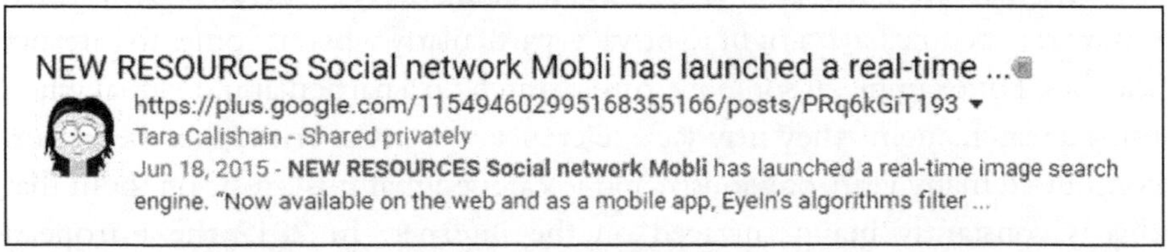

NEW RESOURCES Social network Mobli has launched a real-time ...

https://plus.google.com/115494602995168355166/posts/PRq6kGiT193
Tara Calishain - Shared privately
Jun 18, 2015 - **NEW RESOURCES Social network Mobli** has launched a real-time image search engine. "Now available on the web and as a mobile app, Eyeln's algorithms filter ...

Figure 9.1 *A Google+ reference to an article arising from a search for search engine social networks*
Google and the Google logo are registered trademarks of Google Inc., used with permission

Before we leave standard search engines behind it's just worth pointing out that the image search function might be useful as well. If you're not sure if the 'Phil Bradley' that you're after is male or female, run a swift search through an image engine just to check. This is also useful if you're dealing with a foreign name that you've perhaps not heard before, and who knows – you may get lucky and find a photograph of the actual person that you are looking for. You might also try the video search function as well – given that it is so easy to add video to the likes of YouTube, many people will have their own channels.

E-mail search engines

Some search engines are simply databases of names matched to e-mail addresses. The data is collected from a variety of sources such as newsgroups, social media sites, web pages, people who directly register and so on. Some of these are independent search engines while others are associated with an existing engine. The USA is generally well served for search engines that will provide details on individuals, such as 411 Locate at www.411locate.com/people-search, Address Search at www.addresssearch.com and the Zaba search finder at http://e-mail.iaf.net/e-mail-search.html. The rest of the world is rather more limited, however, and so it may well be necessary to try different types of search engine to locate individuals. However, one last possibility might be to research the company or organisation that you think they work for, see how e-mail addresses are used and try sending an e-mail to the account that you hope is active, and cross your fingers! One word of caution – many of these services are commercial in nature, so before you can find all of the information on a person that you are interested in you may need to pay for the privilege.

People finders

A people finder attempts to do more than just provide an e-mail address. When possible they will give you a phone number, street address and so on. Furthermore, once you have that type of information you could then begin to use one of the street mapping services to take a virtual drive along their road and take a look at their house. This does get us dangerously close to the 'stalker' level of research, but I would seriously suggest that you do attempt to find yourself on the internet, just to see how much personal information is available, much of which you will not be aware of! If you do happen to find material that you're not happy about there isn't a great deal that you can do, as it depends on who owns the data. For example if a friend has mentioned you on Facebook, you could ask them to remove the reference, or if you appear on Google Streetview and your face isn't already blurred, they will do it for you. Goodwill is the key issue here, so a polite 'softly softly' approach would be advised.

192

192 (www.192.com) is a good example of the people finder type of service. If you have a vague idea of where a person lives, simply search on their name and 192 will return address details, a view of the road in which they live via Bing, their telephone number, electoral roll details, information on their house and so on. The majority of this data costs money, but it is available, perfectly legally. A similar American product is Anywho, at www.anywho.com/whitepages, and in Canada, you could try Canada 411 (www.canada411.ca), while the WikiWorldBook, at http://wikiworldbook.com/free-people-search, takes a more global perspective, and also links into social media networks.

Pipl

Pipl, at http://pipl.com, is also a global search engine, and this one pulls similar information together, and tries to create a variety of profiles of individuals for searchers, making it easier for them to identify the particular person that they are after. A search for my name, for example, found LinkedIn accounts, Amazon accounts, YouTube videos, Facebook accounts, and so on. The problem with Pipl was that it found too much information for me – I didn't realise that there were quite so many namesakes! This isn't really that surprising, given that it provides information on over 3 billion people. However, if you want to look for a person globally (while adding in a location, even one as broad as a country) it's worth trying out.

Other people finders

Other search engine options include:

- E-mailSherlock, www.e-mailsherlock.com
- FreshAddress, www.freshaddress.com/find
- Intelius, www.intelius.com/e-mail-search-name
- PeopleSmart, www.peoplesmart.com
- Spock, www.spock.com
- Spokeo, www.spokeo.com
- Xing, www.xing.com
- Yasni, www.yasni.com.

Social media tools

The growth of social media and the irrepressible rise of social networking now provide the people searcher with a whole new raft of tools to use. Some of the early tools, such as Friends Reunited for the UK and MyLife in the USA, have been steamrollered out of existence by Facebook, which has really taken on the mantle of connecting friends with each other. There are other global services such as:

- Alumni, www.alumni.net (a global service)
- Around, www.around.co.uk (a global service)
- Forces Reunited, www.forcesreunited.org.uk/ (a UK service for members or ex-members of the services).

However, these are also becoming less used as time goes on and people continue to gravitate towards Facebook. Having said that, there are still a great many other social networks that focus on particular subject areas, such as literature, parenthood, pets and so on. The Mamuna search engine, at http://mamuna.com, is an excellent tool for identifying such social media networks, and once they have been found the next stage is to visit the site and use any search options that they make available to find the named individuals that you are after.

Facebook and LinkedIn

Of course, there are some social media sites which have become so ingrained into the internet over the past few years there is a very high likelihood that the person that you want will have registered with one, other or both of them, and of course I'm referring to Facebook and LinkedIn. Facebook has over 1.5 billion members worldwide, which makes it the largest 'country' in the world if we were comparing population statistics. We have already discussed Facebook search in Chapter 7, so here I'll just briefly revisit searching for individuals. The search function at Facebook is fairly basic, but you can put in a name, and you are almost certain to get more results than you expect. Some people are quite happy to provide a lot of personal detail, so it may be very easy to identify the person that you are looking for, but other people have their accounts tightly locked down so that it's almost impossible – it really is a case of pot luck, I'm afraid. While there are a few search engines that attempt to search Facebook, they are all very limited and the results that they return are not at all comprehensive, so a search for a person could return zero results but

I wouldn't be confident that they were not using the site.

LinkedIn, at www.linkedin.com/, is often regarded as a 'professional' networking site, with an emphasis on making contacts in your professional sphere of activities, rather than sharing photographs of the family pets. Since the site is widely used by recruiters looking for new staff, search options are quite extensive. You can obviously search on name, keywords, location, country, postal code, title, or the school that someone went to. Furthermore, there are a large number of filters that can be incorporated into a search; industries, seniority level, function and so on. If you have some basic details on the person that you are looking for, LinkedIn is certainly an excellent place to start your search.

Twitter

Twitter, at www.twitter.com, while not having quite the reach of giants such as Facebook, does have many millions of users. There are plenty of different ways to search the resource: the first of those is to actually use Google instead. A search for *site:twitter.com* and then the name of the person that you're looking for will return a list of results that contain not only the name of the person you're looking for in their Twitter 'handle' but also those who are using nicknames but whose real name is a match. Finally, Google can return matches where individual tweets contain the name of your target.

Did you know?
The three most followed people on Twitter are Katy Perry, Justin Bieber and Barack Obama (http://friendorfollow.com/twitter/most-followers).

If you prefer to go directly to Twitter it's worth making the point that you don't have to have an account in order to search it. Simply point your browser to https://twitter.com/search-home and start looking. You can do a simple search on your target's name, although I would suggest putting it into double quotes to make sure Twitter realises that you want to search on the whole name as one element, rather than on two unrelated names. There are also a number of advanced functions that searchers can use in order to find specific people. If you're fairly sure that you have got the right name for someone, try a search string such as *from:philbradley* to see all of the tweets that I have sent (this will work with me, but some people protect their accounts for various reasons, and so this sort of search will return no hits I'm afraid). Alternatively, try *to:philbradley* to see if anyone is talking to the person that you're seeking. You could also try a search *@philbradley* to see instances where I am referenced on

Twitter. With these two options it won't matter that someone has their own tweets protected, you should still be able to locate them via a third party. One final method to try if you're running out of options is to try a geographic search. If you know where the person you're interested in lives (the more specific the better) Twitter uses the search functions *near:* and *within: mi* and so a search would look something like *near:bath* or *within:15 mi*.

You can also use *near:<location>* in conjunction with other search terms, e.g. *near:bath "American Museum"* if you think it's possible to find your contact that way – although, to be honest, if you have that much information on them at that point you should pretty much have found them using other methods!

Finding people that you don't know

At first glance this seems a bit weird, but it's something that we do all the time. I may need to find a trainer who can run a session on mobile technology, but I don't know anyone off-hand who could do that for me. So it's really simply just a case of finding people with a certain amount of authority that you can then research in more detail.

Obviously you can use a lot of the resources that have been previously mentioned in this chapter. Search for the subject that's of interest and add in other keywords such as 'expert' or the awful 'guru'; you'll almost certainly come up with some names in the SERPs. On the other hand, try searching a resource that has a lot of user-generated input, such as Twitter. Run a search using appropriate keywords and see who is tweeting about that subject. Take a look at their biography, look at their other tweets, see who they follow and who follows them and in a fairly short space of time, you should have a small number of useful names. It may also be worth looking at some Twitter search resources that identify experts in particular areas by using Followerwonk, at https://moz.com/followerwonk/bio, which allows searchers to access Twitter accounts by searching through biographies. Alternatively, visit Buzzsumo at https://app.buzzsumo.com and run a search, then view the 'Influencers' tab to see who is involved in a particular subject area. Figure 9.2 on the next page shows a list of influencers for the subject 'CILIP', and includes well known names such as the CEO and various groups, including details such as their followers.

Facebook isn't a great deal of help directly, but if you can find a Facebook group for your area of interest, it may be worth spending time 'hanging out' in the group to see who posts material, who responds and so on. If all else fails, you could always ask a question yourself to see if anyone can suggest recommendations.

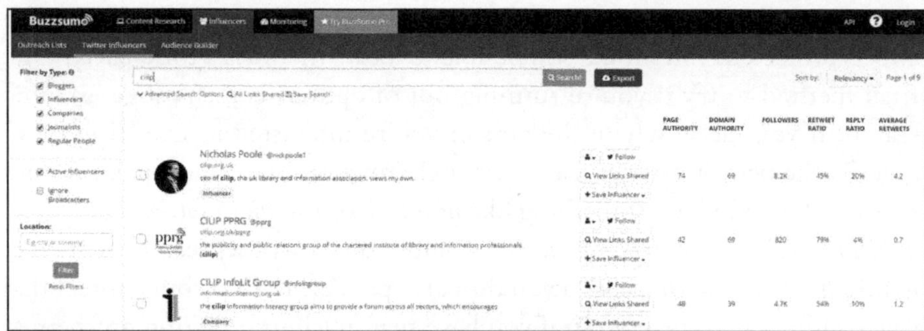

Figure 9.2 *Influencers in the subject area of 'CILIP' on Buzzsumo*
Reproduced with permission from the Buzzsumo app

Another approach that often pays off is to search one of the many sites that host presentations. Conference organisers will often put PowerPoint presentations online and so a Google search for an appropriate keyword and *filetype:ppt* will focus a search, and adding in a type of site, such as *site:.ac.uk*, will narrow it even further. Alternatively, visit sites such as Slideshare at www.slideshare.net or Authorstream at www.authorstream.com to identify individuals who are sharing slides on a subject that is of interest to you. Also consider using YouTube, at www.youtube.com, to see if people have posted appropriate videos in your area of interest; another video search engine, eHow (www.ehow.com) provides links to a lot of videos produced by experts. Finally, since we're looking at presentations, take a look at Lanyrd (www.lanyrd.com), which lists conferences that are taking place around the world. You can often see details on who is taking part, links to their presentations and so on.

There are some search engines that are worth considering if you're looking for experts. Profnet, at www.prnewswire.com/profnet, is designed for journalists who are looking to get quotes from experts, and the site is designed to match both together. Expertclick, at www.expertclick.com, lists thousands of experts in a wide variety of different categories; of course, the definition of 'expert' will differ, but it's a good starting point. Allexperts, created in early 1998 at www.allexperts.com, was the very first large-scale question and answer service on the net. They have thousands of volunteers, including top lawyers, doctors, engineers and scientists, waiting to answer your questions. All answers are free and most come within a day, and they are reasonably comprehensive. Once again, of course, you should check the answers (and the experts themselves!) to ensure that you're satisfied with their level of authority. A similar site, Quora (www.quora.com), hosts questions and answers, which often turn into interesting discussions. Anoox, at www.anoox.com, is another site which allows people to ask questions and then see answers. Of course, the answer could be provided by anyone from an expert to an individual who knows next to nothing, so it's worth taking anything with a pinch of salt and as nothing more than a starting point. Surprisingly, given that Yahoo! is divesting itself of anything to do with search, it still runs the Yahoo! Answers resource at https://answers.Yahoo!.com, and it's possible to search for a subject, see what questions have been asked and, most importantly, what the answers are. Once again, however, there's no way that they can be considered as authoritative, so keep that in mind.

A search engine vanishing act

I am often asked if it's possible to erase yourself entirely from the internet, and quite frankly these days I don't believe that it can be done. However, there are a number of things that you can do to at least limit what people can find about you. Now in some senses this has very little to do with internet search *per se*, so feel free to move straight onto the next chapter (I won't mind), but, equally, learning how to reduce your internet 'footprint', as it were, does provide useful knowledge about some aspects of search that don't get mentioned elsewhere.

If you have a Google account, log into your 'My activity' dashboard at https://myactivity.google.com/myactivity and you will see that there is a record of every YouTube video that you have watched, the Google searches that you have performed, when you search, favourite websites and much more. The dashboard does allow you to adjust your privacy settings; this doesn't cover everything, but at least it's better than nothing. You should also check your web search history at the same time at www.history.google.com to either delete individual entries or the entire history. If you find yourself on pages that Google has cached, as mentioned previously, ask the person who has put the information online to delete it. If they comply, you can then check the Google cache to make sure that the old page is no longer available, and if it is, you can request that Google removes the cached version. Details of this are available at http://support.google.com/webmasters/bin/answer.py?hl=en&answer=1663691. Of course, this is entirely useless if the person who has referred to you chooses not to remove the content in the first place, as is their right of course (unless you have been libelled, which is going to be a painful and probably expensive thing to prove); all that you could do in that case is try and push that particular page down the rankings by ironically adding more information about yourself, written in such a way as to make Google believe that the new page(s) have more value than current ones and ranking them more highly; most people never check on the second page of Google results, don't forget!

If you are unhappy with your Facebook presence there are plenty of privacy settings that can be changed, but since Facebook is constantly tinkering with these I'll simply surrender at this point and say 'find the options yourself'! Two important points, though – don't post material publicly where it can be picked up by search engines and if everything else fails, you can always delete yourself entirely from Facebook.

If you have spent much time online you may well have created accounts on a variety of social media sites, and a quick way to find these is to use the NameChk site at http://namechk.com. This links to over 150 social media sites and you can simply type in your username. The search engine will then display a list of the sites that have that username registered – it may not be registered to you, of course, but it's a useful starting point.

Finally, there are a number of companies that will do the hard work for you, if you feel that you're unable to do it yourself, or you don't have the time. You will need the money, however, as these services can cost hundreds or even thousands of pounds. A search for *reputation management* will find any number of them for you.

Summary

Looking for specific people on the internet is a hit-and-miss affair. People are understandably concerned about their privacy and many will go to extreme lengths to protect it, making them very difficult to find. Others will change e-mail addresses on a regular basis as they move from provider to provider, and may change their name or details on social media websites. Finally, even if you do have the right name, that's seldom going to be enough detail to track someone down, as there will be hundreds, if not thousands, of people who share the same name. The more information you have, the easier it will be to find someone, but there's little to beat an accurate and current telephone number!

CHAPTER 10

News-based search engines

Introduction

There are several questions that arise when looking at the concept of news search. First, what exactly does news mean now? Global and national news is a fairly clear concept, and we can take that down to the next level of local news. However, is it 'news' that your next door neighbour has painted their fence? To you it may well be very interesting and valuable to know what product they used and how effective it is, because you can then go and buy some paint yourself from the same manufacturer if you have been shamed into painting your fence, too. However, your friend at the other end of the country may well not regard this as news at all, though if you paint your fence, it may be – so we could perhaps define 'news' as being fresh information that is of particular interest to us and our friends and colleagues.

Given the ease of use of social media-based tools where we can share updates so easily it is perhaps understandable that people will view the concept of 'news' in a very different way now than they did prior to this ease of access. Indeed, with cameras – both still and video – in most people's pockets in the form of their smartphones, everyone can suddenly become a journalist, and it's quite usual these days to see video footage appear on news channels which started off in a smartphone, or images in newspapers that have been taken (sometimes with, sometimes without, permission) from Flickr and other photograph-sharing websites. Tools such as Periscope, at www.periscope.tv, allow you, in its own words to 'explore what the world is seeing'. I visited the website and I was able to see live streaming of a person showing me the traffic passing an intersection in New York City, the sunrise in California and a musician singing in a bar in Dublin. I could also follow along with the speeches at the Scottish Nationalist Party Spring Conference, learn how to bake cream cheese tarts and watch a protest in respect of immigration rights. All of this is news to some, of mild interest to others and boring to yet another group!

> **Did you know?**
> 2017 is the first year in which half the world's population was connected to the internet (https://thenextweb.com/insights/2017/01/24/digital-trends-2017-report-internet).

On a professional level, speeches and workshop discussions can also easily be shared, so while it's of no international or even national interest, what a speaker thinks about a subject is still going to be important news to the people who are dedicated to that particular subject. So 'news' now has to be seen rather more in the context of what an individual defines as news.

Secondly, what sort of time period are we looking at here? Books can have a production cycle of several months, magazines and journals perhaps a month, newspapers will define as news anything that happened since they last published, so let's say that's roughly a day, and search engines can update their indexes as often as needed to reflect the changing content of news sites. We then have the news sites themselves, which try their best to keep up with the breaking stories of the day, and closely allied to that we have blogs; once again, we're talking about hours or minutes. Finally we have the greatest news pipe of all – Twitter, which can present a news story that is seconds old.

> **Did you know?**
> The word 'Internetted' was first used in 1849, meaning interconnected or interwoven (https://en.wikipedia.org/wiki/Internet).

Thirdly, we have to consider the idea of authority as well. In 'the old days' it was relatively easy to work this out – we could assume that an academic article had been peer-reviewed prior to publication, a book had been edited, and that newspapers had a particular bias that everyone was aware of. However, if I get a news item off a blog, or as a tweet, it doesn't necessarily have the same type of authority that it would have had otherwise. In the early days of Twitter, the only way that one could be certain that a celebrity was actually the famous person you thought was tweeting was if Stephen Fry rang them up, asked them and confirmed it in a tweet. While it's slightly amusing that he was acting as a *de facto* validation source, the rather more important point is that we now need to consider the context of the news item – not just who said it, when and where they said it, but who their friends are, and the extent to which their extended network can validate them. Unfortunately, it's not really that easy; the need to get a story out as quickly as possible can sometimes take precedence, as a daily tabloid found out some time ago. It ran a story based on a tweet from Steve Jobs, which stated that he was going to have to withdraw the iPhone 4 due to technical problems. The journalist working for the newspaper had built up a story based on a single tweet and hadn't checked the actual biographical details of the account, which made it perfectly clear that it was a fake/parody account. At the other end of the spectrum, someone can tweet something which they don't even realise is news. Sohaib Athar started tweeting descriptions of events that happened close to his home in Pakistan, and it was only later that the world realised that he was live-tweeting the attack on Bin Laden by US forces. So – can we, or should we, trust the established newspaper and professional journalist, or should we trust someone who is reporting exactly what they are seeing in front of them? Of course, it's not really that simple, but the concept of authority, validity and trustworthiness becomes more important every day. End-users probably will not realise this, and indeed they may unwittingly perpetrate a myth – in January 2012 there were reports that Cuban leader Fidel Castro had died. This story was tweeted and retweeted hundreds of thousands of times, but it wasn't true. So simply because a large, indeed huge, number of people say something, it's really meaningless.

Finally, we have to consider how we can deal with news that we're not supposed to have. Wikileaks, for example, is a not-for-profit media organisation which provides a way for sources that wish to remain anonymous to leak information to the Wikileaks journalists. This may sometimes be highly sensitive information that should not be in the public domain. There are times when in the UK superinjunctions have been used by celebrities to keep details of legal cases that they're involved with out of the press, but details of which have appeared in social media resources such as Facebook or Twitter. What are our ethical and moral duties here? If we are faced with a request for information, and we're able to get the information which has appeared in the public domain, should we use it, provide it with a caveat, regard it as entirely unreliable and ignore it, or something else?

The concept of 'news' is therefore fraught with many and varied difficulties, and there are very few answers, so perhaps all that we can do is to keep an open mind, educate our members and just do the best we can. Having raised several spectres I will now take a step back from them and turn my attention to the actual tools that you can use in order to find newsworthy information.

General search engines

Many of the major search engines such as Google, Bing, Yahoo! and DuckDuckGo will provide access to news stories. Consequently, it's very easy to use your preferred search engine as a one-stop shop when it comes to news information, but it does help to have an indication as to the sources that the engine uses, how the stories are rated, if there are any inherent biases towards the subject matter, and the extent to which you can get a rounded and comprehensive view of a particular story.

In my opinion, of the general search engines Google provides the best news coverage, and you can find it at https://news.google.com. This was my view in the last edition of this title, and I haven't changed my mind since, even though other news resources have come along. It provides some really good functionality and users of the service have a great deal that they can customise. As well as the 'look and feel' of the page, users can choose what resources they have displayed on the page by personalising it with various sliders, so that for example if World News is really important the slider can be shifted to the right, resulting in more stories and the Entertainment slider moved to the left to decrease information on celebrities. However, it's also possible to add in any news topic that is of interest, and Google also offers the option of adding in ready-made sections such as social networking, space, physics and so on. Therefore, users can create custom sections to locate news items that are local to them, they can add country editions and can even decide how the news is presented – sorted by most users (of a section), highest rated or newest for example.

News stories are displayed clearly, with different news sections to the left of the main stories and recent items, local items and editors' picks to the right, forming an interesting and effective triptych. Each news item has its origins clearly marked and related stories can quickly and easily be pulled up, to add in-depth coverage to a subject. If available and appropriate Google will also display video news clips from major news sources such as BBC News. Google News has an advanced search function, and search terms can be limited to particular elements of the news coverage, such as the title, the source or the country the article is published in. However, it's only available as an option when a search has been run, which is quite irritating if you know exactly what you want, but have to run a search in order to get you to a position where you can do the exact search that interests you.

When searches have been run, the searcher can create an e-mail alert for the subject that they have searched for. They can choose the terms of the query, the type of information that's returned to them, such as news, blogs, video or discussions, how often they get an e-mail (as it happens, once a day or once a week), how many results, and the e-mail address the alert should be sent to. There is no limit to the number of alerts that can be set up, and they can be as simple as an individual word, or a much more complex search query. Searchers can also save the search as an RSS feed, which can be incorporated into their newsreader.

Bing's options, at www.bing.com/news, are a little less 'full on' than Google's, and the news page is far less busy, with a search box, some leading headlines and then below that leading headlines in a variety of different subject areas such as World, UK, Business, Politics and so on. Those subject areas can be expanded if preferred so that the engine just displays all the leading stories from a subject section. Finally, users can of course search for whatever interests them, with results displayed either as the best match or the most recent. However, it's not then possible to limit further without more work, since stories on the subject of community libraries, for example, will return all stories on the subject, regardless of country, which is an annoying limitation of the service.

Yahoo! News, at https://uk.news.yahoo.com/, is another busy screen of news. Under the search bar the engine presents a variety of news categories such as UK, World, Technology and so on, and then presents news stories, with an emphasis on image rather than text. Added to that is a series of advertisements which are not always clearly indicated as such, leading to some confusion. The rest of the news screen is a mixture of images and textual summaries for different categories, 'most popular' news items, latest videos, a poll on a current news story, editor's picks, slideshows, weather and so on. The Yahoo! news resource can obviously be searched, with results being displayed and filtered by either relevance or time. Searchers can then further filter by source and/or time. The search can also be saved as an RSS feed as well.

DuckDuckGo has a small dedicated news section, with half a dozen stories displayed in tile format culled from various global sources. However, it also uses the *!n bang* option, which pulls results directly from Google's news feed. Due to the nature of the search functionality that DuckDuckGo offers, there are a wide variety of other news-based search functions. Users can search via key broadcasters, such as *!bbc*, and they can search international resources, by magazine, newspapers, speciality sources and weather channels.

Specialised news search engines

There are a small number of search engines that simply report on the news – gathering data from news websites such as television stations, newspaper sites and so on. They have a single focus, which is to get news to you as quickly as possible. You may therefore find them to be a rather more appropriate choice if you just need global or national news which is regularly updated.

Infonary

Infonary, at http://infonary.com, is described as a 'real time news digest'. It has a very basic home page, with a small number of headlines, and it also takes headlines from leading UK resources such as television news and newspaper sites. There are a variety of video news items from different video sites such as YouTube. As well as the normal search box several categories of news are available, such as Politics, Sports and Technology. It is also possible to view news via country or alphabetically by subject. Once users move away from the category approach and into personalised searching for key terms Infonary finds results from news sites, search engine news, YouTube, blogs and Twitter. Infonary is updated regularly and provides a good service, although it's rather let down by the very sparse interface.

Newsmap

Newsmap, at www.newsmap.jp, is at first glance a very confusing page, because it has a large amount of headline content contained in different sized squares across the page, all in different colours. However, given a few minutes perusal it all becomes clear. First, users need to locate the tab across the very top of the screen which gives them a choice of country – about 16 options, heavily biased towards the West. The next thing to check is the bottom of the screen, which has a colour-coded index, so headlines with red backgrounds are world news, purple backgrounds are health news and so on. Finally, the lighter the colour, the more recent the news, and the larger the square, the more important the news. This sounds terribly convoluted and messy, but it's a very quick concept to pick up, and the system does provide a considerable amount of granularity, so that with a couple of mouse clicks a user can visually focus on technology stories from the USA, or health and sports stories from Argentina. The colour and size focus really does come into play when running a keyword search, however, as the main stories can leap out of the page at the searcher, helping them to quickly isolate lead stories.

News Now

News Now (www.newsnow.co.uk/h) was launched in 1998, and is currently visited by over 14 million users a month. It's an aggregation service, so it matches breaking news stories in real time against keyword-based topics. In common with other news services it provides small 'boxes' of information on particular topics, which can be clicked on as appropriate, with the original story opening in a new browser tab. News Now also offers a menu of subject areas such as hot topics, science, sports and arts and culture which break down into narrower subjects. It's therefore really easy to go from Sport to Football to the Premier League, to a club and then to transfer news and details of particular players. At every point in this focusing process the searcher is shown how many new stories are available, which is very effective. Searchers can simply type in their topic(s) of interest and the engine will provide information arranged by time; the last hour, two hours, back to the last seven days – if preferred, other date ranges can be chosen. News stories are taken from over 40,000 sources and auto-refresh every five minutes.

There are of course plenty of other alternatives available if you're unhappy with any of the ones that I've discussed above. Try:

- Rocket News, www.rocketnews.com
- World News, http://wn.com
- Daily Earth, http://dailyearth.com
- Headline Spot, www.headlinespot.com
- News Lookup, www.newslookup.com.

Newspapers and traditional media resources

An obvious place to look for news stories is where we've always looked for news in the past – newspaper and television websites. There are quite simply thousands of news sites which go from the tiny local newspaper site that's updated once a week to the huge news resources from organisations such as the BBC which are updated minute by minute. Obviously each of these resources has their own bias, but that is to be expected. Nowadays we can expect each resource to update continually throughout the course of the day with new information and breaking stories, and to include video reports as and when necessary, and even live reporting as needed.

Did you know?
Print-only is still the most common way of reading newspapers in the USA (www.journalism.org/2016/06/15/newspapers-fact-sheet).

Some newspaper sites

Having apparently dismissed these tools in a paragraph, there are some sites that I would like to particularly draw your attention to. The Newseum site, at www.newseum.org/todaysfrontpages, shows over 2000 front pages from 91 countries. It's enlightening and frustrating by turn, since the front page IS all that you get, but to be fair, there's a link to the newspaper's website itself. Consequently it has limited value, but it's a good way to see how subjects are treated around the world.

Google has a newspaper archive of hundreds of broadsheets, some going back to the early 1800s, and it is international in scope. It is arranged alphabetically, so the searcher needs to have a fairly good idea of exactly what they are looking for, but there is a search function that allows users to jump straight to a particular article in a journal. Google also provides a very handy 'related articles' link to similar stories. Perhaps the most interesting aspect of this collection is that the newspapers are provided visually, so it's possible to move around a newspaper, looking at the advertisements, for example. Unfortunately Google has decided not to continue developing this resource, but they are leaving it online for researchers, so if you are looking for archival information, this could be a good starting point.

If your needs are more current, The Paperboy, at www.thepaperboy.com, has a searchable collection of over 6000 online newspapers and e-papers. Content is displayed in magazine format style, but users can click on a world map, choose by country or simply enter a search term.

If you are serious in a desire to read news, the British Library provides access to the British Newspaper Archive at www.britishnewspaperarchive.co.uk and thousands of new pages are scanned every day – the current figure is at 18,729,440 pages. However, this is a commercial product, and does not have a free option.

The RefDesk site, at www.refdesk.com/paper.html, also has a useful listing of American and national newspapers from around the world, neatly divided into US state and country. It provides excellent coverage and links to almost 50 UK newspapers, for example. They are, however, slightly outdone by the Internet Public Library site, at www.ipl.org/div/news, which lists almost 120 UK resources, as well as magazines. Unfortunately the ipl.org site is no longer being maintained and updated, but is still available with links, so it's worth taking a look at, although as time moves forward 'link rot' will firmly take hold as sites change addresses, so look at it sooner rather than later!

Finally, the Library of Congress has a newspaper and current periodical reading room at www.loc.gov/rr/news/oltitles.html, which links to newspaper archives, indexes and morgue resources. As you might expect, there is a strong US bias to the content, but there are also plenty of international references and links.

Good news sites

On a lighter note, you may be interested to know that there are a large number of news sites that are devoted to positive news stories. When talking and teaching about news search I often have discussions about how grim all of the news appears to be, so it's quite nice to be able to highlight a few sites that focus on good news. I certainly wouldn't consider replacing any of these with the tools that I have previously mentioned, but if for some reason you're feeling a little down, take a brief look.

Good News Network, at www.goodnewsnetwork.org, has various news sections, just like regular news sites, with top stories, RSS, a subscription service, inspirational quotes and so on. Good News Broadcast, at http://goodnewsplanet. com, is a very busy site with an emphasis on YouTube videos, and very feel-good, though in my opinion not quite so many 'news' items as the previous one. Gimundo, at http://gimundo.com, provides interesting and uplifting stories on a regular basis. The Great News Network, located at www.greatnewsnetwork.org/index.php, has news by category, region, submit news, and an RSS feed. In its 'About' section it really does clearly define exactly what the role of this type of news resource is all about: 'The Great News Network is meant to supplement your daily news sources – not replace it. Its role is to show that there is hope, people are making a difference, and that a lot of things are getting better.' Positive News is a UK-based site at http://positivenews.org.uk. It's the web-based version of a paper-based quarterly. Not so much current affairs, more feel-good, sustainable-future type of information. Yes! Magazine, at www.yesmagazine. org, again looks like a website of a paper-based newsletter/magazine; more on political issues than current affairs from the look that I took. As a brief aside, when researching this section I looked at a lot of different sites, as you can imagine, and I followed up links to find resources that were quite often several years old. While several more 'traditional' news sources had closed, all of these 'positive' news sites were still all in existence, so there's a message in there for us all somewhere!

News curation tools

Of course, the definition of what is 'news' is going to be different for each and every one of us. Up until now I have looked at national and international news resources, but there are two other types that we should consider. The first is news relating to individual subject areas, which while not of national or international interest may still be very important for each of us in our jobs. The second type of news is going to be rather more personal; what our friends and colleagues are looking it, highlighting and sharing.

I don't expect to find a great deal on the BBC news about developments with search engines, new and interesting Web 2-based utilities or things that are happening within the library world. I could of course quite easily set up my own RSS feeds and news alerts to keep me informed, but once again, because much of this information will not appear on the news, or via news sites, these tools can only provide me with a snapshot. It's at this point that my colleagues and their activities come into their own. I have already looked at the value of social media search engines in Chapter 7 and the role that colleagues can play with them, and this is a subject that I'm returning to again.

We are all familiar with the Facebook 'Like' button, the Google +1 button, blogging about resources, adding them to bookmarking services and so on. Even if we don't always do this ourselves, friends and colleagues do. It can be very useful to see what others in your social circles are looking at, commenting on and sharing, because if they like something or find it interesting, there's a high chance that you will experience something similar yourself. However, it's simply not possible to spend all day checking out these resources, looking through friends' profiles and so on – there simply isn't enough time. This is where news curation services become useful. Simply put, you can provide a resource with access to your Twitter account, or perhaps your Facebook account, and let it gather data on the likes and references to resources that contacts find and make. These can then be presented to you in an easy-to-use format, allowing you to very quickly skim through that highly personalised news. While there are a few of these available for the browser, they have particularly come into their own in various apps for smartphones and tablets, though in some cases they are available for both. It's worth pointing out that although a lot of these products ask for your Facebook or Twitter details and then access data produced by your contacts, they are really only acting as a mechanism from drawing together information that these contacts are already sharing with you.

Addict-o-matic

Addict-o-matic, at http://addictomatic.com, has as its strapline 'Inhale the web; instantly create a custom page with the latest buzz on any topic'. It pulls in results from a variety of news resources such as Bing News, Silicon Alley Insider and Cnet's Tech Blog. This is a slightly different product to the other engines in this category in that it doesn't provide a home page of global or national news; it has a category approach but the user is expected to know what they're after, and to create a search for themselves. The user is in control of the resources used, since a pulldown menu of sources is available and it works on a toggle basis, so that different sources can be turned on and off as necessary. News items are displayed in small news boxes which can be moved around or even deleted as necessary, thus creating a very personalised version of the news, which can then be shared with other people if necessary.

Flipboard

Flipboard, at http://flipboard.com, is the one that you'll probably be aware of, if you are at all familiar with this type of resource. It's made up of small subject cubes, so that when you open the app you see a display of squares, which you can tap on to take you into more detail, with stories displayed in a similar cube or magazine format. When you swipe across the screen, you do get a quite pleasing flip effect as the page 'turns'. Clicking on a story opens up the original tweet or status, displays the story on the screen, and links to the full story on the website. An upward swipe loads it directly for you to read. New sections can be added easily, and they're just a tap or two away. It's a very well regarded resource, and it makes excellent use of the visual and touch screen elements of tablet devices. You can link your Flipboard account to your Facebook and Twitter accounts, for example, as well as news feeds and search results for tweets covering specific subject areas.

Paper.li

The Paper.li service, at http://paper.li, is a content curation service. Users can publish and share their own newspapers based on the topics that interest them, and to which others can share. It can automatically find and curate stories of interest based on feedback from users, and from the stories shared by the people that an individual user follows. It provides social network content aggregation from the major sites such as Twitter, Facebook and YouTube, and also has a professional paid-for version.

My newspaper is 'The Phil Bradley Daily' and you can find it at https://paper.li/Philbradley#. It includes headline news, photographs, videos and information on science, technology and business, as well as other categories. In a matter of seconds I can catch up on what the people I'm following on social media platforms are looking at, sharing and commenting. As the paper is freely available for other people to see, you too can read the same content. It isn't the easiest resource in the world to search but if you use your favourite search engine to add in some keywords and run a *site:paper.li* filter you will very quickly pull up newspapers that may interest you. I ran a search for *librarian site:paper.li* and got over 6500 results, and the first 50 were all exactly on topic.

Scoop It!

A web-based tool, Scoop It!, at www.scoop.it, is designed to act as a personal aggregation tool that is designed to let users bookmark stories of interest to them using the bookmarklet, and to share these stories with friends and colleagues. It's simple to create a topic, and when a user finds a story that would fit well into their magazine they can 'scoop it' and add in any commentary that they wish, or simply leave it as it stands. I have two separate pages on the site; 'Internet search' at www.scoop.it/t/internet-search and 'Privacy and search' at www.scoop.it/t/privacy-and-search (two pages are the limit if you have a free account; a commercial account currently allows people to create five pages). I can use Scoop It! in a variety of ways. First of all, when I'm going around the web and I see a page or article that's of interest to me, I can 'scoop it' with the use of a bookmarklet on my browser bar in a matter of seconds. That's then added to the appropriate page, and I can go back and view it again at any time I wish; it's rather like a bookmarking service. Secondly, as you have seen, I can make the page(s) publicly available for other people to view and make use of. Finally, Scoop It! provides me with suggestions for good content; it learns what I am interested in (I can like or discard its suggestions, so that in time it becomes more accurate) and so keeps me up to date in my subject areas. I can filter suggestions by type (articles, documents, pictures, videos or social networks) and I can manually add sources to further focus my interest.

Scoop It! also has a general search box, so people can obviously just search for what is of interest to them, and once they have found a good resource, visit it again in the future.

Storify

If you wish to curate and share stories by bringing together content that is scattered across various social media sites, then Storify, at http://storify.com, is a useful tool to consider. Users can build a consistent creative narrative, pulling in content from sites as diverse as Twitter, Facebook, YouTube and Flickr. Status updates can be dragged and dropped, reordered and edited as necessary. The story can then be embedded anywhere on the web.

Nuzzel

The Nuzzel site, http://nuzzel.com, is another that provides access to 'top news stories and feeds'. Users have to sign in using their Twitter credentials and Nuzzel can then show you news from your friends – that is to say, links to what people you are following are tweeting about and linking to. It's updated every hour, so the news is always fresh, and the headlines are arranged by the number of friends who respond to particular stories. When I checked my account there were articles on how physical books are outperforming digital titles, books for girls, reading lists and information on fake news. It's also possible to respond directly to the tweets from inside Nuzzel, making it quick and easy to get involved with a story and the person you're following.

Nuzzel can also create news collections based on the lists that you have created for yourself on Twitter; collections of people that you follow that you have tagged to specific collections. You may therefore be interested in taking a look at the top news stories from 'Search engines' at http://nuzzel.com/Philbradley/searchengines. Nuzzel also has a search function and links to stories that it has found on social media, based on the keywords that you have searched on. Finally, Nuzzel can send you a daily digest of news stories, so it's really easy to keep up to date with what's going on in your world.

Other tools

As I am sure you expect by now, these are far from the only news curation tools that are available on the web. While they work in a variety of ways, they all exhibit characteristics similar to those previously mentioned. So if none of those attract you, it's worth exploring resources such as Bagtheweb (http://bagtheweb.com), Feedly (www.feedly.com) or Summify (http://summify.com).

Fake news

There has always been incorrect, inaccurate and just plain wrong information on the internet. There's a famous cartoon of a man furiously typing away on his computer and his wife's voice comes from upstairs 'Are you coming to bed?' and as he continues to type he says 'No! Someone said something wrong on the internet.' For many years we've had sites such as Snopes, at www.snopes.com, as the definitive reference source for urban legends, folklore, myths, rumours and misinformation, and before that 'The Straight Dope', a question-and-answer column published in the *Chicago Reader* since 1973, now with a website at www.straightdope.com. However, these sites have always tried to take a story that may perhaps have once had a grain of truth in them and sort the wheat from the chaff. Many of these stories have been handed down, passed on as 'a friend of a friend said' and shared on social media. While these stories may well be fake they are the result of misunderstandings and entertainment, rather than anything more sinister.

However, in the last couple of years we've seen an increasing reference to 'fake news', particularly around events such as Brexit (Britain's referendum on leaving the European Union) and the 2016 US Presidential Election, although there have been plenty of fake stories that cover many other subject areas. The current definition of fake news, which I'm taking from an article in *The Guardian* newspaper in December 2016, says:

> Fake news is a type of hoax or deliberate spread of misinformation, be it via the traditional news media or via social media with the intent to mislead in order to gain financially or politically.
>
> (Hunt, E., 'What is Fake News? How to spot it and what you can do to stop it', *The Guardian*, 17 December 2016; retrieved 15 January 2017)

There are two key points here: financial or political gain, neither of which are found by spreading stories surrounding mystery hitchhikers or ghostly apparitions, which sites such as the aforementioned Snopes take delight in debunking.

Financial gain

'For the love of money is a root of all kinds of evil' is the often misquoted sentence that can easily be turned into 'money is the root of all fake news'. As we've seen already, Google makes billions of dollars every year from advertising clicks; a company contracts with Google to pay the search engine a certain sum of money every time a paid for advert is clicked on. If the link is actually on another website, but supplied by Google, the web author will get a proportion of the money, rather like a finder's fee. If lots of people visit a website, perhaps 1–2% will click on an advert, which admittedly isn't much, but 8000 visits may lead to 80 clicks, which soon adds up to a reasonable income. Consequently, if the link to a story is contentious or salacious enough, people will click to visit it, and the fake news provider is one step closer to making some money. These stories can be about, quite literally, anything at all. I've seen headlines saying that the British monarch Queen Elizabeth is dead, that a certain celebrity is moving to a town close to where I live, that certain health foods are actually cancerous (when they're obviously not) and so on. There is absolutely no truth in any of these stories, but people can't but help click on the link, look at the story, and then perhaps click on an advert before leaving the site.

Unscrupulous people will create websites that claim to have been in existence for years, or that they are the online version of a newspaper that has apparently been publishing for years (when in actual fact the newspaper doesn't even exist), and they'll create Facebook pages to bolster the site. They can then visit a celebrity Facebook page, post a story, link to their own Facebook page, then link back to their bogus website in the hope of tricking people into believing the story, visiting and clicking advertising links.

Malware attacks

Another reason for getting people to click onto websites by providing them with fake news headlines is to try and get them to install malware. Malware is short for 'malicious software' and it's designed to disrupt your computer, get sensitive information such as bank details, get access to private files and so on – rather different to a virus, which is more likely designed to replicate itself and destroy your software and erase your data. People can be tricked by a site asking them to view a video, but in order to do that it's necessary to install another piece of software (the malware) in order to view the salacious material.

Biased information

There are plenty of fake news stories that appeal to people who have particular political or religious viewpoints. The *New York Times* reported in November 2016 that Facebook, Twitter and other social media outlets have exposed millions of Americans to false stories asserting that Hillary Clinton's campaign pollster, Joel Benenson, wrote a secret memo detailing plans to 'salvage' Hillary Clinton's candidacy by launching a radiological attack to halt voting, the Clinton campaign senior strategist John Podesta practised occult rituals, and that Mrs Clinton was paying public pollsters to skew results. There are many other examples, from all sides of the political spectrum, and just as many that attack different religious groups for various reasons.

It doesn't help that Google (for example) has linked to fake news sites. It was heavily criticised in the wake of the US Presidential election for linking to a site called 70news (https://70news.wordpress.com). This site headlined the news that Donald Trump had won both the popular and electoral college vote, when in actual fact he lost the popular vote by about 3 million votes. It's still not clear why Google linked to this site, but they did. Google responded by saying that they were going to fact-check and label sites with a 'Fact check' link to a reputable resource, but I have only ever seen this once or twice. Facebook has also stated that it is going to add warning labels to stories to say that they are 'disputed', but again, there's been little evidence of this actually happening.

In summary therefore, I don't believe that users can trust 'the news' that they find, and that they never should have done. A survey in 2015 by Ofcom (the UK Office of Communications) (https://nakedsecurity.sophos.com/2015/11/23/1-in-5-kids-believe-search-engine-results-are-always-true) found that only 60% of adults think that some websites will be accurate or unbiased and some won't be, 23% think that information returned by search engines is true and unbiased and 14% simply don't think about it.

Evaluating the news

When working with other people – and indeed when doing our own research – we really do need to stay on the ball. This is particularly the case when we find information that confirms our own bias towards something; we may well be far more inclined to believe it without question, since we live in our own 'filter bubbles', which are explained in more detail in a TED talk by Eli Pariser (www.ted.com/talks/eli_pariser_beware_online_filter_bubbles).

There is a simple, and easily remembered acronym that we can use when it comes to evaluating what we find, and it's CRAAP. Currency, Relevance, Authority, Accuracy and Purpose. I'll briefly go through each of these in turn, but an online search for the acronym will return many useful sites that are able to go into more detail than I have space for here.

Currency

It's not always clear when something has been published. The page may well have today's date on it, but that's simply due to a computer program designed to do exactly that. The actual article may well be weeks, months or even years old. This is particularly the case when you see news items on Facebook; they can be regurgitated stories that surface to corroborate some other event that's happening in the news. An easy way to check is to go to a search engine that allows you to search on, or rank results based on, time periods. Filter by material that's been added to the engine's database in the last 24 hours, or perhaps the last week. That should hopefully start to weed out more dated material. Run a search on the exact phrase that's used in the headline or the main body of the text to see if it's been used elsewhere and when. If there are any particular names or places mentioned in the article run separate searches for those as well, to see when and where they are mentioned.

Relevance

Is the information that you're finding relevant to the query at hand? Does the information make sense to you, or is it far too technical, using terminology that you don't understand? Does the information that you're looking at match information that you've found on other sites? Explore the website in some detail to see if it has a particular bias towards any one view, and look at the contributors to the site. Check their own background to see if they have published material elsewhere or, to be really cynical, do they actually exist, or are they completely fictitious?

Authority

This leads us neatly onto a proper investigation of the author of the piece or article that you're looking at. What are their credentials, and where do they work? Are they cited anywhere else? Take a look at their social media presence and see how many people they follow on Twitter, and perhaps more importantly, how many people follow them back. If you're really concerned, see if any of their followers are fake; sites such as Status People, at https://fakers.statuspeople.com, will let you run some free searches to see how many followers are fake. It's not a perfect tool by any means, but if any more than 10% of followers turn out to be fake it's worth proceeding with caution. Once again, check the website that is hosting the information, and take a look at the URL; is it one of the top-level domains, such as .ac, .gov or .edu? If it isn't, dig more deeply into the site; the Wayback Machine, which I talk about in Chapter 12, will be helpful here.

Accuracy

Check some of the statements on the page to see if they are accurate by cross checking with other sites. Cut and paste some of the text to see if it has been copied wholesale from somewhere else. Are there any spelling errors or problems with punctuation or grammar? As a rule of thumb, the more errors you find, the less likely the information is to be accurate, although it's worth suspending some level of disbelief if the author's original language isn't English.

Purpose

Why has someone produced the information that you're looking at? Is the information there to entertain or amuse, in which case you may well be looking at one of the many satirical sites that exist and their purpose isn't to spread fake news. However, many people can get taken in by the information found in sites such as The Onion (www.theonion.com) and in good faith spread the information that they find far and wide – usually to their friends on Facebook, who send it onto their friends and so on. Does the article reference or present different viewpoints, and is there any obvious bias or prejudice, perhaps around the choice of words used to represent individuals, racial or religious groups? Can you find other information that hasn't been included which might weaken the case or claim of the author?

Check, check and check again!

One advantage of social media and user-generated content is that anyone can write anything that they want to quickly and easily. However, this is a major disadvantage as well. There are plenty of reasons why fake news is on the increase, and however much search engines or social media platforms try and do to stop this, they are doomed to failure; fake news will always get through. Trust no one, not even your friends (even if they come from an information background!), and keep checking your sources until you're absolutely convinced that the information you have got is sound.

Summary

Searching for news is already becoming one of the most interesting and fastest-moving areas of internet search – mainly because no one really knows what it means anymore! Consequently we're seeing the development of news search engines, the collation of content, the delivery of content and even the definition of that content changing continually. People are becoming journalists, so as well as reading the news we're more capable than ever of recording and publishing it, which brings the associated difficulties of authority and validity. With the ever-increasing use of mobile phones we will see news being brought to us all of the time, and it's going to be tailored down to where we physically might be located, with a search engine working in tandem with the GPS option on the smartphone. News really is all around us now.

CHAPTER 11

Multimedia search engines

Introduction

In the earlier days of internet search video and multimedia was very much the poor relation. Most people used dial-up connections to access the internet and the equipment needed to create video or make voice recordings was either expensive to purchase or complicated to use – often both. By 2016, 81% of UK households had a broadband connection (either fixed or mobile) and 42% of users had taken up the option of superfast fixed broadband by the end of 2015 (www.ofcom.org.uk/about-ofcom/latest/media/facts). The total number of global broadband subscribers had grown to 10% of the world's population by the end of 2014; in the developed world this figure was 27% (https://en.wikipedia.org/wiki/Global_Internet_usage). Due in part to the cheap availability of webcams and more importantly the increased sophistication of smartphones, 400 hours' worth of video is uploaded to YouTube every minute (up from the 72 hours I referenced in the previous edition of the book), and more than 1 billion hours of YouTube footage is watched every day, which is a tenfold increase since 2012. That means that if you wanted to watch an entire day's worth of uploaded video it would take you approximately 65 years to do so (https://youtube.googleblog.com/2017/02/you-know-whats-cool-billionhours.html). Meanwhile, on Facebook an average of 100 million hours of video was watched every day in January 2016, and over 8 billion views daily (http://expandedramblings.com/index.php/by-the-numbers-7-amazing-facebook-stats).

I think we can safely say that sharing and watching video on the internet

Did you know?
It is expected that online video will account for 74% of all internet traffic in 2017 (www.digitalinformationworld.com/2016/12/infographic-video-marketing-statistics-2017.html).

has become a serious business. Of course, a large amount of the content shared and viewed is simply for entertainment (although how one defines that is of course open to question; what is entertainment for one person may well be serious research for another), but with news items being shared on video sites, 'how-to' videos, educational material, television programmes and so on, content found on video has to be taken into account when searching. In this chapter I'll look at some of the ways in which searchers can utilise the flood of content that's available and suggest some search engines to use in order to retrieve it.

Traditional search engines

As we have seen in previous chapters, most search engines have a 'video' option. Google is perhaps a little bit greedy with two choices – their own 'Videos' resource, which can be found in the general menu, or visited directly at www.google.com/videohp or at YouTube. Google Videos is the poor relation of the two and has a chequered history, in that it's been listed for closure, then saved; it's still available but it's not a tool that I would want to rely on. It also has a very small collection, relatively speaking; a search for *dog* on Google Videos returned 11,400,000 results, while the same search on YouTube gave me 65,300,000; an entirely unscientific test, but it's a general indication of the different amount of resources available. Consequently, as Google owns YouTube, that's where I'll focus, but as YouTube is a separate site in its own right I'll return to it later in the chapter.

As previously mentioned in Chapter 4, Bing provides access to videos via the menu bar at the top of the search screen, but it also has a link at www.bing.com/videos/search. The video search option provides immediate links to top videos, viral videos, TV, news, celebrity and so on; much of the offering is primarily focused on the entertainment market. A search results in an infinite scrolling list of videos with a thumbnail, the length of the video, title, date of the video and where it's located. Videos can be viewed directly on the search engine website, but links are available which take the viewer directly to the originating site. Bing provides links to related searches, and there are filters for length, resolution and source. One quick word of warning, which not only relates to Bing's offering, but to many others: you may well be advised to have some filtering or safe search option in place, as even an entirely innocent search will return pornography.

DuckDuckGo, of course, utilises the 'bang' search option and simply links searchers to other video sites, so a search for *dog !video* runs a search at Google video, and *dog !vimeo* takes the searcher directly to results at Vimeo. Exalead has a video search option, available at www.exalead.com/search/video, or above the search box. Results can be sorted by relevance, newest, oldest, rating, length or view count. Searchers can filter results by source or category. However, since my *dog* search gave me a paltry 346,000 results, it's one that I'd only use in desperation.

Video-specific search engines

Most search engines will have a video search option, as we've seen from the previous examples, but in most cases they are simply indexing other resources such as YouTube, so it makes sense to go directly to the specialist search engines themselves. There are a great many engines of this type, some of which attempt to provide access to any and all videos, while others tend to specialise in a particular type of video, such as educational or historical. Let's take a look at a few of them, but I should warn you in advance that you may find this section to be a huge time sink, as you explore one collection, think 'I'll just watch one more' and you find that several hours have passed!

Did you know?
More video content is uploaded to the web in one month than TV has created in three decades (www.clickbank.com/5-video-marketing-trends-every-digital-marketer-needs-to-know).

blinkx

blinkx has a video search site at www.blinkx.com. It provides a search home page with the usual search box and also 19 categories from news and politics to health, sports, celebrity and travel. Content in each category is arranged chronologically with links to featured contributors such as the Huffington Post, ITN and Reuters. When I started typing in a *library* search, blinkx gave me news articles from sites such as the *Washington Post*, the Today Show and Associated Press. The results that I obtained were all news-related, the most recent being a few hours old. Each result took up most of the screen as a large thumbnail with details on it of the time it was uploaded, the source, the title, an option to add as a favourite and a link to sharing the video. Underneath the thumbnail was a brief summary. Unfortunately there was no indication as to how many videos were available, and since the results were on an infinite scroll I couldn't even count page numbers. blinkx provided some basic Boolean functionality such as *NOT* and *OR* as well as the option for phrase searching via double quotes, but there wasn't an advanced search option. The channels option was not well documented, but since blinkx offered me ones from the Library of Virginia and the Library Channel I am assuming that they are user-generated resources – they certainly contained appropriate content.

Dailymotion

Dailymotion, at www.dailymotion.com, attracts over 300 million users from around the world, who watch over 3.5 billion videos on its player every month. It has over 40 localised versions in 16 different languages, and is based in France. The content is varied, with an emphasis on entertainment, but there are lots of useful news clips from global news corporations such as CNN International. Videos can be browsed via categories such as news, sports, arts, music and so on, or searched via the search box. My search for *library* returned over 600,000 videos and they were a mixture of news-based, anime and humour. I was offered access to 69 different 'channels' from different providers (many of them library services) over 160 playlists or compilations of videos around a specific aspect of 'library'.

Dailymotion did not provide an advanced search function, but it was possible to use their basic category approach to narrow down results to specific selections such as 'most viewed today' or 'tech' or 'movies'. The engine offers an option to register for an account for a 'tailor-made' video experience.

Internet Movie Database

The Internet Movie Database, or IMDb for short, at www.imdb.com, isn't strictly speaking a video search engine of the type that I'm referring to in this chapter, but since its focus is on films, television and news items, this is a sensible place to discuss it. It describes itself as

> the world's most popular and authoritative source for movie, TV and celebrity content. The IMDb consumer site (www.imdb.com) is the #1 movie website in the world with a combined web and mobile audience of more than 250 million unique monthly visitors. (www.imdb.com/advertising)

IMDb offers a searchable database of more than 130 million data items, including more than 4 million movies, TV and entertainment programmes and more than 7 million cast and crew members. This makes the search engine a prime tool when searching for video-based information. There is of course the ubiquitous search box, but it comes with a pulldown menu to limit search to titles, TV episodes, keywords, characters, quotes and plots. There is also an advanced search function, which allows access to title search, name search and collaborations and overlaps. It's also possible to browse titles by genre, country, language, year and keyword, while people can be browsed by gender and star sign. Text from the plot summary can be located using the search option as well as, trivia, quotes, goofs, credits, locations and more. Name search can be limited to biographies, quotes and trivia.

The IMDb also provides current affairs information about the film and television industry, listing new movies, coming soon, top news, television news, celebrity news and even movie showtimes. Although it's not possible to view videos at IMDb, it does link to trailers, and since it is owned by Amazon, options to purchase the films themselves, or to rent them by post.

YouTube

I have already mentioned some of the quite frankly mind-boggling statistics surrounding YouTube, so I shan't repeat myself. Suffice to say, if you need to find a video, YouTube is probably the best place to start. A search will return a listing of videos in the main section of the screen with a thumbnail shot of a frame, an indication as to the length of the video, the title, authorship, upload date, number of views and a brief summary. Videos can be filtered by upload date, result type (which is to say by video, channel, playlist, film or show), duration, features (high definition, closed caption, Creative Commons, 3D or live) and they can be sorted by relevance, upload date, view count or rating. These filters can be chosen after a search has been run, or alternatively used within the search itself by the use of the comma. So if I was interested in finding videos that referenced 'library', were in HD format, had closed captions and were of a short duration I could actually just type into the search box the search *library, HD, short, CC* and immediately get results filtered appropriately.

Videos can be viewed in full screen or embedded on the YouTube page, and the viewer can obtain more information on the video if it's available, read or contribute to comments, like or dislike a video, obtain a transcript, view

Did you know?
The equivalent of 110 years of live video is watched on Periscope every single day (https://medium.com/periscope/year-one-81c4c625f5bc).

statistics and flag videos. Finally, if you have registered with YouTube you can subscribe to a particular channel to keep up to date with any new videos that are uploaded. The ability to search by channel is very helpful – once you know that one exists of course. It may be necessary to do a straightforward search to begin with, such as *CILIP*, but this will then return videos that have been uploaded by the user 'CILIPMarketing' and a second search will return all of their video uploads. Alternatively, it's worth just searching for an organisation or a person – a search for *phil bradley* will highlight my own channel as well as videos of the country and western singer for example.

Since Google owns YouTube it's possible to use some of its search functionality. It will come as no surprise to learn that searchers can use phrase searching and the minus or exclude function, and users can force any word to appear in the video title using the *intitle:* operator. For an even more precise search it's possible to add in the *allintitle:* search function instead. Of course, you could always go direct to Google and use *site:youtube.com* as a search parameter and then add in extra query terms to find material that will be of interest. The asterisk also works, as you would expect, so a search for *national library of* * returns results that include the National Library of Sejong City, the National Library of Australia and the National Library of Technology. By adding in the search term *channel*, searchers will be able to limit their results to specific channels, vastly reducing the number of results that they get. So for example, a search for *football association* will result in almost 3,000,000 results, but a search for *football association, channel* reduces this down to 16,600 results. By searching for football association as a phrase search, *"football association", channel* we are further reducing the results to about 3000, and further reduction is of course possible by adding in yet more filters. YouTube also started to support the hashtag in 2016, so it's always worth trying this out if you're returning too many results. For example, *library* returns almost 10,000,000 results, while *#library* only gives us 272 results; the value of this of course does depend on people sensibly using particular hashtags, so some detective work might be needed to identify the most appropriate hashtags.

If you want to find videos taken at or around a specific location at a particular period of time the YouTube search function isn't really the best of tools. However, there is a very nice little geo-search tool that you can use and it's at http://youtube.github.io/geo-search-tool/search.html. It's very basic, but powerful. Users can search for a location such as a city, town, village, intersection or address within a timeframe of between one hour and one year, with specific keywords within a particular radius. Searchers can also limit results to Creative Commons licensed material, embeddable results or live-only material. It's nice and easy to focus in on the location, or choose a video and see where it was taken. Of course it's going to be very useful if you want to see what videos were taken of, say, a protest against government cuts to public services if you think that it hasn't been properly covered by the media. Or if you want to see what video was taken of a specific place at some period of time in the past, this is a good tool to try out.

Amnesty International has released an excellent tool that allows you to see when a video was uploaded, called Citizen Evidence, at www.amnestyusa.org/citizenevidence, so that you can check the validity and authority of the videos that you watch. You can extract the metadata to get information that YouTube doesn't give you. If multiple versions of a video have been uploaded you can check out the earliest version, and you can also see all of the thumbnails associated with the video. You can then do a reverse image lookup to see where else they appear on the web.

Vimeo

Vimeo, at http://vimeo.com, has as its focus the individual user who wishes to upload video to share with friends – it's a little bit like Flickr in this respect. Consequently a lot of the videos will have limited or no professional interest to searchers in most instances. Having said that, there are a large number of videos available – my basic search for *library* returned over 90,000 results. The engine does have some advanced search options, so I could narrow this number down by searching for all videos, just ones that I had uploaded or videos from my contacts (thus emphasising the social networking nature of the site). I could also limit by refining my results to particular categories, such as instructionals, animation, narrative or any of over a dozen others. I particularly liked the options for documentaries, reporting and journalism, which gave me quick access to news-related videos in a way that was superior to YouTube's search functionality. Vimeo also offers options to refine by date uploaded, duration, price and Creative Commons licence.

Educational video search engines

BBC Video Nation

BBC Video Nation (www.bbc.co.uk/videonation/archive) is subtitled 'your views and experiences on camera and online'. Content is divided into over 40 categories, such as age, anger, disability, memories, school and work. There are also feature sections such as Africa, D-Day, Mother's Day and Teachers, with local sites around the UK by county. Unfortunately the resource has now been archived, but it's still available for use, it's just not being updated any longer. However, it still contains really useful information.

CriticalPast

CriticalPast can be found at www.criticalpast.com. The videos tend to be focused on the 1940s with over 57,000 videos in total, and with over 7 million images. From my browsing, there did seem to be a fairly heavy US bias as well. The search options are not perhaps as flexible as one might like, but you can filter by colour, sound, language, date or location. There was a nice option to show clips from specific dates in history (which they link to suggesting that searchers put their own birthdate in, but of course it could be any day), and I tried this myself. I had one video clip from 1918, nine from 1930–39, eighteen for 1940–49, seventeen for 1950–59 and eight from 1960–69. Fifty were monochrome and 3 in colour, and 35 were silent. You can see, therefore, that the emphasis really is on the past, rather than current content. Once a clip has been chosen to view it's also possible to pull out still images from it. While both films and photographs can be viewed for free, they carry a heavy watermark and the price to purchase the film or still can be quite expensive. However, for viewing on the screen with a group of people this site is quite useful. It's an interesting collection, and if you're into US history from the 40s, it's made for you. Other people may have rather slimmer pickings though.

eHow

The eHow site, at www.ehow.com, has the subtitle 'Fix. Build. Create. Learn. Life made easier'. It has a dozen categories, such as food, tech, personal finance and pets, with over 2 million articles and videos on how to do things. It has a very practical focus, rather than entertainment. Rather than choose to browse the available categories searchers can simply use the search box. A search for *library* returned informative videos on teaching library skills, using your local library for reading activities and the placement of a home library.

TeacherTube

TeacherTube, at http://teachertube.com, is designed to support the educational community with instructional videos. It's a safe venue for teachers, schools and home learners to share knowledge and information. Members of the site upload educational material, but they are also able to make constructive comments, rate videos and flag videos if they feel that they are inappropriate. The search engine provides access primarily to videos, but searchers can limit to audio, photographs or documents, for example. The site is entirely free and no registration is required to use it, but it does contain a considerable amount of advertising.

TED Talks

TED Talks, at www.ted.com/talks, is another superb resource which provides access to over 2400 talks ranging from two or three minutes to 20 minutes in duration. Search options include talks subtitled in different languages, events, date filmed, most viewed and – rather quaintly – options to limit searches to talks that are 'courageous', 'funny', 'informative' or 'fascinating', for example. It's an extremely useful site to find short videos for use in training sessions, motivational work, education, or to keep up to date with developments in different subject areas.

Videojug

Videojug, at www.videojug.com, is also a 'how-to' video site and calls itself 'the home of how-to videos'. It provides expert advice with over 60,000 free, professionally produced guides. Users can search via categories such as 'health and wellbeing', 'family and education' or 'technology and cars', or they can use the usual search box. The majority of videos will assist in practical tasks such as how to wire a plug, face-paint children or create meals using particular ingredients.

Other video search tools

Break, at www.break.com, is an entertainment site and search engine, as indicated by what was trending on the site when I looked – dogs, cute cats, funny babies and news bloopers. I tried a search for *library*, more in hope than expectation, and the majority of videos returned were either humorous in intent or mildly pornographic. (It's worth noting that in most instances the 'family filter' seemed to be of very limited use on this engine.) Having been mildly critical of the site I should also point out that it did have a fair selection of filtering methods – by video, picture, games or users, an option to sort by newest, views, rating or comments, the ability to search in specific channels and related genres.

Crackle, at www.crackle.com, specialises in movies, television programmes using the slightly unfortunate phrase 'in guys' favourite genres – like action, sci-fi, horror, crime and comedy'. Surprisingly I found 49 links to videos with my *library* search, but the majority were cartoon or anime. However, since the site really is designed for entertainment purposes, it would be unfair to be critical of it on that point.

FindAnyFilm, www.findanyfilm.com/search, is a database of films that are available in the UK. It's supported and funded by the UK Film Council and is very impressive. They claim that they have every film available in the UK. Nice simple interface – just type in the film that you're interested in, or browse by genre, A–Z or advanced search. Once a film has been located you get to see the trailer (if one is available), a full summary and film viewing options. The resource will find places where a particular film is showing; at the cinema, on TV, on DVD or Blu-ray, if it's available for download, watching online or in other formats. There is also an 'alert me' function for each of those options as well. FindAnyFilm also links to related titles, 'have you considered' options, most popular, new, and so on. Advanced search allows searchers to limit to title, actor, director, keyword, genre (20+), language, release date and certificate. It will also find cinemas that are close to you, show you what's on, provide a map and website link and give you filtering options. They claim:

> In true film nerd style, here at FindAnyFilm, we're committed to becoming the UK's most comprehensive film-watching search engine. That means we're increasing the number of titles and choice of reputable retailers all the time. So if a film is not listed, you can be sure we'll be working behind the scenes to make sure it will be soon. (www.findanyfilm.com/about-us)

Giphy, at http://giphy.co, is designed to help users find animated gifs; quite short animations that continually repeat in a loop. In early October 2016 Giphy passed 100 million daily users, who send 1 billion gifs per day, and viewers watch more than 2 million hours of gifs per day. To be honest, the search engine isn't that great – you're pretty much stuck with single word searching, so don't expect anything elaborate. There are a few basic categories that you can browse through, but it's not brilliant. Giphy does, however, have some extra tools that you can use to create your own animated gifs on your smartphone or tablet device, and you can upload them onto the site to share with other people. In summary, a poor search engine in terms of functionality, but great for finding funny and amusing images.

Tellyads, at www.tellyads.com, is a fun site, listing over 20,000 adverts and

927 vintage TV commercials to date. It has a very simple interface – a search box and an A–Z listing – so you really do need to know exactly what you're looking for, and it's probably fairly rare that you'll need a site quite like this, but it's worth knowing that it's there.

What Is My Movie, at www.whatismymovie.com, will try and identify specific films for you. Simply type in some basic concepts and it will try and find matches for you. I tried several and it found them every time. For example, I tried *gunslinger looking for gold in the American Civil War* and it came back with *The Good, The Bad and The Ugly*, *man looking for family in the Civil War* gave me *Shenandoah*, *two men on holiday in the lake district* resulted in *Withnail and I*. You can also try it with film quotes: *all the towns in all the world* came back with *Casablanca*. They say of themselves:

> Whatismymovie.com is a showcase of the technology of Valossa, which is a spin-off company of the University of Oulu, Finland. We aspire to create a new, descriptive way of searching video content. Our technology understands the contents of video files itself. Ranging from text to pattern recognition, we reach down into data that has not been searchable in the past.
>
> (www.whatismymovie.com/about)

You can help improve the engine by clicking on the buttons for a good or bad match. You can also run searches on titles, actors, directors and traditional search. It's not clear to me what that last is, but you can use it! The display of results is really nice – you get a picture of the movie – usually a film poster, a nice abbreviated synopsis, a link to 'more like this' and you can also click on a link to watch the film, which runs an Amazon.com search and returns a price as well.

Even more options

It will come as no surprise to realise that there are plenty of other video search engines that attempt the same job as YouTube. Due to the sheer size of the Google-owned resource there are going to be few reasons to try elsewhere, but of course an expert searcher will want to have alternatives to hand. With that in mind, a short list of other general video search engines is given below.

- Aol Video search, www.aol.com/video
- Mefeedia, www.mefeedia.com
- Metacafe, www.metacafe.com
- Veoh, www.veoh.com.

Audio search engines

As we've now looked at text, graphics and video in this book, it's logical to also cover audio search. If we exclude music search options, audio is something of a poor relation; while there are some search engines available they are quite few in number. Any attempt to properly cover music search engines would require at least a single chapter by itself, if not more. While there are obviously times when music searches are required, a lot of engines are general in nature, and it would be repetitious to cover them in detail. Moreover, many of these resources focus on playing music for entertainment purpose (which is very logical, of course) and they tend to get shut down due to copyright violations, so I hope that you will forgive me if I leave you to find these for yourself.

Findsounds

FindSounds, at www.findsounds.com, has a 17-year history, which makes it a very august resource. It's a sound effects search engine and it provides access to animal sounds, birds, household noises, musical instruments, the noises that people make, television and movie sounds and vehicles. Search options include file formats and the number of channels – mono or stereo. Perhaps unsurprisingly no sounds had been labelled 'library', so I used a fallback search, *dog*. This provided a total of 200 results, with a link to the original source, a visual interpretation of the sound wave of the file and an opportunity to listen to the sound itself.

The Macaulay Library

The Macaulay Library resource, at http://macaulaylibrary.org, is the world's largest and oldest scientific archive of biodiversity audio and video. It focuses on ornithology, and has as its mission 'to collect and preserve recordings of each species' behavior and natural history, to facilitate the ability of others to collect and preserve such recordings, and to actively promote the use of these recordings for diverse purposes spanning scientific research, education, conservation, and the arts.' Users can search recordings by species, and results indicate the waveform, species, sound type (such as call or song), location, date and length. There is also an option to view video results as well. This is obviously a very specialised search engine, but cannot be bettered in its area.

PublicRadioFan

The PublicRadioFan site, www.publicradiofan.com, features listings for thousands of public radio stations and over 1900 podcasts. The majority of these are entertainment stations playing various types of music, but there are also links to news resources as well. Searchers can filter and limit to programmes by category, source, name, by station, or excluding music.

Soungle

Soungle, at http://soungle.com, returns sound effects and musical instrument samples. Keyword searches retrieve effects with minimal information other than bitrate, waveform, time and brief descriptions. While it's quite basic in search terms, it does have a wide variety of files available, so if you were ever asked to find the sound of a creaky door, this would be a useful site to visit.

Soundjax

Soundjax, at http://soundjax.com, indexes and renders waveforms and catalogues audio from the internet. Results are displayed with their waveform and an option to listen to it on the page, as well as download it. Each waveform also has mono/stereo data, filetype, playtime, bitrate and size associated with it as well. Search options appear to be quite limited – when you type in a search Soundjax will provide suggestions; typing in *dog* gave options such as 'dog growling' and 'Prairie Dog', for example.

Podcast search engines

A podcast is an audio file that is available on the internet and can be downloaded onto a computer, mobile device or smartphone to be listened to. They are usually available as a series or in support of a television or radio programme, either repeating the same content or providing slightly different information. There are podcasts that cover every conceivable subject area possible, from hard science through to comedy, from murder mysteries to real-life murder enquiries. They are an excellent way to keep up to date with things that are happening in your own particular subject area of interest, or if you need to research a subject. You're probably already thinking the words in your head that I'm about to say, but I'll say it anyway – there are lots of different podcast search engines out there, far too many to cover in detail. Consequently I'll just focus on one or two of the major ones and provide links to others for you to explore for yourself.

Audiosear.ch

The Audiosear.ch website, at the easily guessed address www.audiosear.ch, is a full-text search and intelligence engine for podcasts and radio, according to their 'About us' page. They transform speech into text, analyse it and index it. The engine has indexed 16,545,790 minutes, 391,412 podcast episodes and 9,640 shows. The SERPs provide a thumbnail of the podcast, a title, subtitle, length, date and summary of each result, with the addition of keywords. The option to download the podcast is also available, and in some, but not all instances a transcript is available. People can then hover over a bar and see where the search terms are mentioned and in what context, as can be seen in Figure 11.1.

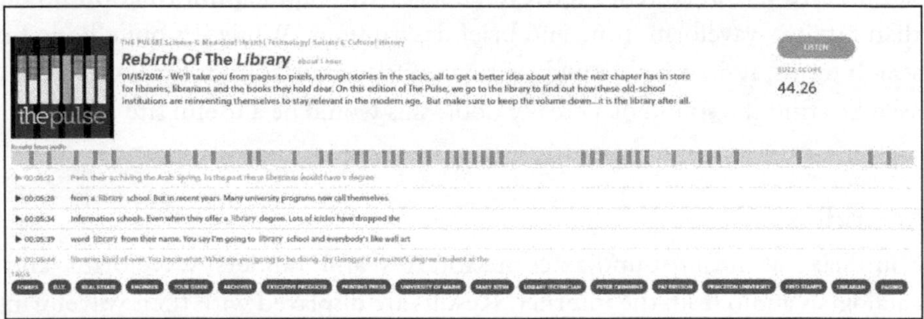

Figure 11.1 *The transcript of a podcast listing references to the search term library in Audiosear.ch*
Courtesy of www.audiosear.ch © 2017

Audiosear.ch can also send registered users an e-mail alert whenever a specific word or phrase is mentioned in a podcast that they index. Searchers can either do a simple free-text search or they can choose to find specific podcasts and filter results by network or by subject category. Finally, Audiosear.ch provides lots of useful information on the daily iTunes Chart and in-depth show statistics, so that people can really investigate which podcasts are currently popular, what's losing importance and what's attracting people's attention.

Stitcher Radio

The Stitcher list, at www.stitcher.com/stitcher-list/all-podcasts-top-shows, provides a weekly ranking of the most popular shows on the site. Searchers can click on links to particular podcasts and learn who created the podcast, what it's about, read episode summaries and listen to them directly from their device or download them to listen to later. There is also a link to a table of 'top movers' and 'most shared' as well as a category or directory listing. Clicking on any of the categories will display a new list of tables for top shows, top movers and most shared podcasts. As a result, it's very easy to find good-quality podcasts with limited browsing.

Stitcher also has a search box which provides auto-complete options, so in my search for *librar* (even before finishing the word) I was given suggestions for 'Free Library Podcast', 'New York Public Library' and 'The Wicked Library'. Having completed my search for *library* the SERPs gave me options to see all results, shows only and episodes only. I could then choose to listen to the podcast there and then or download it to listen to later. Stitcher provided an impressive list of podcast shows from or about libraries. Unfortunately the results were provided in the form of an infinite scroll, so I have no way of telling just how many shows were listed, but I gave up once I'd reached the three-figure point. That alone, in my opinion, makes it a good-quality resource and helps explain why it's one of my 'go-to' resources when I'm looking for this type of material.

Apple iTunes podcasts

If you're interested in listening to podcasts on an Apple device such as an iPhone or iPad, the appropriate app can be downloaded from the iTunes store at https://itunes.apple.com/gb/app/podcasts/id525463029?mt=8. As you would expect from Apple, it's a well designed app, offering top charts, featured podcasts and a search option. Once an appropriate podcast has been identified the app allows users to download it and update with new episodes automatically. Android users can download a similar app from the Google Play Music website at https://play.google.com/music/podcasts/publish.

Other podcast search engines

- AllPodcasts, www.allpodcasts.com
- iPodder, www.ipodder.org/directory/4/podcasts
- NPR Podcast directory, www.npr.org/podcasts
- Podcast Alley, www.podcastalley.com
- Public Radio Fan, www.publicradiofan.com/podcasts.html.

Summary

The internet is now, more than ever, a platform for multimedia-based content. All too often, however, it's one area that remains largely untapped, perhaps because it's been difficult to find exactly what is required from resources that have always been difficult to index. This is less of a problem as technology is catching up with the requirements that we have, so, for example, we can now pull words directly out of a podcast and index them. Whatever you might happen to be looking for, it's worth considering a search to see if there's a news item or video on the subject or an expert interviewed in a podcast, so cast your search net even more widely these days; not only different search engines, but different types of data!

CHAPTER 12

Specialised search engines

Introduction

It's an unfortunate fact of life that not everything can be put into neat little accurately labelled boxes, and search engines are no exception to this rule. Much though it grieves me, it really is necessary to have a chapter that looks at search engines that don't fit neatly into any of the other categories that I have used in the book. It may be because the search engine is so unusual that it defies any sort of categorisation (as you'll see later, Bananaslug fits that description perfectly), or because it covers content that isn't included elsewhere. Whatever the reason, there are several engines that really deserve inclusion in the book, so this chapter is where you'll find them.

Did you know?
There are over 10 million domain names that end in .uk (http://research.domaintools.com/statistics/tld-counts).

Academic search engines

Academia

Academia is part social network, part database, part search engine and you can find it at www.academia.edu. It defines itself as a 'platform for academics to share research papers. The company's mission is to accelerate the world's research.' Almost 50 million academics have joined the service (up from the 2 million mentioned in the last edition of this book, illustrating how quickly the service has grown), adding almost 18 million papers and listing over 2 million research interests. Academia offers a simple search box, with instant suggestions as you type. Results are broken down into a variety of areas; people, documents, journals and jobs for example. Documents may range from papers that have been uploaded by individual researchers, which can be downloaded and read in a PDF format, through to links to web pages or to other social media sites such as Pinterest. If you need to find an expert in a particular area, this is a good place to start, as you can quickly see their interests, what they have published, who they are following and their recent activities on the site.

BASE

BASE, or the Bielefeld Academic Search Engine (www.base-search.net) provides access to over 100 million documents pulled from over 5000 sources, with the full text of about 60% of the indexed documents being available. The sources included are selected and reviewed by BASE staff to ensure, as they put it 'data garbage and spam do not occur'. Searchers are presented with a search box from which they can choose to search an entire document, or title, author and subject fields.

Results are displayed in field order, including title, author, description and publisher, with links to the originating URL and content provider. Search results can be sorted by relevance, author, title or date. Furthermore, BASE offers options to refine results by various fields such as author, subject, Dewey Decimal Classification number, content provider and so on. Records can be checked in Google Scholar, e-mailed, exported or added to a list of favourites. Searchers can also get an RSS or ATOM feed for their search, they can save the search and add a search plug-in to their browser's search box, if it has one.

BASE also has an advanced search function with six different field options, which can be combined, content sources – which are geographical, publication dates from and to, and document types, from books to sheet music. I particularly liked the option to filter by terms of re-use; that is to say, by Creative Commons licence or works that are in the public domain.

LexisWeb

LexisWeb, at www.lexisweb.com, is the home of LexisNexis, which is a global provider in the area of legal, risk management, corporate, government, law enforcement, accounting and academic markets. It provides customers with access to billions of documents from over 45,000 sources. Search results are – in common with other engines in this area – very comprehensive and they provide searchers with far more than a few words of summary. Searchers can obviously run straightforward searches, but can set their 'search scope' by limiting to over 60 practice areas. Results can then be narrowed by site type (news, government, commercial, law firms and so on), related topics, citations, legal terms, jurisdiction, source and file format, to name a few.

Did you know?
In order to store all of the data on the internet you would require 5 million terabytes (www.lifewire.com/surprising-facts-about-the-web-3862898).

Obviously, LexisNexis is a very well known company which has made a business out of providing researchers with the information that they need, so it will come as no surprise to learn that much of the material they make available is via a commercial arrangement. Searchers can either subscribe, or they can buy individual articles, each individually priced. However, each record does provide a useful excerpt and bibliographic details, which means that it may be possible to track the article down via interlibrary loan. However, there are many records that use as their source web pages, which makes it far easier to get access to them!

LibGuides

Although this chapter can only really provide a taster of some of the many thousands of resources available for specialised searching, I would be entirely remiss if I didn't include at least one tool that has been created by the library and information science community, so the obvious choice was the LibGuides Community, at http://community.libguides.com. Over 130,000 librarians have produced over half a million guides to different subject areas. These can be searched by all institutions, academic, public, special libraries, K-12, partner sites or guide authors. Results are displayed by title, summary, author, source, date and tags. The guides themselves are produced using the commercial product Libguides produced by Springshare (http://springshare.com/libguides), so there is an element of consistency in the guides, but since they are produced by different librarians, covering different subjects for different readers, do expect considerable variety. I ran a quick search for *fake news* and came up with some really useful content from a variety of different academic sites; it was a quick, easy and effective way to get immediate access to authoritative information.

OAIster

OAIster, at http://oaister.worldcat.org, is a union catalogue of over 30 million records representing digital resources from more than 1500 contributors. It's a multidisciplinary search engine which searches the collections of many libraries worldwide using WorldCat, the world's largest network of library-based content and services. Search is based on the 'two pane' system, with results in the main, central window and a menu in the left. Searchers are provided with a simple search box, but with instant suggestions as they type. Results include an image, title, author(s), language, publication data, editions and formats, libraries that own the item and in some instances the ability to view the item there and then. Searchers are able to narrow their results in a variety of ways, such as by downloadable archival material or articles, by image, ebook, map, audiobook or even musical score. Alternatively, this can be done by author, year of publication, language or topic.

Since OAIster works hand in glove with WorldCat, it's also possible to search for items in local libraries – if their collections have been included in the database, obviously.

Science.gov

Science.gov, at www.science.gov, has as its strapline 'Your gateway to US Federal Science'. It searches over 60 databases and over 2200 websites from various Federal agencies, providing access to over 200 million pages of authoritative US government science information. Consequently it's a rather nice example of a meta-search engine, searching across all resources to find appropriate results. The results summaries are very helpful – title, database, author(s), source and date. There is also an excellent summary section for each result which is far more than the few words that we're generally used to seeing; commonly in the range of 50 or more words.

Science.gov also provides searchers with a helpful filtering menu; by topic, authors and dates, for example. There is also an excellent clustering visualisation tool for the results in the shape of concentric circles, which breaks the subject of the search down into narrower elements, with narrower ones under those, and even narrower again. A search for *dyslexia* can be broken down into Learning disabilities, Students, Processing, Developmental Dyslexia and Children with Dyslexia. If I choose to narrow the last of these down I have a choice of five options, include Words, and this itself can be broken down into narrower categories, such as Phonological awareness. It's one of the very best visualisation tools that I've seen, and it's both simple to use and visually appealing. Science.gov also allows searchers to limit by source, or to sort by rank, date, title or author, or to choose textual results or multimedia-based results. There is a link to the Wikipedia entry for a subject, alerts can be created for the search, and individual results can be marked for later printing or e-mailing.

Sweetsearch

Sweetsearch (www.sweetsearch.com) is a search engine for students. It limits results to about 35,000 websites that its staff of research experts and librarians have evaluated and approved. It helps students find good-quality, authoritative information quicker and more effectively. Sweetsearch is powered by Google's custom search engine resource and so you will already be familiar with the search engine functionality; it's really the choice of authoritative sites that makes this engine of particular use.

Zanran

Zanran, at www.zanran.com, has been described as the Google of statistical information, since it's used to search the web for data and statistics. It claims that 'Zanran gets you more meaningful numerical results than any other search engine'. Examples of the kind of searches that work well on Zanran are *diabetes prevalence in America*, *5 year survival rates lung cancer UK by stage*, *obesity France* and *aviation emissions United States*.

The SERPs provide the title of the graph, table or report and the journal that it's been taken from, together with date of publication, summary and URL. To the left of each result is a small icon, which when hovered over with the cursor will display a full page from the article, illustrating appropriate graphs and tables. The results can be filtered by geographic region, by specific site, by date and by file type. In order to download any of the 100 million graphs it is necessary to register, but this is at no charge.

Other academic search engines

Of course it's impossible to list all of the engines that fall into this category and I've really only chosen a few to look at in order to give readers an indication of what is available. As usual, there are plenty of others out there, so I'm including a list of a few more:

- Anthropology Review Database, http://wings.buffalo.edu/ARD

- Behavioral and Brain Sciences, www.cambridge.org/core/journals/behavioral-and-brain-sciences
- CiteSeerX, http://citeseerx.ist.psu.edu
- ERIC, https://eric.ed.gov
- Ethnologue, www.ethnologue.com
- FindZebra for rare diseases, www.findzebra.com
- Jurn, www.jurn.org
- Microsoft Academic, https://academic.microsoft.com
- Psycline, www.psycline.org
- Science Direct, www.sciencedirect.com
- Social Science Research Network, www.ssrn.com/en
- Sociosite, www.sociosite.net
- Sparrho, www.sparrho.com.

Search engines for children

In all of the time that I've spent researching and exploring search engines I have acquired a few 'holy grails' that I have never been able to find, and unfortunately one of those is an excellent search engine for children.

Having looked at one end of the academic spectrum, I wanted to also take a look at the other, and provide a listing of search engines that are suitable for children. I looked at dozens of different engines but unfortunately for a variety of reasons I really couldn't find any that I felt that I could confidently recommend; they all had something that I thought made them unsuitable. Rather than simply limit my coverage to a single paragraph, however, I thought that I would briefly cover some of the things that I looked for when assessing these engines, so that if you decide to take a look for yourself, you'll have a template to work from.

First of all, what age is a child? A search engine for children below ten should look very different to a search engine for young teenagers, but a lot of engines really didn't seem to take this on board at all. Obviously the younger the age group, the more basic the search, the simpler the results and there's probably going to be a design element of bright bold colours, pictures of animals and so on.

I did obviously search for specific words and terms, just to see if the search engines provided unsuitable results. To save you having to think of some yourself, I tried *dogging*, which is a British term for a certain type of sexual practice that generally takes place in car parks (but which is also the name of a children's book, so they might search for the term), *blue tits* – for obvious reasons – and *schoolgirl* – again for obvious reasons. I could have chosen a lot of other terms, of course, but I think that these three were enough to point out the extent to which a child can surf safely.

Some engines were capable of filtering content so that I could get material on birds, for example, without adult images, but many took the easy way out by blocking the term entirely. Some search engines merely returned no results, but others did flag up that an incorrect search had been run. These error screens were just poor, with no idea that the terminology they used would be either inappropriate, or indeed incomprehensible, to children or worse, that the children would quite likely feel as though they had done something wrong and had looked for 'bad words' when they were innocently searching.

I was also disappointed that while some engines were able to work out the difference between blue tits as a description of a physical situation or as a type of bird, too many were not, and just didn't give any help at all. Very few provided alternatives but, as we can see with search engines that provide a clustering approach, this is not actually that difficult to do. It wouldn't be that hard for an engine to return a result that said something along the lines of 'We couldn't find anything on blue tits, so we did a search for birds instead'. If a child isn't helped at this crucial point, this is just going to turn a child off searching, rather than encourage them.

There was also the really big problem of Google adverts. While the domain owners seemed to take care to try and limit inappropriate results, they don't seem to have given much thought to adverts, which are as objectionable as the content they're trying to block, and which lead directly to inappropriate sites for children. Completely unacceptable at all – either block adult sites, or do as some of the others have done, which is not have advertising at all, or screen it correctly.

Many of the engines that I looked at were simply using the Google custom search engine function with safe search turned on. In my opinion this is a fairly lazy way to provide a resource, since it relies on a third party to get everything right, and as we've seen with Google before, it doesn't always do that. A very quick way to test this out is to run a search for *martin luther king historical examination* and the engine will probably return the racist website www.martinlutherking.org, which – although I may well be biased – is not an acceptable site for children to view.

In summary, therefore, while lots of children's search engines are available, it's next to impossible to find one that correctly filters material, provides a range of materials, gives sensible help and advice screens and doesn't show inappropriate advertisements. Perhaps the best solution is for an adult to sit down with their child and search with them, teaching them good practice and reassuring them if and when they go wrong.

Other specialised search engines

We are now reaching a miscellany heaven or hell in this chapter, because there are still a lot of search engines that I want to bring to your attention which still don't neatly fit into any particular categories. Some readers may look through this section and shrug their shoulders and move on, while others will shout 'Eureka!' as they find exactly the tool that they've been looking for. I hope that you're in the latter category!

BananaSlug

BananaSlug, at www.bananaslug.com, takes a rather different approach to the concept of search. The searcher types in their search, and BananaSlug runs the search on Google and adds in a random word to provide an element of serendipity to the results. BananaSlug offers several categories of words for the user to focus the amount of serendipity used, and these categories vary from Archetypes to Jargon words and Themes from Shakespeare, for example. I couldn't honestly recommend this for serious searching, but for a few moments of fun it's worthwhile.

Fagan Finder

Fagan Finder, at www.faganfinder.com, is a wonderful tool, linking to a large number of different search engines; it's like a meta-search engine of search engines. It provides a search box and links to various engines; simply click on the one that's of interest and it will give you a larger selection to choose from. So, for example, if I'm interested in running a search for a particular quotation Fagan Finder gives me access to over 50 different specialised search engines, to say nothing of the extra additional resources that it links to. Fagan Finder has links to specialised search engines in the areas of word reference, biographies, audio, translations, products, academia, news, maps, search engines and images. Just to take one of those sections, video, there are over 100 links to different video-based search engines. It is an absolute treasure trove and one that is certainly worth keeping bookmarked.

Fanchants

Fanchants, at http://fanchants.com, is a search engine that will provide users with access to recorded football chants. It's probably news to both you and me, but football chants are taken very seriously by some fans, and this database has a collection of thousands of them; over 13,000 in the UK alone. The search engine provides access by country and by team. However, it's also possible to search by a number of options such as anthems, classics, funny, vintage and the delightful sounding 'avin a go. The chants are available to listen to as MP3 files, lyrics are provided and brief background history. Chants have been recorded directly from the terraces and so they give listeners a really atmospheric sound.

FindHow

FindHow (www.findhow.com) rather gives the game away with its name – it is a search engine that helps you to find out how to do something – from changing a tyre to citing an article in a paper. It's obviously very practical in nature, but other than that the remit is wide, covering subjects as diverse as careers, money, writing, pets, hobbies and the automotive industry.

Knowem

Knowem, at www.knowem.com, is a useful engine if you are heavily into using social media tools. It allows you to check over 550 different social media websites, such as Twitter, Blogger, Typepad, Delicious and Pinterest, to see if a particular name has been taken. If you have been tasked with securing your brand name this tool will prove to be invaluable, or if you want to protect your own name and ensure that someone else with the same name doesn't get to register it first, Knowem will check the websites for the name that it's been asked to search on. The first search will highlight popular social media sites, greying and crossing out icons where the name has been taken, but providing a link to any resource that hasn't had the name taken, together with information about the site. It's then possible to narrow the search to look at aspects of social media such as blogging, bookmarking, design and entertainment. Furthermore, Knowem will also provide details on the availability of domain names and trademarks. Figure 12.1 on the next page shows the result of a search that I ran on my own name to see if it was available on different social networks. This could be quite useful if you're attempting to track down a particular individual; rather than waste time looking for a name on a particular site where it hasn't been registered the search can instantly be focused on social networks where it has.

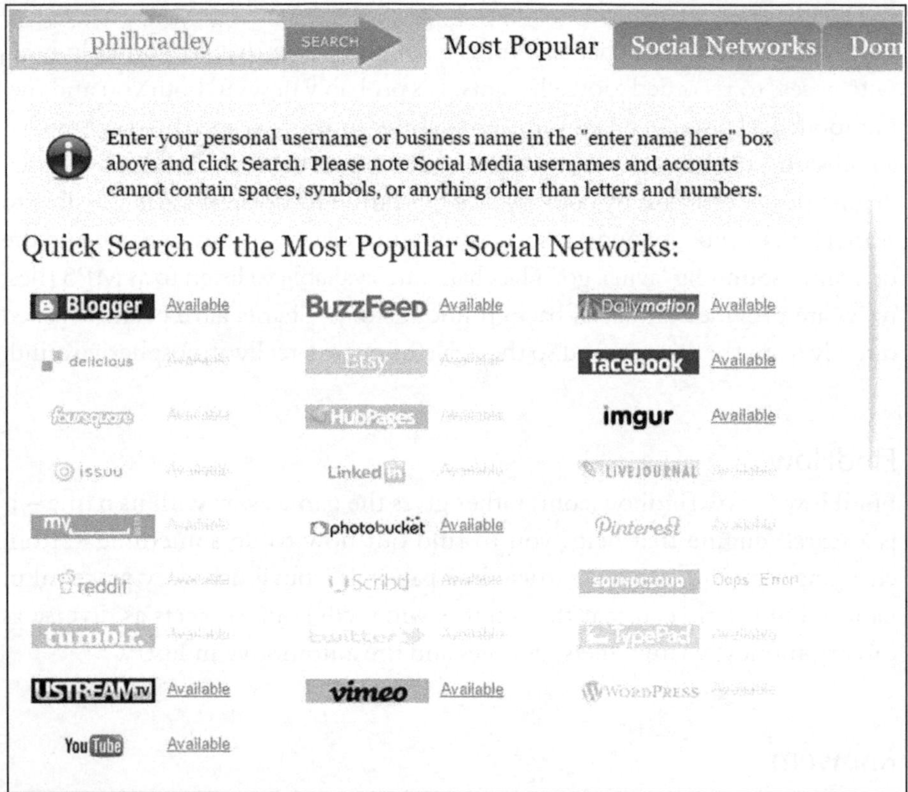

Figure 12.1 *A search on Knowem. Only a small number of sites haven't got a Phil Bradley registered on them!*

MillionShort

MillionShort is an engine that may well cause some consternation when first viewed, at http://gb.millionshort.com, because what it has done is remove the 1 million most popular websites from its index. Alternatively, you can choose to remove the top 100, top 1000, top 10,000 or top 100,000 sites instead. We're all aware of the 'fact' that most searchers never look beyond the first page of results, and this engine is giving people an opportunity to really dig down much further to find the gems that might be hiding dozens of pages down in the results. It's not entirely clear to me how they are defining their figures, because I am sure that some of the sites that I saw are certainly within the million most popular sites on the web, but I still found lots of information that I wouldn't have done without using MillionShort, so that small criticism aside, it was an interesting experience!

Stands4

The Stands4 network of search engines is another excellent resource. It's a leading provider of free online reference and educational resources, currently made up of 15 different search engines. These cover biographies, definitions, lyrics, phrases, poetry, quotes, references, rhymes, symbols and synonyms. The company was founded in 2001 and has steadily grown, adding more search engines into its stable as it has. Each of the sites has its own URL, but you can see them all by following the on-page links from the Abbreviations tool at www.abbreviations.com.

Eat By Date

The shelf life and expiration date guide at www.eatbydate.com is a useful search engine that tells you for how long you can safely eat food past its sell-by date. Simply type in the food item that you're interested in (yoghurt, bacon, etc.) and this site gives you an interesting new perspective. As well as providing information on the varieties of food (canned, fresh, opened) it tells you how to tell if something shouldn't be eaten, how to store it to extend its life and other useful information. This is an interesting search engine which does one simple job very well.

SymbolHound

SymbolHound, at http://symbolhound.com, is an engine that some people will just look at blankly, while others will jump up and down in excitement about. It's an engine that – as the name suggests – searches symbols for you. Google has started to expand into the area of symbol searches, but if you want something like *===javascript* or *ruby $$* this is going to make life much easier for you. It has an advanced search function with the usual suspects such as all terms, any terms, exact phrase and so on. Results are clear – with URL, summary and title. So, if you need to search for symbols such as &, %, and π, this is one engine that you really need to check out.

US Zip

This will obviously have a limited value on one side of the Atlantic, but for my readers in the USA, US Zip, at www.uszip.com, is going to prove to be a really useful tool. Simply type in a location to see all of the relevant zip codes, or type in a zip code to find the specific place that you're looking for. Once you've found the place that interests you, that's where the real value of the search engine comes into play. There is a wealth of knowledge about the location at your fingertips. Total population, housing units, land area, demographic information (gender, age, race), public school and library information, universities, colleges, hospitals, crime rates; all nicely presented with useful charts and graphs. This is a really nice tool and one worth keeping in mind.

The Wayback Machine

The Wayback Machine, or to give it its other title 'The Internet Archive', at https://archive.org, is a tremendously powerful tool. It works in the same way that a free-text search engine does, by sending out robots to spider websites and copy the content back to home base. However, that's where the similarity ends, since the Wayback Machine then archives this information and stores all of the pages online, in chronological order, for users to view them. Figure 12.2 shows the archived data that the engine has on my website.

> **Did you know?**
> The original website for the 1998 film You've Got Mail is still live at http://youvegotmail.warnerbros.com.

Users can simply click on a particular date and view the collection of pages that the Wayback Machine has archived. This can be particularly useful for a variety of reasons. If you need to check the history of a particular site, you can see who has owned it and the web page content over time. If you needed to

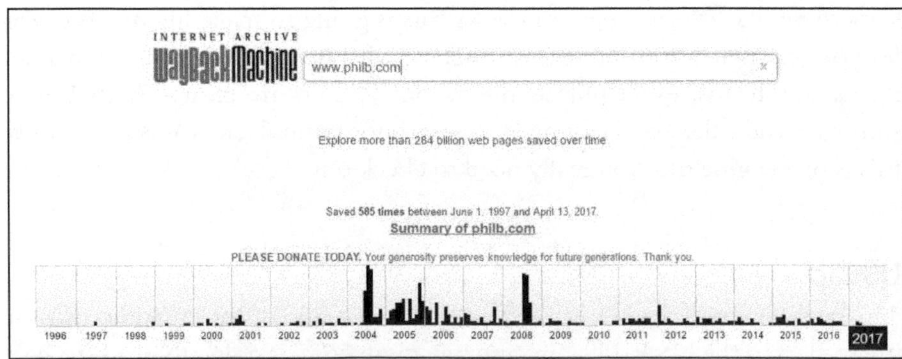

Figure 12.2 *The Wayback Machine's archive of the author's website*
Reproduced with permission from https://web.archive.org/

know the name of the CEO ten years ago you may be able to find it by trawling the current site, but it would simply be quicker and easier to visit the archived version for the date that you're interested in, and see if the name was listed. You can see how people viewed a particular event at a specific moment in time by reading their reports or news items. You could check the development of web page design or other web-based technologies by checking appropriate sites.

Unfortunately you cannot be sure that you'll find the site that you're interested in. The Wayback Machine doesn't especially advertise itself, or tell web authors that it has archived their site, so many people are unaware that previous incarnations of the site are still online, but they can ask for their pages to be removed from the 284 billion web pages stored.

Wolfram|Alpha

Wolfram|Alpha, at www.wolframalpha.com, is a rather different search engine. In fact it's not a search engine at all in most senses of the word; it calls itself a 'computational knowledge engine'. Many searchers, when exploring a new search engine, will often start by looking for themselves. We normally know where we're referenced, how many references there are and so on, so it's a useful starting point. However, if you do this over at Wolfram|Alpha you get information about the names 'phil' and 'bradley'. We learn that Phil and Bradley are male given names, latest information for US births (Wolfram|Alpha is currently using data produced in the year 2011 for this), history of US births from 1880 to date, estimates for current US population and estimated current age distribution. The source data for this comes from six different places, all of which are listed. It's a shame that we're only getting content from the USA – adding in UK or England just confuses the engine, and we get no results.

Trying a date also gives really different information (remember the computational element here), because if I type in a date such as 9 April 1865 I learn a lot about the date – that it fell on a Sunday, it was 144 years, 1 month and 10 days ago. (Lovely little cut and paste function there which I only discovered when trying it!) It's also the 99th day of the year, the date that the American Civil War ended, and sunrise/sunset information and the phase of the moon are also given. A search on the same date in Google emphasises the historical information, rather than anything else.

Another example of the computational element – a search for *population England China India France Germany* provides a summary of the total population for those countries, highest and lowest, tabular data, population history, and a huge slew of data on the demographics. This content is taken from many different (listed) sources, and they're fairly current. However, while it did give the population for my local town, this was dated to 2004. On the other hand, the same search in Google gives me a more recent, but much less precise, figure.

There are plenty of other things that the engine can do which more traditional search engines cannot. For example, it can work out probabilities. A search for *24 coin tosses* will provide a result that shows the likelihood of all the flips coming down as heads, tails, 12 heads and 12 tails or at least one head or tail. If you're interested in comparing websites, simply type in a couple of URLs that you're interested in, such as *facebook.com vs google.com* and Wolfram|Alpha will provide you with a comparison of daily page views, visitors, site ranking, history, subdomains, views per visitor and so on. If you need to know what the weather was like on a particular day in a particular location, a search for *weather in London June 21 1980* will give you the temperature, conditions, humidity and wind speed, as well as historical temperatures for the date as well.

Wolfram|Alpha can also provide you with a great deal of information about you, based on your Facebook account. If you allow the engine access to your account it can do a huge amount of number crunching and will serve up a fascinating array of facts, such as exactly how old you are, average post length (words and characters), total likes, total comments, word frequencies, significant words (also available as a basic word cloud), most liked post, most liked photograph, most commented on post, top commentators, check-ins, weekly app activity and interface activity by device. Not only that, but information on friends' genders, friends' relationship statuses, ages, oldest friend, youngest friend, friend locations, spoken languages, religious and political beliefs, birthdays, common names of your friends, friends with most mutual friends, and friend networks!

I've produced a short video which shows some of the things that Wolfram|Alpha can do, and how powerful it can be when used in conjunction with other search engines; it can be found at http://youtu.be/3IL9Vo8h2Ic. Suffice to say, if you are a reference librarian, and/or ever have a need for facts and figures about a subject (which is most of us at one time or another), this is one search engine that is really worth getting to know inside out.

2lingual Google Search

2lingual Google Search, at www.2lingual.com, is a dual-language search engine that makes it easier to search across Google in two different languages. It currently supports 37 different language options, and when it is searched it will perform the 'normal' search and a cross-language search in the language of the searcher's choice. Results are presented side by side in two different panes. It obviously makes more sense if you can speak the language that you're searching in, but since 2Lingual does an initial translation for you, it's still possible to get some useful material. It's also helpful to see just how different the results are between two language sets.

Summary

The problem with a chapter like this is that, quite frankly, it could go on almost forever. There are going to be more search engines available than I'll ever be able to cover, and indeed one of your favourites may not have been mentioned by me at all, for which I apologise! However, I can almost guarantee that whatever you want to find, regardless of the subject, format or age, there's going to be a search engine that is available to you. It's just a question of using another engine to find the one that you want. Then you simply need to evaluate it and start using it.

CHAPTER 13

Hints, tips and the future

Domain names, URLs and web pages

Domains

Become familiar with the major domain identifiers, such as .com, .co.uk, .org and country codes. Organisations usually try and register memorable combinations of names and identifiers, but these days if they are registering a domain for the first time they may have to take whatever they can get, so if you're not finding the site that you expect at a .com address, try the .org or even the .org.uk, version for example. In the last few years the number of different domain names has increased, so we now have ones such as .accountant, .club, .help, and .science. A complete list is available on Wikipedia at https://en.wikipedia.org/wiki/List_of_Internet_top-level_domains. You can use the *site:* search function to limit your search to any of these new domains, and it should give you a smaller set of results, but you'll probably still need to do a more general domain search to find everything that you need.

Did you know?
The first website in the world is still online, at http://info.cern.ch/hypertext/WWW/TheProject.html.

It's worthwhile checking to see who a domain is registered to, if you have any doubts about the validity or authority of a particular site. In the UK the organisation responsible for domain name registrations is Nominet and they have a very useful *Whois* tool at www.nominet.org.uk/uk-domain-names/about-domain-names/domain-lookup-whois/whois-tool that you can use to check a domain – as long as it has .uk in the address. You can see who a domain is registered to; either a person or an organisation, their address, when the domain was registered to them and when it is going to expire. It's not a foolproof method, because a registrant can pay extra to have their details redacted and it won't find addresses that end in .com either – even if they are based in the UK. If you have no luck with Nominet, do a simple *whois* search within your favourite search engine and it will return a variety of tools that you can use to explore domain ownership.

While on the subject of domains, please do check very carefully, and make sure the domain that you're looking at is the one that you think you're looking at. For example www.twitter.com is not the same address as www.tvviter.com (2 v's do not a w make!) and the University of Southampton website can be found at www.southampton.ac.uk and not www.southamptonuniversity.co.uk. You may also find that if you receive an e-mail with a link in it, the link that is displayed on the screen is not necessarily the link that your browser will click on. It's therefore worth warning members of your library not to simply click on a link in an e-mail, but to type the URL directly into the browser themselves. Tricks like this are known as 'phishing' and are designed to get people to pass on details of their accounts, passwords and so on to a third party who can then use those details for nefarious purposes.

Site not found

If you click on a link and get taken to what is known as a '404 error page', which is the way that the remote server tells your browser that it can't find the right page, it's always worth checking the URL and chopping a little bit off the end, up to the last forward slash. Keep doing that until you get to a page that does work, and see if you can trace the right page that way – or just go straight to the home page of the site and see if they have a search function. Alternatively, using the *site:* functionality that some engines offer is always a good way to find a page that might have been moved on a site. If that fails, try to identify the page via the *cache:* option on a search engine or use the Internet Archive, at www.archive.org, to find the information that you need.

Get the most out of your browser

The browser is a very powerful piece of software, but one that is very often overlooked. Considerable development goes into making the browsers better, faster and more efficient than previous versions, and indeed, superior to the competition.

Customising your browser home page

When your browser opens, the page that appears on the screen is what is known as the home, or start page. This may be a page that takes you to your organisation's home page, it may take you directly to a search engine, the home page of the computer manufacturer or some other page, which may or may not be helpful. However, there's no technical reason why you have to put up with this, and you should give some thought to producing your own home page. There are a great many tools available that will assist you in this, and a good example is Netvibes, at www.netvibes.com. It's a free resource and is designed around the concept of modules or widgets that you can create, with bookmarks, search engine search boxes, RSS feeds, news items from newspapers or the media and so on. All of your information is therefore kept in one place for you, and because your page is hosted on their server (rather than stored locally on your specific machine) you can get access it to from any computer anywhere in the world. It's a very fast and effective way to keep on top of subjects that are of interest to you and provides helpful shortcuts to your favourite search engines. Alternatively try a similar start page at a site called Symbaloo (www.symbaloo.com) and you can see my page of search engines at www.symbaloo.com/mix/searchengines34, which you're welcome to use if you create your own account at Symbaloo.

Bookmarking

Another option related to bookmarks is to use one of the many bookmarking services that are available. Examples are Delicious, at www.delicious.com, and Diigo, at www.diigo.com, which allow you to store your bookmarks on their servers and add in your own preferred keywords and summary of the page. It's then simply a matter of returning to the site when you want to find a web page that you need to view again, and find it using their search option. These tools are excellent when it comes to research, as it's an easy job to visit a lot of pages, store them and use them for future reference. If you have pages that you visit regularly, however, you may wish to add them to your start page, or set your browser up so that it opens a specific set of tabs every time it starts.

If you have a number of searches that you run on a regular basis, there's no point in continually retyping in the search over and over again. Simply type it in once, get the results and bookmark the page. It's the search that is saved, not the set of results, and you can simply add in a time option to pull back the most recent searches, or indeed add in the option for displaying just the most recent hour or a day's worth of results to further narrow the search and simplify your life.

When you click on a result and visit a web page you often have no real idea as to where you'll locate the term(s) that you're looking for. A very simple approach here is to use the Control key in conjunction with the F key. This will bring up a dialogue box at the bottom of the browser window and you can type in anything you wish at this point, and the browser will highlight the combination of characters that you've typed in. You can simply jump from one to the next until you find exactly what you're looking for.

Printing web pages

When printing off a web page it can be very irritating to waste ink and paper with content (particularly adverts) that you don't want. There are plenty of tools that can be used to make it easier to read a page, or to print the page off. A good tool to try out is Print What You Like, at www.printwhatyoulike.com. You can simply add a bookmarklet to your browser bar, and when you need to print off a page it will create a printer-friendly version of the web page.

Multiple browsers

It's worth having several browsers on your computer. You can then set each browser up exactly how you wish, perhaps to open an entirely different set of pages for you, to load different variants of your user name and so on. If you want to compare the personalisation of results, for example, have one browser that logs you into your Google account, and another browser that doesn't. Run the same search in both browsers and see what different results are returned to you. Ideally, if you can have two actual monitors this makes life even easier – while it sounds like an unnecessary luxury, a two-monitor setup will save you large amounts of time. I'm using such a system myself, so I can have one screen open to a page of search engine results in the left-hand monitor, with my word processor open in the right-hand one, and I can easily just look back and forth while I'm typing. The alternative is to constantly switch from one resource to another, which is a slow and tiresome approach.

Browser shortcuts and extensions

Check to see what shortcuts your browser will offer you. For example, in Firefox, pressing Control and N will open up another version of the browser, Control and I brings up a search box for your bookmarks, Control and H displays your history and Alt and D puts your cursor into the address bar.

Pressing the Home and End keys takes you to the beginning of a page or the end of it, respectively.

Check to see what extensions can be added to the browser. There are literally thousands of these available, and they do all manner of things to make your searching and browsing life easier. Simply run a search for (browser name) extensions in order to see what's available to you, but keep an eye on the time, because searching for extensions can become quite addictive.

You can create very useful start pages for your browser as well. These are pages that open as soon as you start your browser. Obviously you could have links into pages such as NetVibes or Symbaloo, but you can also use utilities such as Bookolio which is a Google Chrome extension and available at https://chrome.google.com/webstore/detail/bookolio/lbgmbgopjppdjfopndcni omnhpodajba?hl=en. If you install it and you open a new tab on your browser, Bookolio will provide you with a search bar, links to various different search engines and access to some of your bookmarks. You can see it in action in Figure 13.1.

Figure 13.1 *The Bookolio browser page*
Reproduced with thanks to The Bookolio Team

As you can see, I have mine currently set to search Google, but I can simply click on any of the circular icons beneath the search bar to change the default to another engine. It's a really easy and effective way to remind yourself that the world does not revolve around any one search engine. If you don't like or use the Chrome browser you could try the All in One extension for Firefox, which works in the same way, although it has the additional feature that you can add in your own search engines. It's available at www.allinone.ws.

Searching

Hopefully you've got a very good handle on the whole search experience now, but it's always worth reiterating a few things. Although it's tempting to just use the same search engine all of the time, you'll be aware that there are plenty of them out there. Try using one of the 'blind search' tools such as BlindSearch, at http://blindsearch.fejus.com, to compare results and then see which engine you actually do like the most.

Keeping up with the changes

Keep up with the changes to search engines; there really isn't a day that goes by without a new search engine starting up, one closing down or another changing what it does. I try to keep on top of this myself in my own blog at www.philbradley.typepad.com but there are also other sites that you should consider looking at, such as Search Engine Land, at www.stateofsearch.com. If you really get bitten by the search bug, there are lots of communities that you can join on LinkedIn or Facebook. I'm loathe to add in too many personal recommendations, since what I find useful may not be useful to you, but I would also suggest that you will find it very helpful to visit the sites of some of my colleagues in the search engine industry, such as Karen Blakeman's site, at http://rba.co.uk. Karen is just as fascinated with search as I am, but she also has an excellent collection of resources in the area of business information. Tara Calishain maintains the Researchbuzz site at https://researchbuzz.me, which is phenomenally useful and updated multiple times during the course of the day, and I learn a huge amount from it. Gary Price runs an extremely informative blog called Infodocket at www.infodocket.com, which covers a wide variety of different subject areas, but all related in some way to librarianship, information science, the internet and search.

Privacy when searching

There may be times when you really want to stay anonymous when browsing, for a whole host of reasons. Most browsers nowadays have a privacy option available, and there are plenty of extensions that can be added to the package to ensure that no one knows who you are or what you're searching for. However, there are also a fair number of tools available on the web which help in this process as well. Hide My Ass, at www.hidemyass.com, has what is called a free 'proxy' service which hides your IP address and protects your online identity. Anonymouse, at http://anonymouse.org, does the same job, as do many others – just search for 'anonymous browsing' to get a list of some.

Viewing more results

Don't forget to look beyond the first page! It's really easy to forget that the first 10 results are just that – the first 10, and there are plenty more after that. A cartoon that I saw recently made a very good point; 'Q: Where's the best place to hide a body? A: On the second page of Google'. It's worth checking with the options in your favourite search engine and changing the default number of results from 10 to 20 or even 50 if you can.

Choosing keywords

Always put your most important keywords first in the search string. Many search engines will just search for all of the words however you have typed them in, but others will actually provide different results, once it realises what you're really interested in.

Being cautious

Please don't forget to be distrustful. It's a horrible thing to have to say, but when you are searching for news events some people will have created web pages that are seeded with malware, and even the mere act of clicking on a page may cause you problems. So even though you desperately need news of a specific event quickly, don't just mindlessly click on the first result that comes up – search engines do try and ensure that dangerous links are removed, but there's always a risk that one might get through. If you need information on breaking stories, use a news search engine or go directly to one of the national or international news sites and search there. This is a particular problem when it comes to URLs that have been shortened with excellent services such as Bit.ly. Simply because you're told that the link will take you to the site of your dreams, it could quite easily take you to a site full of malware and leave you in the middle of a nightmare instead. Don't forget to use the DuckDuckGo option to expand out that shortened URL so you can see exactly where you're going to end up (mentioned in Chapter 4). Alternatively try a tool such as the one found at www.checkshorturl.com.

Other search tips

If you are out and about, don't forget that you can still search for whatever you need to find by using any of the many hundreds of apps that are available to you on your smartphone or tablet device. If you have a favourite search engine, do check to see if it has an app available – many of them do these days, and I can't see them becoming unpopular in the future – quite the opposite.

Set a time limit for a search, and stick to it. It's all too easy to keep searching for something long after you should have stopped. Have an internal clock ticking and if after 5 or 10 minutes you've not got what you were after, change your tactics.

Don't forget to leverage your contacts. If I'm having real difficulties finding something I'll often go straight to Twitter and ask my question there. Since I follow and am followed by lots of librarians, someone can usually come up with a great tactic or strategy for me to use – or even the answer that I need if I'm lucky!

Here's a search that we can all appreciate. You can recall a particular book – about the American Civil War for example, but you can't quite remember the exact title, or even who the author was. However, you can remember that the colour of the book was a mauve/purple colour with a photograph of a cannon on the front of it. Simply go to a search engine with an image search function and run a search for *"American Civil War"* and then limit the results to photograph and choose the closest colour, and lo and behold, some books that will hopefully jog your memory. It's always worth remembering that you can now search for things by colour and type of image – perfect for hunting down that elusive book!

Finally, don't forget that old and trusted method – printed resources! Despite all of the wonders of the internet age, with information at your fingertips remember that books, journals and newspapers – or even microfilm or microfiche – may well hold the answer to your question.

Finding confidential information

Surprisingly, this is extremely easy to do, since people forget that Google will index a high proportion of material that goes online, and if they have not been careful about where material has been stored on a server, search engine spiders may well find it. Obviously I'm not expecting people to go off and start hunting down what should be private and confidential information, but it's worth knowing how to do it, so that you can check your own site or that of the organisation you work for, just to ensure that everything is as it should be.

There are a variety of search terms that may be helpful to use here. 'This document is confidential', 'Not for distribution', restricted, private, personal and classified are a few terms to consider, but I'm sure that you can think up many more. The *filetype:* option is a good approach to start looking for information of this type, since phrases will be embedded within documents, and may be overlooked. So a generic filetype search in Google as a starting point would look like this:

filetype:rtf OR filetype:ppt OR filetype:pptx OR filetype:csv OR filetype:xls OR filetype:xlsx OR filetype:docx OR filetype:doc OR filetype:pdf

This gets us a collection of filetypes; there are plenty more of course, but these are the most likely to yield useful results. Then it's a question of simply adding in appropriate terminology. The addition of *"this document is confidential"* returns about 150,000 hits of a very wide variety. Some of the hits contain information that really should be confidential, while others refer to documents which are confidential ones – a false hit in other words. The addition of further qualifiers, such as *site:.gov.uk* still returns over 9500 hits though, which some may view with concern. The *filetype:* operator can also be used in conjunction with the *inurl:* search option, so we can run a search for *filetype:xls inurl:"e-mail.xls"*, which returns a listing of documents in a spreadsheet format with e-mail details.

The use of the *intitle:* operator can sometimes identify material that should not be available for all and sundry to see, especially if used in the format *intitle:login inurl:passwd site:.co.uk*, as you can imagine. More generally, *intitle:index of* will sometimes return results that display a listing of files, which can then be viewed, and checked to make sure that there is no embarrassing data available. Many people have webcams connected to their systems, and these can be identified by searching for strings such as *intitle: "active webcam page"*, while searching for something such as *intitle:"login password"*, *intitle: "Index of" passwd* or *inurl:password* may pull up documents where passwords are stored in plain text. If you ever need to check to see if music files were being stored on a system, a search for *intitle:index.of mp3 beatles* would display websites that had that music stored in such a way that it could be downloaded. You could always replace the *mp3* with some other file format, of course. Alternatively, a search for *intitle: "Index of" config.php* will return sites that have config.php files available, and if we skip over the technical details this file may contain username and passwords for specific types of database.

Searches can get much more complex and sophisticated however, as we can see with a search for:

-inurl:(htm|html|php) intitle: "index of" "last modified" "parent directory" (jpg|gif).

To break this search down a little bit – we've told Google not to search in the

URL field for various common file types, but we do want the phrase 'index of' in the title field, plus the terms 'last modified' and 'parent directory' and images that are either .jpg or .gif. This search will then return matches that present the user with lots of directories that they can look through which contain images that they could, in theory, simply download. Of course, by adding a *site:* function into the search you can just limit it to checking out your own site.

There are obviously many more searches that could be run, but since this isn't a book about hacking into websites, I think it best to stop at this point. I should also like to make the point that searching for other people's information is morally and ethically unsound, if not illegal in some situations. You may also discover to your cost that if you start to download any of the material that you find by searching in this way you have little or no guarantee that it does not contain a virus, so I would again caution you against exercising too much curiosity. Limit your excursions to your own sites to ensure that they are not compromised!

Another hint, which in some ways completely contradicts what I've just written, and that is to try not to be too clever when running a search. Never forget that Google (for example) isn't your friend, and it quite simply doesn't like long or complicated searches; too many search terms may result in lower results with less quality. Unless you are absolutely certain that a complex search is going to work, keep it reasonably simple, and try different combinations of short searches. Rather than a search for 'term1, term2, term3 term4' try searching for 'term1 term2', then another for 'term 3, term4' and so on, in combination. It will take longer, but you may get more accurate results in the end.

Other resources to test your searching skills

If you're a very sad person (like me) you may find that you really do actually enjoy trying to answer difficult search queries just for the fun of it. Luckily there are one or two places that you can visit which will help you scratch that itch. As you might expect, Google has produced a series of lesson plans, with various categories such as Culture and Science. Most of the questions are fairly straightforward and designed for children, so are ideal to incorporate into lesson plans, but some are really fun in their own right and may well test your skills. You can find the Google lesson plans at www.google.com/intl/es419/insidesearch/searcheducation/lessons.html. There is also the 'A Google a Day' challenge, with trivia questions, a timer and points to be won; again, it can be quite addictive and you think 'I'll just try one more'. Finally, Google runs an 'Advanced Power

Searching with Google course' at various times through the year. Not only is it a useful course that is done (for free) online to give delegates a better understanding of Google, but it's a valuable way of keeping on top of changes to search and getting people to think more widely about the subject area. Details are available at their website at www.powersearchingwithgoogle.com. These are all a great ways of testing your own search abilities, and making sure that you're still on top of your 'Google Fu', as it's colloquially referred to.

Another useful site to hone your skills is the SearchReSearch site, at http://searchresearch1.blogspot.co.uk, and it's run by Daniel Russell, who is a Google employee, but this is his own personal blog. Daniel usually asks one question per week and encourages people to provide the answer, methodology and the time it took in comments on the blog. His questions usually relate in some way to what he is doing, or where he has been, and I certainly took inspiration from him for the earlier questions that I asked! The questions are generally reasonably hard to do and you really have to think laterally in order to get the answer, but they're always a real challenge of your ability to search Google.

Mobile search

Did you know?
When people search for something 'near me', 88% are doing so on a mobile device (www.seo.com/blog/23-search-engine-facts-and-stats-you-oughta-know).

I haven't spoken at any great length about mobile search because quite frankly I can't do the subject justice in much under the length of a book. However, that certainly doesn't mean that I don't want to talk about it. There are many similarities and differences between searching on a mobile device such as a phone or a tablet and searching on a laptop or desktop in a fixed location. More than 50% of search queries globally now come from mobile devices (http://searchengineland.com/report-nearly-60-percent-searches-now-mobile-devices-255025). Google takes into account the look and feel of websites when viewed through a mobile device, and the better the experience, the higher the ranking for that site becomes, so we have yet another algorithm to add into the relevance ranking mix mentioned in Chapter 3. Many mobile or cell owners use location-based services and are interested in local shopping, weather information and personal advertisements, and so this is obviously of interest to local businesses, which need to produce sites and content that more closely match the interests of people running local searches. The importance of digital assistants such as the iPhone Siri cannot be underestimated, as we're now in a position to simply ask our devices for the information that we need, rather than having to type it in. As a result, search tools need to be smarter at understanding general conversation and natural language instead of a series of tersely written keywords.

Did you know?
20% of mobile queries are voice searches (www.seo.com/blog/23-search-engine-facts-and-stats-you-oughta-know).

Now you can, of course, simply use an existing browser app for your device, such as Safari, Chrome or Opera, and if you wish to, you can synch your bookmarks to ensure that you have a similar experience when using the internet, irrespective of device. On the other hand (or indeed as well), there are plenty of search apps available that can be installed on the device. There may be limitations due to the software that is supported, and the type of device you're using; while most apps will be available for both iOS and Android phones and tablets, the options may be rather more limited if you're using a Windows-based machine. However, there will be plenty of apps available to help you search.

Major search engines such as Bing, DuckDuckGo and Google have their own apps, and these work in a very similar fashion to the way that the websites work, so there's going to be no real surprise there if you decide to try them out. Other sites that have apps are StartPage and Wolfram|Alpha, so if there's a search engine that you particularly enjoy using it's worth visiting its home page or 'About us' page to see if there's an app available for you to install. There are plenty of other apps that you can use, but please be aware that it's a highly volatile market; search engines on the web start up almost weekly and disappear just as quickly, but they seem to have a very long life in comparison to apps. In preparation for a course that I ran recently I downloaded half a dozen different search apps and by the time I came to actually run the course several of them had ceased operation. Although the app still opened, nothing happened when a search was typed in, but it was only by trying to reach the website that I could definitively confirm that the app was dead and no longer being supported.

AllSearchin1 by Avatar Apps (available on both iOS and Android devices) allows users to run a search and then view the results using Google, Bing, Yahoo!, Baidu or Wikipedia from within its own browser window, or results can be loaded directly into the Safari browser if preferred. It's very basic, but it does a reasonable job of acting as a multi-search engine, although the choice of Baidu, which is a Chinese-based engine, is rather unusual.

Just Search, available on iTunes, is an engine that gives access to various search engines chosen by the user. This is a really nice feature, since it's possible to add just about any search engine of choice, which will then be displayed on the search screen. All that users need to do is to type in their search term and then choose the engine that they want to run the search on. Users can arrange the order of the search engines by pinning their favourites into the first four spots on the display, and other choices are arranged automatically, based on recent usage. Just Search also keeps a list of recent searches on the screen, so it's really easy for users to revisit searches if necessary.

picTrove Pro for both iOS and Android is a picture search engine. It will automatically search nine different engines and sites such as Google, Flickr, Facebook and Photobucket, then display the results on the screen. Users can then simply click onto the set of results that interest them and then onto the specific image that they want to look at in detail. It's a very fast engine and results appear on the screen almost instantly.

Search by TapMedia, at www.tapmedia.co.uk, is another multi-search engine app. A search will return links to different search websites such as Google, Google Images, Pinterest and eBay and by clicking on the resource the app will take you to that engine and automatically run the search. It also links to YouTube, Wikipedia, shopping sites, recipe sites, books and tweets. It's a very basic tool, but it does an acceptable job, and it is free.

The future of search

It's almost impossible to predict where search is going to go into the future, since it's such a volatile world, but there are a few obvious signposts. With the seemingly unstoppable rise of mobile technology, user-generated content is going to continue to grow at mindboggling speed. I've occasionally indicated this growth in previous chapters by including statistics from the last edition, and by the time you read this yourself the current statistics are going to be woefully out of date.

The internet is increasingly becoming a visual place, with images, video and sound files being uploaded in favour of text-based data. I suspect that we'll see more tools that can 'listen to' this content and index it before making it available for searching.

We'll continue to see search being integrated into our daily lives. For example, the Alexa product from Amazon is a physical device that is capable of voice interaction, playing music, keeping lists and answering questions. Users can simply ask it questions such as 'Alexa, what is the weather like tomorrow?' or 'Alexa, how tall is Mount Everest?' and get an immediate answer. We already have access to personal digital assistances with our smartphones, and it's becoming second nature to just ask for the information that we need. Furthermore, we're now moving into territory where we are given answers to questions that we haven't actually asked. Google 'cards' that pop up on smartphones can provide you with information about where you are, what you're interested in, and remind you about things you need to do.

Did you know?
It's estimated that there will be more than 24 billion devices connected to the internet by 2020 (http://uk.businessinsider.com/what-is-the-internet-of-things-definition-2016-8).

The internet of things – devices connected to the internet, such as fridges, sensors, vehicles and other items – will continue to increase exponentially. They will interconnect, talk to each other, increase automation, collect data and automatically perform actions on our behalf. The possibilities promised are virtually limitless and are hopefully beneficial!

Interestingly, I don't often see the phrase 'Google killer' mentioned any more. In the last decade search engines were often described using this phrase, and they seldom lasted a year before you would see the inevitable 'this domain name is for sale' sign on the website. I think that Google is going to be the predominant search engine well into the future and nothing is going to challenge it. However, we'll continue to see other search engines rise and fall as they try and find their own particular niche in the search engine world; some will succeed and others will disappear. If pushed, I think the major competition to Google will come from Bing, with its huge backing from Microsoft; DuckDuckGo will continue to keep its place as the most important of the privacy-based search engines, and Yandex will become the home of people who wish to do serious research.

As far as Google search goes, I don't have a positive attitude. Rather than improve search functionality they have increasingly disabled what the search engine can do; while it's a cynical view I truly believe that if it doesn't make them money, they're not interested in supporting it. They believe firmly in the 'good enough is good enough' viewpoint, and as long as most people are reasonably satisfied with what they get from search, that's acceptable. Meanwhile all the slightly more complex functions such as synonym search, reading age and the *link:* option are being removed from search. I don't think that this will be the last, and it would not surprise me in the slightest to see other search functionality removed in the next couple of years.

However, let's not end this chapter, and indeed this book, on a depressing note. We are truly lucky that we still have quite literally hundreds of different search engines at our fingertips, and between them – with enough skill and expertise – we can find literally anything that's available on the web. We really are in a true golden age of information, and as expert internet searchers the world really is our oyster. We are fortunate to be in a position to help so many people so quickly and easily – long may it continue!

Index